Crisis? What crisis?

Manchester University Press

Crisis? What crisis?

The Callaghan government and the British 'winter of discontent'

John Shepherd

Manchester University Press

The right of John Shepherd to be identified as the author of this work has been asserted by him in accordance with the Copyright, Designs and Patents Act 1988.

Published by Manchester University Press
Altrincham Street, Manchester M1 7JA, UK
www.manchesteruniversitypress.co.uk

British Library Cataloguing-in-Publication Data is available

Library of Congress Cataloging-in-Publication Data is available

ISBN 978 1 7849 9115 9 *paperback*

First published by Manchester University Press in hardback 2013

This paperback edition first published 2015

The publisher has no responsibility for the persistence or accuracy of URLs for any external or third-party internet websites referred to in this book, and does not guarantee that any content on such websites is, or will remain, accurate or appropriate.

Printed by Lightning Source

For Jan – again – and Emma, Francis, Louise, Caroline, Cato and Orla

Contents

Illustrations

Illustrations appear between pages 58 and 59.

1. Delegation of Ford strikers led by Cllr Johnny Davis at the Labour Party conference, Blackpool, 1978. (Courtesy Cllr Johnny Davis.)

2. Public service workers demonstrating during the National Day of Action, London, 22 January 1979. (Ken Goff/Time & Life Images/Getty Images.)

3. Merseyside gravediggers and crematorium workers on strike, Liverpool, February 1979. (Source: *Workers News*, 6 February 1979; every effort was made to trace the copyright holder.)

4. Surrey shoppers at almost empty supermarket shelves during the road hauliers' strike, January 1979. (Ken Goff/Getty Images.)

5. 'Labour Still Isn't Working': Conservative Party poster, 1979 general election. (Conservative Party Archive Trust/Getty Images.)

6. Prime Minister James Callaghan leaves 10 Downing Street after 1979 election defeat. (Popperfoto/Getty Images.)

Acknowledgements

I am pleased to acknowledge that this book contains material copyright to Lady Thatcher; reprinted with her permission. I would like to thank Chris Collins, Margaret Thatcher Foundation, for his kind assistance. I am also most grateful to The National Archives at Kew for permission to use copyright material and to the following for permission to quote from material for which they hold the copyright, including their publications: Lords Bernard Donoughue, Roy Hattersley, Kenneth O. Morgan, David Owen, Geoffrey Goodman and Sir Robert Worcester. Every effort has been made to trace copyright holders and to avoid infringement of copyright. I apologise unreservedly to any copyright holders who have inadvertently been overlooked.

I have received expert and generous assistance from the staff of many libraries, archives and record offices: Bodleian Library; British Library; British Library of Political and Economic Science; Cambridge University Library; Julie Parry and Darren Treadwell at the Labour History Archive and Study Centre; Manchester Central Reference Library; Modern Records Centre, University of Warwick; The National Archives; The National Library of Scotland; The Working Class Movement Library. I am greatly indebted to Sir Robert Worcester and Kerry Colville at Ipsos MORI. My special thanks to Dr Allen Packwood and Andrew Riley and their colleagues at the Churchill Archives Centre, Cambridge, for help and hospitality over many years. Libraries and their staff in Australia who also receive my sincere appreciation for their help include: The Bob Hawke Prime Ministerial Library, Adelaide; Brisbane State Archives; The National Library of Australia, Canberra; The National Library of New South Wales, Sydney; and the Noel Butlin Trade Union Centre, Canberra. I am also indebted to Australian friends Professor Russell and Gwen Lansbury; Paul Monro; Professor Greg Patmore; Dr Mark Hearn; and also to Ralph Willis in Melbourne, for a transatlantic phone call, as well as a most enjoyable dinner in Melbourne, with Carol Willis, Prof. John and Wendy Langmore.

I am very grateful to the British Academy for awarding me a valuable research grant under their Small Grants Scheme. My thanks also to Dr Tara Martin for sending me a copy of her excellent thesis.

My research has benefited greatly from opportunities to present papers and talks at universities and learned societies, including the Faculty Research Seminar, Anglia Ruskin University, Business and Labour Historians Seminar, University of Sydney, Cambridge, Reading and West Yorkshire branches of the Historical Association. I was especially pleased to accept the kind invitation of the University of Huddersfield to present my inaugural professorial lecture at the University on the 'winter of discontent'. My thanks to Pro Vice Chancellor Professor Tim Thornton, Professor Martin Hewitt, Jayne Jefferies, Samantha Bridge, Philippa Morgan and Steve Shepherd.

I am also most grateful to Dr Jon Cruddas MP, James Brown, Margaret Mullane and Ben Grubb for their support and hospitality. Deepest thanks are also extended to Lord Professor Kenneth O. Morgan for his friendship, support and encouragement with this project. Learned colleagues have generously read and commented on the work in progress, notably Mark Dunton, Contemporary Specialist, The National Archives, who generously shared his unrivalled knowledge and insights with me. Also, Dr Janet Shepherd and Professor Chris Wrigley read and commented on the complete typescript in preparation and provided considerable valuable feedback. I owe them both an incalculable debt of gratitude. Any remaining errors and omissions are entirely my responsibility.

At Manchester University Press, I have been most fortunate in my Senior Commissioning Editor, Tony Mason, who has given me invaluable advice, guidance and constant encouragement throughout this project. I am extremely grateful to Ralph Footring, who handled the copy-editing with expertise and unfailing good humour. I am also most grateful to Denise Hayles, Beverley Harding and Dr Janet Shepherd for their expert secretarial and technical assistance.

I am most indebted to the University of Huddersfield and the Vice-Chancellor, Professor Bob Cryan, for awarding me a Visiting Professorship followed by a Professorship to continue my research interests in the highly stimulating environment of the School of Music, Humanities and Media. My special thanks to the Dean, Professor Mike Russ, and his successor, Professor Martin Hewitt and to my fellow historians Professors Barry Doyle, Keith Laybourn and Paul Ward; and Drs Sarah Bastow, Pat Cullum, Janette Martin and Andy Mycock in Politics. I am also most grateful to Julia Laybourn and Professor Keith Laybourn for their generous hospitality in Pudsey on my visits to the University of Huddersfield. Particular thanks to Professors Keith Laybourn and Paul Ward for their expert support.

I would like to thank the following for their support, help and hospitality with research visits in Australia and Britain: Kelly and Reg Chapple; Jenny and John Childs; Pat and Lee Hahn; Anne and Nick Lampe; Professor Russell and Gwen Lansbury; Sue Lusted; and Carol Probert. In addition, I also wish to thank Roy Hattersley, Cynthia Shepherd and the Rev. John Shepherd for their assistance with my work.

My special thanks to the many people who very kindly gave of their time and granted me invaluable interviews: Jeff Baker; Brendan Barber; Lord Joel Barnett; Tony Benn; Rodney Bickerstaffe; Frank Bland; Professor William A. Brown; Jim Clark; Michael Cockerell; Dr Jon Cruddas MP; Cllr Johnny Davis; Lord Bernard Donoughue; John Edmonds; Geoffrey Goodman; Lord Ted Graham; Roy Hattersley; Walter Harrison; Patricia Hewitt; Fred Jarvis; Lord Neil Kinnock; Sir Tim Lankester; Lord David Lea; Lord David Lipsey; John Mallinson; Lord Tom McNally; Lord Matthew Oakeshott; Lord David Owen; Lord Jim Prior; Lord Giles Radice; Lord William Rodgers; Sir Clive Rose; Lord Tom Sawyer; Robert Shepherd; Baroness Ann Taylor; Brenda Treadwell; Stephen Wade; Michael White; Lord Larry Whitty; Ralph Willis; Baroness Shirley Williams; Sir Robert Worcester.

My last debts are most important to me. I am especially grateful to my two daughters, Emma and Louise Shepherd, and their partners, Francis Mallinson and Caroline Blake, for their constant help and encouragement, and to Cato and Orla for making me smile. My appreciation also goes to other family members for their assistance and support: Bob and Sandra Shepherd; Dan Shepherd and Patrick Murphy; Sue and Colin Drummond; Debra, Stephen, Eleanor-May and Alastair Wade; Karen, Carrick and Findlay Livingstone; Jessica Livingstone, Dan, Mya and Stanley Woodhouse.

Finally, while this volume is dedicated with heartfelt thanks to members of my family, I would particularly like to acknowledge the constant help and advice of my wife, Dr Janet Shepherd. Without her unstinting support, this book would certainly not have seen the light of day.

John Shepherd
Dry Drayton
Cambridgeshire

Abbreviations

ALP	Australian Labour Party
APEX	Association of Professional, Executive, Clerical and Computer Staff
ASLEF	Associated Society of Locomotive Engineers and Firemen
AUEW	Amalgamated Union of Engineering Workers
BL	British Leyland
BP	British Petroleum
CBI	Confederation of British Industry
CCU	Civil Contingencies Unit
COHSE	Confederation of Health Service Employees
CPS	Centre for Policy Studies
CPSA	Civil and Public Services Association
CSU	Civil Services Union
EEC	European Economic Community
EY(P)	Ministerial Committee on Economic Strategy, Sub-Committee on Pay Negotiations
FBU	Fire Brigades Union
FDA	First Division Association
FT	*Financial Times*
GMBW	General Municipal Boiler Makers' Union
GMT	Greenwich Mean Time
GMWU	General Municipal Workers' Union
HGV	heavy goods vehicle
ICI	Imperial Chemical Industries
IMF	International Monetary Fund
IMWF	International Metal Workers' Federation
IPC	International Press Corporation
IPCS	Institute of Professional Civil Servants
IRA	Irish Republican Army
ITN	Independent Television News

MDP	measure of domestic progress
MORI	Market and Opinion Research International
MP	Member of Parliament
MRC	Modern Records Centre (University of Warwick)
NALGO	National Association of Local Government Officers
NASUWT	National Association of Schoolmasters Union of Women Teachers
NATO	North Atlantic Treaty Organization
NEC	National Executive Council
NHS	National Health Service
NJNC	National Joint Negotiating Committee (Ford)
NOP	National Opinion Poll
NUM	National Union of Mineworkers
NUPE	National Union of Public Employees
NUR	National Union of Railwaymen
NUT	National Union of Teachers
OPEC	Organization of the Petroleum Exporting Countries
PM	Prime Minister
PPB	party political broadcast
RHA	Road Haulage Association
RHWC	Road Haulage Wages Council
SALT	Strategic Arms Limitation Talks
SCPS	Society of Civil and Public Servants
SFPS	self-financing productivity scheme
SNP	Scottish National Party
TGWU	Transport and General Workers' Union
TNA	The National Archives
TSSA	Transport Salaried Staffs' Association
TUC	Trades Union Congress
TULRA	Trade Union and Labour Relations Act
UPW	Union of Post Office Workers
USDAW	Union of Shop, Distributive and Allied Workers
VJ	Victory over Japan

Chapter One

The 1970s: 'winters of discontent'

On 10 January 1979, Labour Prime Minister James Callaghan landed by VC10 at Heathrow airport on his return from an international summit on the Caribbean island of Guadeloupe, hosted by the French President Giscard d'Estaing, with US President Jimmy Carter and German Chancellor Helmut Schmidt. Unfortunately, to Callaghan's chagrin, some of the British press reported this high-level meeting on the second round of the US–Soviet Strategic Arms Limitation Talks (SALT II) as more of a foreign junket for the world leaders and their wives.

Callaghan returned from the warm shores of Guadeloupe and a short holiday in Barbados to one of the worst winters of post-war years, which seemed in tune with the industrial chaos of strikes, go-slows and work-to-rules in Britain, subsequently dubbed by the press the 'winter of discontent'.[1] Four national rail strikes made travel a nightmare for many people. Even within cities and towns, commuting was hazardous, with ungritted roads

---

1   The phrase 'winter of discontent' originally appeared in the opening couplet of William Shakespeare's *Richard III* (1594): 'Now is the winter of our discontent / Made glorious summer by this sun of York'. The eponymous role was mordantly performed by Sir Laurence Olivier in a 1955 British film. The modern coining of the term 'winter of discontent' is usually attributed to the editor of the *Sun*, Larry Lamb, who claimed: 'That incidentally (with apologies to Shakespeare) was the *Sun's* own label, though it was to be widely adopted'. Larry Lamb, *Sunrise: The Remarkable Rise and Rise of the Best-Selling Soar-Away* Sun (London: Papermac, 1989), p. 159. Yet, while the newspaper did not use the phrase until shortly before the 1979 general election (*Sun*, 30 April 1979), Alan Fisher, General Secretary of the National Union of Public Employees, had warned about a 'serious winter of discontent' over six months before (*Daily Telegraph*, 18 September 1978). David (later Lord) Lipsey, part of the Downing Street Policy Unit, had used the phrase in an official memorandum to the Prime Minister: 'But could we win an election after a *winter of discontent*...?' (emphasis added). David Lipsey to Prime Minister, 5 October 1978, The National Archives (henceforth TNA), PREM 16/1610. See also below, pp. 32–3. For other examples of the phrase that pre-date the actual 'winter of discontent', see Alwyn W. Turner, *Crisis? What Crisis? Britain in the 1970s* (London: Aurum Press, 2008), pp. 264–7; Andy Beckett, *When the Lights Went Out: What Really Happened to Britain in the Seventies* (London: Faber & Faber, 2009), p. 140.

during strikes by local authority workers. Even those too young to have lived through those months can often readily cite a familiar compilation of iconic media images and popular memories, such as the mountains of uncollected municipal rubbish in London's Leicester Square and elsewhere, union pickets at hospitals blocking entry to medical supplies and, probably above all, the refusal of the Merseyside gravediggers to bury the dead in Liverpool – with the rumoured possibility of interment at sea instead.[2]

The weather during the 'winter of discontent' was extremely cold and comparable to the severe climatic conditions experienced in Britain during the infamously harsh winters of 1947–48 and 1962–63. As weather presenters Ian McCaskill and Paul Hudson recalled, snow had fallen during November and early December 1978, followed by heavy rainfall in different parts of Britain. London had 'its wettest December since records began'. However, the main impact of the treacherous weather – with heavy snowfalls spreading from Scotland followed by more freezing weather – was felt in January and February 1979. At Westminster, MPs devoted parliamentary time to the appalling weather.[3] The succession of blizzards sweeping England formed a bleak backdrop to a series of escalating industrial disputes. The combination of unusual, almost arctic weather and industrial disorder in different parts of Britain, reported in graphic detail, particularly by the tabloid press, helped to ensure the 'winter of discontent' became etched in the national psyche.[4]

As the Prime Minister returned from his international summit in 1979, the temperature had dropped to −7°C at Heathrow and −17°C at Linton-on-Ouse in Yorkshire. The sun-tanned Callaghan's tetchy response to a reporter's question about 'mounting chaos' at a somewhat disorganised Heathrow conference with the British media was misreported by the press the next day with the classic banner headline 'Crisis? What crisis?'[5] It seemed to put in a nutshell an out-of-touch Prime Minister and a hapless government battling trade union power as the temperature of industrial relations in Britain soared.[6] At the airport, the Prime Minister actually said: 'I don't think other people in the world will share the view that there is mounting chaos'. However, Denis Healey later recalled that that infamous headline, 'Crisis? What crisis?', would become indelibly associated with

---

2 These iconic images, and the industrial conflict that produced them, are discussed in detail in the present volume, particularly in chapters 5 and 6.

3 *Parliamentary Debates* (House of Commons), fifth series, 19 February 1979, vol. 963, cols 28–40.

4 For the weather conditions, see Ian McCaskill and Paul Hudson, *Frozen in Time: The Years When Britain Shivered* (Ilkley: Great Northern, 2006), p. 140; John Kettley, *Weatherman* (Ilkley: Great Northern, 2009), pp. 82–3.

5 *Sun*, 11 January 1979, p. 1.

6 The *Sun* did print Callaghan's actual words on its front page, but in a much smaller typeface. The Heathrow press conference can be seen at 'Jim Callaghan press conference 1979' on YouTube. For a transcript, see 'Interview with the Prime Minister ... at Heathrow Airport ... 10 January 1979', TNA PREM 16/2050.

James Callaghan in British folklore, much as 'The pound in your pocket' became associated with his predecessor, Harold Wilson, at the time of the 1967 devaluation or Healey himself with his own 'Squeeze the rich until the pips squeak', in fact a misquote from a speech he made in Lincoln during the February 1974 general election.[7]

At Heathrow Callaghan was also questioned about whether he should have been abroad at a time of serious industrial strife. The 'winter of discontent' had started with a major nine-week strike in the Ford Motor Company in September 1978. This dispute became a catalyst for various forms of industrial strife in the subsequent months. January, February and March 1979 witnessed the height of the industrial disruption in Britain, including the national road haulage strike as the oil tanker drivers' dispute reached a conclusion. On 22 January 1.5 million public sector employees stopped work as part of a 'National Day of Action'. In many places, strikes by public service employees continued well after this date, involving local authority manual workers, health service auxiliary staff and civil servants.

In twentieth-century Britain, the 'winter of discontent' of 1978–79 witnessed a national outburst of strikes comparable with earlier years of industrial protest, in 1915–22 and 1972–74. In 1979 alone, over 29 million days were lost as a result of around 2,000 stoppages involving nearly 5 million workers. During 1978 there were 2,349 stoppages with 9.3 million working days lost, involving directly a total of 979,000 workers. During January–March 1979 – at the peak of the 'winter of discontent' – 5 million working days were lost. The major industrial stoppages involved 20,000 bakery workers (November–December 1978); 57,000 Ford workers (September–November 1978); 7,500 provincial journalists (December 1978–January 1979); 2,200 oil tanker drivers (December 1978–January 1979); 56,000 road haulage drivers (January 1979); 20,500 railway workers in four one-day strikes (January 1979); 1.5 million public service workers in local authorities and in the health service, in various disputes (January–March 1979); 3,000 water and sewage workers in January 1979; and about 2,500 social workers in social care services (August 1978).[8]

---

7 Denis Healey, *The Time of My Life* (London: Penguin, 1990), p. 463. The television impressionist Mike Yarwood said that Callaghan was a difficult politician to impersonate. 'There was not much to latch on to until the day he returned from abroad and pretended to know nothing of the chaos that had taken place in his absence.... After that I portrayed him as permanently believing everything in the garden was lovely.' Mike Yarwood, *Impressions of My Life* (London: Willow Books, 1986), p. 140. In 1974 Healey actually said 'squeeze property speculators until the pips squeak'. As shadow Chancellor in 1973 he had declared: 'there are going to be howls of anguish from 80,000 people who are rich enough to pay over 75 per cent on their last slice of income'. William Keegan, 'The old bruiser who remained the boy next door', *Observer*, 3 December 2006.
8 John Gennard, 'Chronicle. Industrial relations in the United Kingdom November 1978–March 1979', *British Journal of Industrial Relations*, vol. 22, no. 2, July 1984, pp. 268–79.

Crucially, this Shakespearian 'Winter's Tale' seriously undermined Labour's historic relationship with the trade union movement, out of which the party had been born. Within a matter of weeks, after arctic weather had gripped Britain, the minority Callaghan government lost a vote of confidence, on 28 March 1979, by a single vote (310–311). The May 1979 election returned Margaret Thatcher to Downing Street with a comfortable overall majority of 43 and paved the way for 18 years of unbroken Conservative rule.

Ever since then, the 'winter of discontent' of 1978–79, with its dramatic images of industrial conflict – particularly the public sector strikes in early 1979 – has symbolised the Callaghan government's chronic weakness in the face of all-powerful unions. Enduring popular myths were created and continue to be evoked by Conservative opponents and a hostile media. Yet the 1970s as a whole are often remembered for recurrent crises, poor economic performance and industrial unrest. These years followed a so-called post-war 'golden age' of increased prosperity, rising living standards and relative industrial quietism. Then, in dramatically changed circumstances of a world energy crisis, Labour returned to office after the February 1974 general election. Edward Heath's Conservative government of 1970–74 may be recalled for the imbroglio involving the highly controversial Industrial Relations Act 1971, the Industrial Relations Court and the 'Pentonville Five' imprisoned dockers, as well as five declarations of a state of emergency, the miners' strikes of 1972 and 1974, and the 1974 'three-day week'.[9] Faced with this legacy, the Wilson and Callaghan administrations – a minority government for most of its five years – could claim some credit for tackling Britain's economic and industrial problems. As Steven Fielding has argued, 'those few weeks that formed the "winter of discontent" were then *atypical*: despite what Labour's detractors claimed, rotting rubbish and cancelled burials did not define the [Labour] Party's period in office'.[10]

Over 30 years on, the 'winter of discontent' still resonates in people's imagination and can be debated with great passion on all sides. Interestingly, when the Modern Records Centre (MRC) at the University of Warwick officially reopened, after a major refurbishment, on 1 November 2011, the 1978–79 'winter of discontent' was chosen for a special discussion to celebrate the occasion.[11] The thirtieth anniversary of the 'winter of discontent'

---

9 William Brown, 'Industrial relations', in Michael Artis and David Cobham (eds), *Labour's Economic Policies 1974–79* (Manchester: Manchester University Press, 1991), pp. 213–16.
10 Steven Fielding, 'The 1974–79 governments and "New Labour"', in Anthony Seldon and Kevin Hickson (eds), *New Labour, Old Labour: The Wilson and Callaghan Governments, 1974–79* (London: Routledge, 2004), pp. 286–7 (emphasis added).
11 The MRC was officially re-opened by the Rt Hon. Tony Benn and Baroness Warwick, chair of the MRC Advisory Board. It was followed by a discussion on the 1978–79 'winter of discontent' and the possibility of an 'autumn of discontent' in 2011 between Tony Benn and Sir Richard Lambert, Chancellor of the University of Warwick and former Director-General of the Confederation of British Industry, which was chaired

was also marked by a public debate before a packed audience at the British Academy in London on 22 February 2009, with a panel discussion and invited contributions from the floor.[12]

Earlier, in 1987, politicians, trade union leaders, captains of industry and civil servants who had been directly involved at the storm centre of the 'winter of discontent' had gathered at a symposium organised by the Institute of Contemporary British History to mull over the key issues in the disintegration of Labour's social contract and the advent of the winter strife in 1978–79.[13]

By the summer of 2010, a global financial crisis, following the collapse of the Lehman Brothers Bank in New York on 15 September 2008, evoked comparisons to 1978–79 'crisis Britain'. In July 2010, a major three-day conference, 'Re-assessing the seventies', at the Centre for Contemporary British History of the Institute of Historical Research, featured a comprehensive programme of cultural, economic, social and political topics setting re-appraisals of the 'winter of discontent' in a broader context of late twentieth-century British history.[14]

In 1985 at Blackpool, in a direct reference to the 'winter of discontent', Margaret Thatcher, addressing the annual Conservative Party conference and the nation, asked: 'Do you remember the Labour Britain of 1979? It was a Britain in which union leaders held their members and our country to ransom ... the sick man of Europe.'[15] During the 1970s, the unions were often blamed by their opponents for contributing to the downfall of three administrations – the governments of Harold Wilson (1970), Edward Heath (1974) and Jim Callaghan (1979). However, not all agreed with this view of industrial relations in the 1970s. Gerald Kaufman, a minister in the Department of Employment in the Callaghan administration, believed the winter strikes in 1979 had a less damaging effect than the press portrayed, owing to 'the liaison built up between ministers in several departments and the leaders of the unions concerned'.[16]

---

by Rodney Bickerstaffe, former General Secretary of the National Union of Public Employees and Unison.

12 The main paper was presented by Professor Colin Hay. The panel of discussants, chaired by Peter Riddell, were Lords Kenneth Baker, David Lea and David Lipsey. See Colin Hay, 'Chronicles of a death foretold: the winter of discontent and construction of the crisis of British Keynesianism', *Parliamentary Affairs*, vol. 63, no. 3, July 2010, pp. 446–70.

13 Institute of Contemporary British History, 'Symposium: the winter of discontent', *Contemporary Review*, vol. 1, no. 3, autumn 1987, pp. 34–43.

14 Lawrence Black and Hugh Pemberton, 'Reassessing the seventies: the benighted decade', *British Academy Review*, issue 14, November 2009.

15 *Daily Telegraph*, 12 October 1985.

16 Gerald Kaufman, *How To Be a Minister* (London: Faber & Faber, second edition 1997), p. 118.

In particular, the 'winter of discontent' figured large in the Conservatives' 1979 election campaign. The myths and realities of the turbulent events continued to feature in subsequent Conservative election victories, in 1983, 1987 and 1992, as the electorate was reminded of the perils in store if Labour won at the polls. In early January 2012, The National Archives at Kew released under the 30-year rule the 1981 papers of the first Thatcher government. Interviewed on BBC News concerning what the newly available official records revealed about the Conservative government's handling of the 1981 Toxteth riots in Liverpool, Lord Heseltine quickly referred to the 'winter of discontent' during the Callaghan Labour government's period in office.[17]

The 'winter of discontent' represents a decisive turning point in late twentieth-century Britain that led to 'Thatcherism', as well as a landmark in the history of the British Labour Party and trade union movement. In 1997 Labour finally returned to office with Tony Blair as Prime Minister, who accepted the 1980s Thatcherite legislation on trade union reform. Under 'New Labour', the young party leader resolutely declared, there would be no return to the chaotic chapter of Labour's past in the 1970s.[18]

Yet, despite a considerable and expanding literature on the political and social history of late twentieth-century Britain, there is no full-length study of the 'winter of discontent' itself. In subsequent recollection, even mythology, the industrial strife of 1978–79 has often been a symbol of Britain's post-war economic decline and the dominance of over-powerful union barons in British political life.[19] There are a number of excellent works on the troubled industrial relations of 1978–79. Kenneth O. Morgan's magisterial biography of James Callaghan is undoubtedly essential in studying the 'winter of discontent', to be supplemented by his study of Michael Foot.[20] Edward Pearce has also produced a detailed biography of Denis Healey, which, in a total of 52 chapters, comprehensively covers the history of the British Labour Party, and which provides insights into the Callaghan–Healey alliance during the winter unrest of 1978–79.[21]

---

17 Author's knowledge.
18 John Shepherd, 'Labour wasn't working', *History Today*, vol. 59, no. 1, January 2009, pp. 43–9.
19 As has been argued, for example, by Lord Skidelsky and Bernard Donoughue, political adviser to James Callaghan. See Robert Skidelsky 'The worst of governments', in Anthony Seldon and Kevin Hickson (eds), *New Labour, Old Labour: The Wilson and Callaghan Governments, 1974–1979* (London: Routledge, 2004), pp. 316–20; Bernard Donoughue, *The Heat of the Kitchen: An Autobiography* (London: Politico's, 2003), ch. 15.
20 Kenneth O. Morgan, *Callaghan: A Life* (Oxford: Oxford University Press, 1997); *Michael Foot: A Life* (London: HarperCollins, 2007). See also Kenneth O. Morgan, 'James Callaghan, 1976–1979', in Vernon Bogdanor (ed.), *From New Jerusalem to New Labour: British Prime Ministers from Attlee to Blair* (Basingstoke: Palgrave Macmillan, 2010), pp. 123–43.
21 Edward Pearce, *Denis Healey: A Life In Our Times* (London: Little, Brown, 2002).

More nuanced perspectives can also be found than the negative verdicts on the minority Wilson and Callaghan governments, which were minority or mainly minority governments from 1974 to 1979, and on Labour's domestic and foreign policies after the financial crises represented by the sudden increase the oil price instigated by the Organization of the Petroleum Exporting Countries (OPEC) and the intervention from the International Monetary Fund (IMF).[22] In this respect, the period from December 1976 to the late autumn of 1978, before the 'winter of discontent', can be viewed as one of relative economic and social improvement, which has been well chronicled, for example, in the edited volumes on Labour's economic performance by Michael Artis and David Cobham, and by Richard Coopey and Nicholas Woodward.[23] In particular, Chris Wrigley's extensive writings on industrial relations and trade union history are essential for understanding the era of the 'winter of discontent'.[24] Robert Taylor's work on the history of the trade union movement generally and of the Trades Union Congress (TUC) in particular also provides an important commentary from an experienced observer of trade union politics over many years.[25] To this should be added another important collection of trade union essays, co-edited by John McIlroy, Nina Fishman and Alan Campbell, which has now been published in a second edition.[26] In a number of articles, Colin Hay

---

22 For informative accounts that shed valuable light on the precarious nature of the day-to-day life of minority government during the Wilson–Callaghan administrations, 1974–79, see Peter Rose, 'The Wilson–Callaghan government of 1974–79: by-elections (eventually) bring down a government', in Chris Cook and John Ramsden (eds), *By-elections in British Politics* (London: UCL Press, 1997), pp. 215–27; Philip Norton, 'Parliament', in Anthony Seldon and Kevin Hickson (eds), *New Labour, Old Labour: The Wilson and Callaghan Governments, 1974–1979* (London: Routledge, 2004), pp. 190–206; Joe Ashton, *Red Rose Blues: The Story of a Good Labour Man* (Basingstoke: Macmillan, 2000).

23 Michael Artis and David Cobham (eds), *Labour's Economic Policies 1974–1979* (Manchester: Manchester University Press, 1991); Richard Coopey and Nicholas Woodward (eds), *Britain in the 1970s: The Troubled Economy* (London: University College London Press, 1996). See also Robert Taylor, *The Trade Union Question in British Politics: Government and Unions Since 1945* (Oxford: Blackwell, 1993); and Jim Tomlinson, *Politics of Decline* (London: Longman, 2000). For a perceptive reassessment of the Wilson–Callaghan governments, 1974–79, see Kenneth O. Morgan, 'Was Britain dying?', in Anthony Seldon and Kevin Hickson (eds), *New Labour, Old Labour: The Wilson and Callaghan Governments, 1974–1979* (London: Routledge, 2004), pp. 303–7.

24 Chris Wrigley (ed.), *A History of British Industrial Relations 1939–1979: Industrial Relations in a Declining Economy* (Cheltenham: Edward Elgar, 1996); Chris Wrigley (ed.), *A History of British Industrial Relations: vol. 3, 1939–79* (Brighton: Harvester Press, 1996); Chris Wrigley, 'Trade unions, the government and the economy', in Terry Gourvish and Alan O'Day (eds), *Britain Since 1945* (Basingstoke: Macmillan, 1991), pp. 59–87; Chris Wrigley, 'Trade unions, strikes and the government', in Richard Coopey and Nicholas Woodward (eds), *Britain in the 1970s: The Troubled Economy* (London: University College London Press, 1996), pp. 273–92.

25 Taylor, *The Trade Union Question*; Robert Taylor, *The TUC: From the General Strike to New Unionism* (Basingstoke: Palgrave, 2000).

26 John McIlroy, Nina Fishman and Alan Campbell (eds), *The High Tide of British Trade Unionism: Trade Unions and Industrial Politics 1945–79* (Monmouth: Merlin Press, second

has put forward the thesis that the 'winter of discontent' was constructed by the right-wing media and by the New Right in the Conservative Party as a manufactured crisis that depicted a beleaguered state held to ransom by trade union power.[27]

The 'winter of discontent' has also been well chronicled in two valuable published diaries by Tony Benn, Energy Secretary in the Callaghan Cabinet, and Bernard Donoughue, head of the Policy Unit at Downing Street. Both were key participants at the centre of government. Most interestingly, the diarists provide differing political perspectives from the left and right of Labour politics, and with penetrating (sometimes acerbic) insights on the troubled times in the last months of the minority Callaghan administration.[28]

In the main, the 'winter of discontent' has had a largely bad press, with responsibility for the industrial chaos during September 1978 to March 1979 laid firmly at the door of the TUC and the trade union movement. In particular, this blame for the industrial disorder that beset the Labour government has been reinforced by the memoirs of different members of the Callaghan administration. Nearly ten years later, Old Labour's last Prime Minister still wrote about the 'winter of discontent' with a high degree of emotion. Jim Callaghan, 'the keeper of the cloth cap', observed: 'Even with the passage of time it is painful to write about some of the excesses that took place. One of the most notorious was the refusal of the Liverpool grave-diggers to bury the dead, accounts of which appalled the country'.[29] Dennis Howell, Minister of Sport at the time and, like Callaghan, a former trade unionist, castigated the unions: 'transport strikes by lorry drivers, local government strikes, strikes in hospital and, worst of all, strikes by grave-diggers.... Never has public opinion been so bitterly expressed against the unions.'[30] Subsequently, other members of the Callaghan Cabinet roundly condemned union militancy. Former Labour Foreign Secretary David Owen observed: 'Jim [Callaghan] was well aware that indiscipline and what I described as thuggery [of the strikers] were threatening the Government'.[31] As Minister of Transport, William Rodgers provided a detailed first-hand account of the 'winter of discontent' in connection with his handling of the bitter road haulage dispute, which, alongside the oil

---

edition 2007). This edition includes detailed responses to reviewers' critical comments and interpretations of the first edition.

27 Colin Hay, 'Narrating crisis: the discursive construction of the winter of discontent', *Sociology*, vol. 30, no. 2, 1996, pp. 253–77; Hay, 'Chronicles of a death foretold'.

28 Tony Benn, *Conflicts of Interest: Diaries 1977–80*, edited by Ruth Winstone (London: Arrow Books, 1991); Bernard Donoughue, *Downing Street Diary, Volume Two: With James Callaghan in No. 10* (London: Jonathan Cape, 2008).

29 James Callaghan, *Time and Chance* (London: Politico's, 2006, first published 1987), p. 537.

30 Denis Howell, *Made in Birmingham: The Memoirs of Denis Howell* (London: Queen Anne Press, 1990), p. 282.

31 David Owen, *Time to Declare* (Harmondsworth: Penguin, 1992), p. 408.

tanker drivers' dispute, brought the government closest to declaring a state of emergency in Britain.[32] Peter Shore, who was Secretary of State for the Environment, declared vehemently: 'Not only were these [trade union] pay claims massively and incontestably inflationary, industrial action was ruthlessly applied in total disregard of the interest of the public and of the effects on the community'.[33] A more recent example, from Shirley Williams, was written in similar vein: 'In winter all hell broke loose.... Worse still were the reports that the dead lay unburied in hospital morgues up and down the country. The strikes turned into some kind of frenzy, in which otherwise decent men and women outdid one another.'[34]

Greater emphasis is now given, though, to the specific causes of the 'winter of discontent', including the swingeing cuts in public expenditure that helped emasculate the social contract from its broader conception to a mechanism for stringent wage restraint. As former Cabinet minister Barbara Castle declared: 'It was not the unions that broke the Social Contract but the government, as it carried through the deflationary policy Denis Healey had convinced himself was necessary, with further spending cuts, cash limits and all the conventional measures to reduce demand'.[35]

Alternative interpretations have been advanced that challenge some widely held misconceptions that the industrial strife was the direct result of powerful trade union sectional interests pursuing excessive and inflationary wage demands. In a reappraisal of conventional views of British economic failure and industrial disorder in the 1970s, Nick Tiratsoo demonstrates that despite large strikes in mining, transport and car manufacturing, most industrial disputes lasted no more than three days. In fact, despite apocalyptic books such as *Is Britain Dying?*, 1970s Britain was no more strike-prone than Germany, France or Japan, and occupied a middling position in any international league table.[36] During the 'winter of discontent' the predicted shortages and lay-offs caused by industrial stoppages proved grossly

---

32 William Rodgers, 'Government under stress, Britain's winter of discontent', *Political Quarterly*, vol. 55, no. 2, 1984, pp. 171–9. Also see Chris Wrigley, 'The winter of discontent: the lorry drivers' strike, January 1979', in Andrew Charlesworth, David Gilbert, Adrian Randall, Humphrey Southall and Chris Wrigley, *An Atlas of Industrial Protest in Britain 1750–1990* (Basingstoke: Macmillan, 1996), pp. 210–16.

33 Peter Shore, *Leading the Left* (London: Weidenfeld & Nicolson, 1993), p. 118.

34 Shirley Williams, *Climbing the Bookshelves: The Autobiography* (London: Virago, 2009), p. 249.

35 Barbara Castle, *Fighting All The Way* (London: Macmillan, 1993), p. 498. On forming his administration in 1976, Callaghan did not offer a post to Barbara Castle. For a powerful account of working-class consciousness and working-class solidarity in the early 1970s, see Ralph Darlington and Dave Lyddon, *Glorious Summer: Class Struggle in Britain 1972* (London: Bookmarks, 2001).

36 Isaac Kramnick (ed.), *Is Britain Dying? Perspectives on the Current Crisis* (Ithaca, NY: Cornell University Library, 1979). Similar contemporary titles that reflect the mood of 'crisis Britain' in the 1970s include: Robert Bacon and Walter Ellis, *Britain's Economic Problem: Too Few Producers* (London: Macmillan, 1976); Tam Dalyell, *Devolution: The End of Britain?* (London: Cape, 1977).

exaggerated. In particular, in a cautious start to her leadership of the Conservative Party from 1975, Thatcher had no blueprint to solve contemporary British economic and industrial relations problems.[37]

In similar vein, Steve Ludlam in a series of works has given specific attention to key factors that underpinned the breakdown of the social contract and the advent of the 'winter of discontent': falling incomes under the Callaghan government's stringent pay policy, the impact of real public expenditure cuts, as well as sectoral divisions between the public sector unions and major general unions that undermined the role of the TUC and that contributed to the breakdown of the social contract.[38]

In addition, Tara Martin's pioneering research, including interviews with key rank-and-file activists, has revealed the significant role of women trade unionists, particularly in the National Union of Public Employees (NUPE), in their participation in the industrial unrest. Her study demonstrates that their experiences provided an important 'rite of passage' and their activism was a valuable contribution to the development of trade union and Labour politics during and after the 'winter of discontent'.[39]

In 1985 Philip Whitehead's *The Writing on the Wall* provided an illuminating record of the key episodes of the 1970s in the UK, with the different perspectives of Scotland, Wales and Northern Ireland as well as the political events of England and Westminster.[40] Ever since 1979, the 'winter of discontent' has become emblematic for the final days of the Callaghan government and the wider picture of 'crisis Britain' in the 1970s, a country in economic decline. In the early 1979 the strikes by different groups of public sector workers were highlighted, particularly in the tabloid press, for the suffering caused to the old, the sick and the vulnerable in local communities. In this respect, in an extensively reported attack, the Archbishop of Canterbury, Dr Donald Coggan, roundly condemned the strikers for their callous attitude.[41]

---

37 Nick Tiratsoo, '"You've never had it so bad"? Britain in the 1970s', in Nick Tiratsoo (ed.), *From Blitz to Blair: A New History of Britain Since 1939* (London: Phoenix, 1997), pp. 163–90.

38 Steve Ludlam, '"Old" Labour and the "winter of discontent"', *Politics Review*, vol. 9, no. 2, 2000, pp. 30–3; 'Too much pluralism, not enough socialism: interpreting the unions–party link', in John Callaghan, Steve Fielding and Steve Ludlam (eds), *Interpreting the Labour Party: Approaches to Labour, Politics and History* (Manchester: Manchester University Press, 2003), pp. 150–65; 'Labourism and the disintegration of the post-war consensus: disunited trade union economic policy responses to public expenditure, 1974–1979', PhD thesis, University of Sheffield, 1991.

39 Tara Martin, 'The beginning of Labor's end? Britain's "winter of discontent" and working-class women's activism', *International Labor and Working-Class History*, no. 75, spring 2009, pp. 49–67; Tara Martin, '"End of an era?" Class politics, memory and Britain's winter of discontent', PhD thesis, University of Manchester, 2008.

40 Philip Whitehead, *The Writing on the Wall: Britain in the Seventies* (London: Michael Joseph, 1985).

41 *Catholic Herald*, 25 January 1980. For an alternative and more sympathetic Christian viewpoint on issues raised by the 'winter of discontent', see General Synod Board for

Lord Donoughue viewed the crisis of the 'winter of discontent' of 1978–79 from the centre of government at Downing Street and noted the Prime Minister's pivotal role. In observing the break-up of the social contract as a result of trade union militancy, he commented:

> It was James Callaghan who took the brunt of that attack.... Having built his political career with the trade union movement he was psychologically unable to break the link and lead the government and country against the old trade union allies. He stood paralysed while his counter-inflation strategy collapsed.[42]

Today, the label 'winter of discontent' evokes memories of a minority centre-left administration in great difficulties, facing rising oil prices and energy costs, soaring inflation and public sector strikes against the community; these difficulties sealed the downfall of the Callaghan government in 1979.

What were, in fact, the various circumstances that led to the breakdown of Labour's social contract with the unions, the 'winter of discontent' and defeat in the 1979 election? In 1973–74, OPEC had quadrupled crude-oil prices, in retaliation for Western support for the Israel in the Yom Kippur War. The result was a global crisis that shook the Western industrial economies, led to unparalleled worldwide inflation and brought to an end the 'golden years' of the post-war boom (1950–73) based on full employment.[43] In Britain a new term was coined – 'stagflation' – to describe the dual problems (not normally associated) of increased unemployment and soaring inflation; the latter, by the summer of 1975, was to peak at 27 per cent.

Harold Wilson had become Prime Minister (for the third time) at the head of a minority government with a radical manifesto of social and economic transformation.[44] At the October 1974 election, Labour secured only a wafer-thin overall majority, of three over all other parties. In April 1976, James Callaghan, who had held all three major offices of state – Chancellor of the Exchequer, Home Secretary and Foreign Secretary – won the Labour leadership contest and became Prime Minister following Wilson's surprise

---

Social Responsibility, *Winters of Discontent: Industrial Conflict. A Christian Perspective* (London: CIO Publishing, n.d. but 1981).

42 Bernard Donoughue 'The conduct of economic policy 1974–79', in Anthony King (ed.), *The British Prime Minister* (Basingstoke: Macmillan, 1985), pp. 70–1.

43 The oil price hike had been the latest shock to world economies following the strategy of the Johnson administration in the United States of budget deficits and associated monetary policy to fund the Vietnam War in the late 1960s and the breakdown of the Bretton Woods system of fixed exchange rates. See Coopey and Woodward, *Britain in the 1970s*, pp. 3–4.

44 The Labour manifesto included a promise to work towards 'a fundamental and irreversible shift in favour of working people and their families'. Bo Sarlvik and Ivor Crewe, *Decade of Dealignment: The Conservative Victory of 1979 and Electoral Trends in the 1970s* (Cambridge: Cambridge University Press, 1983), pp. 7–8.

resignation in March 1976.[45] Remarkably, the Wilson–Callaghan Labour governments of 1974–79 were to survive for virtually two parliaments without an overall majority (apart for a few months).[46]

During this time, the social contract became the major plank in Labour's alliance with the unions and the cornerstone of its counter-inflation strategy. In the aftermath of Labour's election defeat in 1970, it represented a rebuilding of the Labour–union relations following strong widespread opposition in the trade union and labour movement to Barbara Castle's White Paper *In Place of Strife* (1969), which included changes in union law to counter unofficial strikes.[47] Callaghan had been a leading opponent of the White Paper, which was eventually dropped after the TUC gave its famous 'solemn and binding agreement' about intervention in 'serious unconstitutional stoppages'.[48] At the 1971 Labour Party conference Jack Jones, who had been elected General Secretary of the Transport and General Workers' Union (TGWU) in 1969, had called for a new partnership between the political and industrial wings of the labour movement, which resulted in the establishment of the Labour and Trade Union Liaison Committee in January 1972. Robert Taylor has written: 'By the winter of 1975–76, it was to the Liaison Committee that the Cabinet looked for help and guidance rather than to the Left-dominated NEC which went into relative eclipse'.[49] This pact, dubbed the 'social contract', outlined a future Labour government's programme on industrial relations – mostly enacted in a raft of new labour legislation from 1974 to 1976 – proposals for individual democracy, a wide range of important economic measures and increased expenditure on social policy.

---

45 For a recent informative account of Callaghan's career up to his entry into 10 Downing Street, which draws on the knowledge of the splendid John Cole, *Guardian* and *Observer* journalist and BBC political correspondent, see Paul J. Deveney, *Callaghan's Journey to Downing Street* (Basingstoke: Palgrave Macmillan, 2010). See also Morgan, *Callaghan*; John Cole, *As It Seemed To Me: Political Memoirs* (London: Weidenfeld & Nicolson, 1995).

46 James Graham's inspired and well staged 2013 play at the National Theatre, *This House*, is based on the history of the 1974–79 parliaments, particularly from the perspectives of the Labour and Conservative whips. It captures the turbulent politics and the fascinating personalities at Westminster in the 1970s.

47 *In Place of Strife* followed the report of the Donovan Commission on Trade Unions and Employers' Associations (1968), which recommended that the role of law in industrial relations be very limited. Proposals to restrict the right to strike, 'cooling-off' periods, a ban on closed shops and pre-strike ballots were rejected. For an excellent analysis, see Taylor, *The Trade Union Question*, pp. 151–7. Interview: John Edmonds, Victoria, London, 17 November 2010. Interview: Lord Giles Radice, House of Lords, 26 January 2011.

48 Answer to private notice question by Lord Shackleton (Lord Privy Seal), *Parliamentary Debates* (House of Lords), 19 June 1969, vol. 302, cols 1107–14.

49 Jack Jones, *Union Man: The Autobiography of Jack Jones* (Abersychan: Warren & Bell, 2008), pp. 237–8. Robert Taylor, *Labour and the Social Contract*, Fabian Tract no. 458 (London: Fabian Society, 1978), pp. 2–3.

Labour's critics claimed the TUC side of the bargain on wages policy was less clear. As Chief Secretary to the Treasury, Joel Barnett summed up the arrangement of working closely with the TUC:

> we went much further in the way we co-operated under the terms of the quaintly titled Social Contract, supposedly enshrining a new relationship between government and unions. To my mind, the only give and take in the contract was that the Government gave and the unions took.[50]

Yet Philip Whitehead recalled that 'for their part the unions not only contributed to the funding of the Labour Party, but their leaders acquiesced in a second, and nodded at a third, period of pay restraint'.[51] It was widely acknowledged that the success of Labour's social contract was mainly attributable to Jack Jones, General Secretary of the TGWU, who worked closely with Len Murray, General Secretary of the TUC.[52] After the inflationary wages bonanza of 1974–75 that threatened possible hyperinflation and even the downfall of the Labour government, 'Emperor Jones' (as he had been called), the main advocate of shop-floor collective bargaining, was influential in persuading the TUC to agree a voluntary policy of a flat-rate increase in wages of £6 per week for the next 12 months in phase 1 of the social contract, in the national interest.[53]

Phases 1, 2 and 3 helped to reduce the unparalleled inflation rate from 28 per cent in late 1974 to 7.8 per cent in June 1978.[54] By this point, the wider social and economic measures promised by the social contract had largely been abandoned, leaving only stringent wage control as the main political issue. There was therefore a sign of storms ahead when the highly respected and popular Jones was shouted down at the 1977 TGWU biennial conference on the Isle of Man as he endeavoured to secure a further year's support for the government's pay policy rather than a return to free collective bargaining. There were two portents of what was to come in the 'winter of discontent'. First, from 1976 to 1978, the Grunwick strike about union recognition took place in north-west London at the Grunwick Film Processing Laboratories. The strikers were mainly immigrant East African

50 Joel Barnett, *Inside the Treasury* (London: Andre Deutsch, 1982), p. 4.
51 Whitehead, *The Writing on the Wall*, p. 257.
52 For a recent detailed account of the social contract, see Robert Taylor, 'The rise and fall of the social contract', in Anthony Seldon and Kevin Hickson (eds), *New Labour, Old Labour: the Wilson and Callaghan Governments, 1974–1979* (London: Routledge, 2004), pp. 70–103.
53 The TUC General Council voted 19–13 for the phase 1 £6 flat-rate per week increase with no increases for those earning over £8,500 p.a. except increments. This was endorsed at the 1975 TUC congress and Labour Party conference by substantial majorities.
54 After a complicated negotiation, phase 2 (1976–77) resulted in a 5 per cent limit (minimum increase of £2 per week and a maximum rise of £4 per week). Phase 3 (1977–78) limited wage increases to £10 per week within the 12-month period, though some settlements (including at British Oxygen, Ford and ICI and for oil tanker drivers) exceeded this figure. Interview: John Edmonds, Victoria, London, 17 November 2010.

women who worked long hours for low pay. At its peak, the dispute, which attracted national media attention, involved thousands of trade unionists, often in violent conflict with the police. On 19 May 1977 three Labour ministers (sponsored by the APEX union) – Shirley Williams, Denis Howell and Fred Mulley – had joined the picket line. The Scarman inquiry report upheld the strikers' case, only to be rejected by the employer, George Ward. The Grunwick dispute had significant implications for British industrial relations.[55] And secondly, there was the first official national strike by the Fire Brigades Union (FBU), from 14 November 1977 to 16 January 1978. Callaghan took a hard line by using troops equipped with 'Green Goddesses' (military substitute fire engines) to break the strike.[56] At the start of a bitter dispute in which the FBU challenged the pay policy of its employer, the *Daily Express* foresaw a future 'winter of discontent' in Britain.[57]

In 1978 Professor Eric Hobsbawm gave the annual Marx Memorial Lecture on 'The Forward March of Labour Halted?', surveying the British labour movement over the previous 100 years. During a crisis for Labour, it opened a major debate on the left in the 'winter of discontent' and beyond. His analysis included the growth of sectionalism in the 1970s, with workers pursuing their 'own economic interest irrespective of the rest', which could inconvenience the public as well as employers and weaken class solidarity.[58]

By the late 1970s British trade unionism held a previously unparalleled position in British political and industrial life. At a time of far-reaching structural and occupational changes in the British economy, union membership, which stood at 10 million in 1964, peaked in 1979 at nearly 13.3 million, as unions represented a majority of British workers for the first time. Trade unionism had lost its 'cloth cap' image. Despite the contraction of traditional industries, such as coal, textiles, agriculture and railways, the 'density' of union membership increased. During these years, the decline in Britain's manufacturing base went hand in hand with the expansion in service employment. Forty per cent of British trade unionists were white-collar staff. A key factor in the 1970s was the rise of the new public sector unions, including the National Association of Local Government Officers (NALGO), NUPE under the campaigning leadership of Alan Fisher, the Confederation of Health Service Employees (COHSE) and the

---

55 For two opposing accounts, see Jack Dromey and Graham Taylor, *Grunwick: The Workers Story* (London: Lawrence & Wishart, 1978); George Ward, *Fort Grunwick* (London: Maurice Temple Smith, 1977).

56 The FBU claim was for an immediate 30 per cent award and was settled within the pay policy, though firemen's pay was linked in future to that of skilled manual workers. Victor Bailey, *Forged in Fire: The History of the Fire Brigades Union* (London: Lawrence & Wishart, 1992), ch. 8.

57 *Daily Express*, 10 November 1977, cited in Dominic Sandbrook, *Seasons in the Sun: The Battle for Britain, 1974–1979* (London: Allen Lane, 2012), p. 662.

58 Martin Jacques and Francis Mulhern (eds), *The Forward March of Labour Halted?* (London: Verso, in association with Marxism Today, 1981).

main teaching unions, the National Association of Schoolmasters Union of Women Teachers (NASUWT) and the National Union of Teachers (NUT). In particular, increasing numbers of women, black and Asian workers joined trade unions, which altered the gender and ethnic composition of their membership. By 1979, for example, women formed nearly a third of trade unionists, compared with a quarter of the membership in 1970. Union membership became sought after as a protection against taxation, inflation and unemployment.

In 1976, owing to a major sterling crisis, the Callaghan government had been forced to negotiate a £2.3 billion loan from the IMF in Washington, DC, to defend the British pound. The IMF's terms demanded extensive cuts in government public expenditure, especially in health, housing and education.[59] In his first address as Prime Minister to the 1976 Labour Party conference, Callaghan famously warned his audience and the nation:

> We used to think you could spend your way out of a recession and increase employment by cutting taxes and boosting government spending. I tell you in all candour that option no longer exists and that in so far as it ever did exist, it only worked by injecting a bigger dose of inflation into the system.[60]

The immediate origins of the 'winter of discontent' can be located in the breakdown of Labour's social contract with the unions. In a New Year 1978 radio interview, Callaghan's objective of a fourth round of wage restraint with a 5 per cent pay norm unexpectedly 'popped out' (as he later put it). This figure had not been discussed with the TUC, but it became enshrined in the government's White Paper *Winning the Battle Against Inflation*, published in July 1978. This proposed a significant tightening of the social contract (in reality, no more than wage restraint when inflation, at around 8–9 per cent, was well above the government's 5 per cent pay norm) but was roundly opposed by the majority of the unions, as we shall see, at the annual TUC congress in Brighton in September 1978 and was overwhelmingly rejected at the Labour Party annual conference at Brighton a few weeks later. At the same time, the Prime Minister's astonishing decision to defer the general election, which had been widely anticipated to be held

---

59 On the IMF crisis, see Kathleen Burk and Alec Cairncross, *Goodbye, Great Britain: The 1976 IMF Crisis* (New Haven, CT: Yale University Press, 1992); Morgan, *Callaghan*, pp. 492, 495, 501, 545–7.

60 *Report of the 75th Annual Conference of the Labour Party*, Blackpool, 27 September–1 October 1976, p. 188. This part of Callaghan's speech was written by his son-in-law, the economist Peter Jay, who became British ambassador to the United States. It is debateable whether Callaghan was rejecting Keynesian outright on the road to monetarism, was really a monetarist or whether his address was rhetoric for tougher economic times ahead. For an excellent discussion of Labour's public spending cuts *before* the 1976 IMF crisis, see Steve Ludlam, 'The gnomes of Washington: four myths of the 1976 IMF crisis', *Political Studies*, vol. 40, 1992, pp. 713–27. Interview: Lord Roy Hattersley, Victoria, London, 25 June 2009.

on 5 October 1978, meant another parliamentary term during the winter, with the government defending a rigid and highly unpopular pay policy.[61]

This study examines the causes, character and impact of the 'winter of discontent' in British politics, particularly the strikes of 1978–79 and the role of the government in managing industrial relations. The following chapters also examine how the media reported the industrial strife, the significance of the 'winter of discontent' in the history of the Conservative Party and its impact on the 1979 general election. Particular attention is given in the following chapters to a number of key questions, including:

- What were the main origins of the 'winter of discontent' and could it have been avoided?
- Why did James Callaghan defer the widely anticipated general election in 1978 at a time of improving economic prospects?
- What were the consequences of his decision?
- Why did the social contact between government and unions break down in 1978?
- What were the motivations of workers in the different disputes?
- To what extent did the 'winter of discontent' demonstrate trade union power or weakness?
- How far does the 'winter of discontent' provide an emblematic image of 'Crisis Britain' in the 1970s?
- Was there a paralysis in government in January 1979?
- Why was no state of emergency declared?
- To what extent was the 'winter of discontent' created by the agenda of the media?
- Why does the 'winter of discontent' continue to resonate in British politics?

Currently, the cultural, economic, social and political history of the 1970s is being subjected to increasingly detailed scrutiny by historians and social scientists.[62] From September 1978 to March 1979, the Callaghan government appeared to be swept by a wave of strikes, go-slows and industrial stoppages. The 'winter of discontent' has now become coded shorthand for poor economic performance, over-mighty union barons, industrial anarchy and an ailing Labour administration that, according to its political opponents, made Britain 'the sick man of Europe'.

---

61 For instance the *Daily Mirror*, on 26 August 1978 (p. 1), after being briefed by Tom McNally, Callaghan's chief political adviser, had earmarked the date of the general election as 5 October 1978. Interview: Lord Tom McNally, House of Lords, 23 June 2007.
62 For a recent study, see Lawrence Black, Hugh Pemberton and Pat Thane, *Reassessing 1970s Britain* (Manchester: Manchester University Press, 2013).

Yet there is an alternative to the traditional view of the 1970s as years of political crisis, industrial discord and inevitable decline. In 2004 the think-tank New Economic Foundation published the innovatory 'measure of domestic progress' (MDP), by which 1976, the year of the IMF crisis, was proclaimed to be the best time for Britons since 1950.[63] Similarly, a more nuanced view of the British 'winter of discontent' is possible than often in persists in current folklore or popular representations.

---

63 The MDP used different criteria (notably crime, family stability, pollution and inequalities in income) from conventional economic indicators. Tim Jackson, *Chasing Progress: Beyond Measuring Economic Growth* (London: New Economic Foundation, 2004).

Chapter Two

Election deferred and the collapse of the social contract

On 7 September 1978, James Callaghan made a famous television broadcast to the nation: 'As you know, during the last few weeks speculation has been building up about the possibility of a General Election this autumn', he declared in his avuncular style. The Prime Minister then referred to the end of the Lib–Lab pact that had made 'the [minority] Government more vulnerable to defeats in the House of Commons' and also outlined the improved economic position of Britain – 'some blue sky over Britain today'. Yet his brief survey of the state of the nation concluded unexpectedly: 'So I shall not be calling for a General Election at this time. Instead I ask every one of you to carry on with the task of consolidating the improvement now taking place in our country's position. Let's see it through together.'[1]

A general election in the autumn 1978 had been widely anticipated by politicians at Westminster, trade union leaders, members of the Labour Party and their Conservative opponents, as well as the general public in Britain. While fixing the timing of the next general election has been the right of the Prime Minister until very recent times, in 1978 journalists naturally contemplated the actual date, with the Labour-supporting *Daily Mirror* naming Thursday 5 October in an exclusive.[2] Denis Healey's biographer, Edward Pearce, who was a *Daily Express* leader-writer in 1978, recalled he had already written his copy, with the 'standard comments of a Conservative middle-market paper on the next month's certain general election', before joining colleagues in their editor's office to watch the

---

1 For the full text, see 'A ministerial broadcast by the Prime Minister, the Rt. Hon. James Callaghan, M.P.', 7 September 1978, The National Archive (henceforth TNA) PREM 16/1621. Callaghan also included the complete broadcast in his memoirs: James Callaghan, *Time and Chance* (London: Politico's, 2006), pp. 517–18.
2 In 2010 the Conservative-led coalition government changed to a system of fixed parliaments in Britain with the next general election set for May 2015.

Prime Minister's broadcast. Pearce rapidly 'fled to the typewriter to turn out 550 quite different words at remarkable speed'.[3]

Probably those most stunned by Callaghan's bolt from the blue were his own political advisers, who had been kept completely in the dark at Westminster about the Prime Minister's decision to defer the election. Bernard Donoughue recalled that: 'we all went along to the Press Office [at Downing Street] to watch the television. It was a superb performance by the P.M. Most of the watchers were astonished by the news of no election. [Roger] Carroll and [David] Lipsey were totally speechless. Tom McNally, Callaghan's Chief Political Advisor, said simply: "Either he is a great political genius or he has just missed the boat"'.[4]

Other civil servants had assembled around the television in the Private Office – all the secretaries and Sir John Hunt, the Cabinet Secretary, who came through from the Cabinet Office to watch. Donoughue noted that he 'showed no sign of knowing what the decision was when I talked to him on the way in'.[5] Earlier in the day, the Prime Minister had told his Cabinet that he had written to the Queen to say that he did not propose to ask Her Majesty for a dissolution of parliament that autumn. Roy Hattersley recalled Callaghan's offer to discuss the matter with the Cabinet, although the Prime Minister 'doubted if we would persuade him to send a second message to the Queen, telling her that he had changed his mind'.[6] Tony Benn noted in his diary that Callaghan's decision (made on 17 August) was a *fait accompli*: 'I was most surprised and indeed angry that the Cabinet had not discussed a decision of this magnitude'.[7]

This chapter analyses why Callaghan deferred the general election in the autumn of 1978, which has been the subject of considerable debate, and considers evidence revealed in recently released Cabinet papers. Callaghan's decision is also examined to assess how far a lost opportunity contributed to the collapse of the Labour government's social contract with the unions and the advent of the 'winter of discontent' of 1978–79.

Callaghan spent 4–28 August 1978 at his Upper Clayhill Farm at Ringmer in the Sussex Weald, which he had purchased on becoming Home Secretary. Normally, it served as a retreat from metropolitan politics

---

3   Edward Pearce, *Denis Healey: A Life in Our Times* (London: Little, Brown, 2002), p. 511.
4   Bernard Donoughue, *Downing Street Diary, Volume Two: With James Callaghan in No. 10* (London: Jonathan Cape, 2008), p. 359.
5   *Ibid.*
6   Roy Hattersley, *Who Goes Home? Scenes from a Political Life* (London: Little, Brown, 1995), p. 207. Interview: Lord Roy Hattersley, Victoria, London, 25 June 2009. The Cabinet conclusions do not mention Callaghan's decision (probably because it was deemed a Labour Party matter). The following week there is an indirect reference: 'Now that he [the Prime Minister] had announced that there would be another session of the present Parliament...'. TNA CAB 128/64, Cabinet Conclusions, 7 and 14 September 1979.
7   Tony Benn, *Conflicts of Interest: Diaries 1977–80*, edited by Ruth Winstone (London: Arrow Books, 1991), p. 334 (diary entry: Thursday 7 September 1978).

to a different way of life in the countryside.[8] On this occasion, it became the location for one of the most crucial decisions for the Callaghan government of 1976–79. Hattersley observed that the members of the Cabinet publicly and privately were content to leave the Prime Minister to it. He noted: 'his judgement was certainly better than ours'.[9]

Deciding the date of the next election was the prerogative of the Prime Minister and a key political judgement. Kenneth O. Morgan, who has provided a most comprehensive account of the Prime Minister's deliberations while at his Sussex farm in August, observed: 'Callaghan, generally admired as an almost legendary reader of political entrails, was thought by most Labour MPs and party voters to be likely to get it right'.[10] As his biographer acknowledged, the highly experienced parliamentarian Callaghan remembered from personal experience, for example, that Clement Attlee had got his timing wrong on the February 1950 and the October 1951 elections, which cost the post-war Labour government a further full term in parliament.[11]

After election strategy meetings in late July with David Steel (at the Liberal Party leader's request), Michael Foot, Michael Cocks, the chief whip (who both favoured soldiering on), various government ministers and Callaghan's principal private secretary, Sir Kenneth Stowe, the Prime Minister retired to Sussex in an upbeat mood convinced he could rely on trade union backing for the government's 5 per cent pay policy. Progress had also been made on the devolution front, which meant continued support for the minority Labour government from Plaid Cymru and Scottish National Party MPs at Westminster. At the same time, the main economic indicators, such as a balance-of-payments surplus, a falling rate of inflation, an increase in real disposal income and a levelling of unemployment, had been moving in the government's favour – all pointing to an autumn general election. This provided a suitable 'window', particularly as there were no overseas crises likely on the political horizon, apart from Rhodesia.[12]

---

8 Callaghan, *Time and Chance*, pp. 229–30.
9 Roy Hattersley recalled: 'Jim sent the Cabinet off on its summer holidays with the announcement that he did not wish colleagues to return with advice about … the election … I observed voluntary restraint for almost two months … [and] campaigned for seven days in North Lancashire … [including in the] marginal seats … returned absolutely convinced that we should hold an autumn election…. So I wrote a letter … "I know you asked us not to give you our opinions on the best election date. Had you done so … [my advice would be] 'go now'".' Hattersley, *Who Goes Home?*, pp. 206–7. Interview: Hattersley. For Callaghan later sounding out his ministers (but before his public announcement to defer the election), see note 19 on p. 22.
10 Kenneth O. Morgan, *Callaghan: A Life* (Oxford: Oxford University Press, 1997), p. 626.
11 For more on this point, see Kenneth O. Morgan, *Labour in Power 1945–51* (Oxford: Oxford University Press, 1984), pp. 402–4; Martin Pugh, *Speak for Britain: A New History of the Labour Party* (London: Bodley Head, 2010), pp. 289–93.
12 Morgan, *Callaghan*, pp. 634–8.

According to his biographer, Callaghan took with him 'not the historical biographies or Trollope novels beloved of earlier prime ministers' for summer reading, but copies of the *Parliamentary Companion*, the *Times Guide to the House of Commons*, David Butler's Nuffield election surveys and 'sheaves of materials' from Robert Worcester's Market and Opinion Research International (MORI) reports on voting opinion and the possible outcome of the next election (with a specific focus on English marginal constituencies).[13]

While originally open minded about his decision, Callaghan studied the polling data sent by Bernard Donoughue, which indicated that Labour had pulled back some of the Tory lead in 1978 and that the government's incomes policy was popular with the electorate – 66 per cent supporting it, as opposed to 24 per cent against. However, noticing the regional variations – such as the West Midland marginal seats – Callaghan became increasingly doubtful about the prospects for a Labour victory, let alone an overall majority. Most seriously, Robert Worcester's forthcoming MORI poll had indicated a 2 per cent Tory lead.[14] As Callaghan put it, by his 'own amateur calculations', constituency by constituency, he calculated a likely general election result of Labour 303, Conservatives 304. It would have meant a loss of a few Labour seats, gains for the Tories and a hung parliament.

Callaghan also carried out wider soundings about the possibility of a Labour victory if he called the election in the autumn. As he noted: 'I began to receive advice and opinions from many quarters'. His deputy, Michael Foot, was definitely against an autumn 1978 election. The chief whip, Michael Cocks, revealed that the whips had met privately and were also opposed to the autumn date, by a clear margin of eight to three, with a few uncertain.[15] The Prime Minister noted that a number of his Labour colleagues were in favour of going to the country, 'although their letters conveyed very little conviction that we could win outright'.[16]

Other factors that suggested delaying included a new electoral register – considered favourable to Labour – which would be in force if the election was held in spring 1979 or later. Also, the benefits of North Sea oil would increase from 1979 onwards.[17] In an interview in the *Daily Mirror*, Callaghan revealed that he had made his decision at his farm on 17 August not to call a general election.[18] After this date, he did continue to consult Cabinet

---

13 *Ibid.*, pp. 636–7.
14 Interview: Sir Robert Worcester, Ipsos MORI Head Office, Borough Road, London, 27 June 2011.
15 Michael Cocks to James Callaghan, 1 August 1978, TNA PREM 16/1621.
16 Callaghan does not name his colleagues at this point. Callaghan, *Time and Chance*, pp. 513–15.
17 *Ibid.*, pp. 638–9, also p. 516.
18 *Daily Mirror*, 8 September 1978.

colleagues, although probably just to confirm the vital decision he had already taken by himself.[19]

The recent availability of Cabinet papers for 1978 and 1979 reveals that Callaghan asked the Cabinet Secretary, Sir John Hunt, for 'a note on the main decisions which could be foreseen over the period October [1978] to April [1979] if the present Parliament should run until then'.[20] Hunt's memorandum throws new light on Callaghan's decision to defer the election and the circumstances surrounding his thinking. The Cabinet Secretary declared that he was not giving advice on when the general election should be held: 'I hope however that it is not too presumptuous to offer one or two thoughts which have struck me in compiling this list [in a detailed memorandum].'[21]

Some key arguments were set out for not calling the general election. In his view, clearly the biggest electoral asset was the government's handling of the economic situation and its willingness to take difficult decisions in an uncompromising manner. However, the Cabinet Secretary acknowledged 'the present general expectation that there will be an election in the autumn'. Therefore any change of course must appear 'as a conscious and deliberate decision even if it involves living dangerously'. He predicted that there would be many difficult decisions ahead and 'a Government facing up to them would probably get great credit'. But 'avoiding or fudging' difficult decisions 'because of a pre-electoral atmosphere would do itself no good'.[22] He advised Callaghan that his decision had to be decisive and certainly not give the impression of holding onto office at all costs in the expectation of more favourable prospects.

The comprehensive six-page memorandum flagged up a series of challenges the government would likely face if it stayed in office for another parliamentary year, particularly on the international front, as well as the economy, industrial relations and important social issues.[23] There were

---

19 Kenneth O. Morgan states that Callaghan asked for written views about the election from all his Cabinet (who mostly replied by 30 August to 1 September). 'The numbers showed a majority for an early poll but, probably in Callaghan's judgement, a balance in terms of weight for delay.' Morgan, *Callaghan*, pp. 639–40.

20 Sir John Hunt to James Callaghan, 3 August 1978, TNA PREM 16/1621. The Callaghan memoirs briefly mention the Prime Minister's request that the Cabinet Secretary advise him on 'the items that the Government would need to deal with up to April 1979 … [Sir John Hunt's] summary showed we would have a number of difficulties, but that we had also made a lot of progress'. Callaghan, *Time and Chance*, p. 513.

21 Sir John Hunt to James Callaghan, 3 August 1978, TNA PREM 16/1621.

22 *Ibid.*

23 In the memorandum, the Cabinet Secretary outlined the issues under the following headings: European Monetary System, Demand Management, Foreign Exchanges, Monetary, Public Expenditure, Trade, Pay, Docks, Other Industrial Relations, Industrial, Devolution, Christmas Bonus, November Upratings for Social Security Benefits, Child Benefit, Legislation Programme. Sir John Hunt, 'October 1978–April 1979 memorandum', 3 August 1978, TNA PREM 16/1611.

significant decisions to be made on the European Monetary System. The Bank of England held a more optimistic view about employment prospects and inflation. There was work to be done on monetary and fiscal policy and, especially, over public expenditure, where the government had a good opportunity to demonstrate the continuation of sound economic management. Two other major areas were pay and industrial relations:

> There will be a whole series of difficult cases, starting with Ford, local authority manuals etc.... There will also certainly be the need, as in phase 3 [of the social contract], to face some strikes.... We shall not really know until late October or November how the [pay] round is going.

This was the closest the memorandum came to indicating industrial strife, although nothing on the scale of the 'winter of discontent'.[24] Lord McNally later recalled that another important factor in Callaghan's decision was the opportunity to continue his work with a third year in office. Clearly, Hunt's memorandum indicated there was much to do and gave the encouragement to undertake the challenge.[25]

Interestingly, the views of the 12 party whips (11 men and one woman) are also revealed in some detail in the batch of papers that the Prime Minister took to his farm in August. A clear majority of eight whips, including chief whip Michael Cocks and deputy chief whip Walter Harrison, were definitely in favour of postponing the election until 1979 (plus one somewhat unsure). Only a minority of three supported an October election. Widely acknowledged as an enterprising and redoubtable team that had kept a mainly minority government afloat at Westminster, the constituencies of the whips were spread throughout Britain. Their sure political nous at the grass roots kept them in touch with the best timing of a general election.[26] What quite possibly had tipped the balance in favour of postponing the election

---

24 The most curious item of government business on the long list in the memorandum was the section on 'Dogs': 'The main and growing problem is stray dogs (estimated at 200,000 and, especially when roaming in packs, a serious menace in some areas).' This figure was probably a typographical slip for 20,000. I am grateful for the guidance of the Dogs Trust Charity, London.

25 Interview: Lord Tom McNally, House of Lords, 23 June 2007.

26 Assistant whip Ann Taylor MP stated at the time that she was 'very worried about an October election and can see no substantial pick up of seats.... Tea room talk accepts that October is not inevitable.... Party morale would be improved by concentrating October to March on attractive things in the House.' Michael Cocks, chief whip, to Prime Minister, 1 August 1978, attaching the views of his colleagues, including: 'But to quote Walter Harrison [deputy chief whip] we have in House terms lived on next to nothing for over four years and could have a go at carrying on'. TNA PREM 16/1621. Interviews: Baroness Ann Taylor, House of Lords, 20 June 2011; Walter Harrison, Wakefield, 5 March 2012.

to a spring 1979 contest, based on a stronger record in office, was outlined in Hunt's memorandum as a significant programme for a third year.[27]

On his return from holiday on 29 August Callaghan talked immediately with Ken Stowe, his principal private secretary, about the general election. He asked him what he 'thought it was right to do'. Stowe said he 'would be very tempted to embark on a new session of Parliament and see the problems through another winter'. He thought there were two main reasons for delaying the election: first, there was no major issue to be resolved; and second, the result of an early election would probably be 'a parliamentary stale-mate' (a hung parliament), as 'there was no tide of opinion flowing'. The Prime Minister confided that 'he had 90 per cent made up his mind' and during August he had taken soundings about the minority parties and was confident of gaining a majority on the Queen's Speech. Callaghan concluded most significantly: 'the great issue was economic recovery and the conquest of inflation in which the wages policy was essential and he would much prefer to fight the battle during the winter, hope to win it and then go to the country'.[28]

It seems that Callaghan believed Labour would not secure a clear victory in an autumn election. Instead, further time in office would give him the opportunity to take advantage of a current running in Labour's direction that would return a majority administration probably in the spring of 1979.[29] In his memoirs, the Prime Minister argued on similar lines: 'There was still another twelve months.... Why run the risk of a very doubtful election result in October 1978 if we could convert it into a more convincing majority in 1979? I made up my mind.'[30]

As head of the Policy Unit at 10 Downing Street, Bernard Donoughue was at the centre of government, albeit kept in the dark about Callaghan's decision to postpone the election. He recalled: 'Callaghan did not show his own hand ... [and] did not consult his personal staff, Tom McNally, Tom McCaffrey and myself, and none of us knew his decision until the last moment'.[31]

Lord Lipsey's recently published memoirs throw fresh light on Callaghan's decision making. As a member of the Policy Unit at Number 10, Lipsey had an inside view of Westminster politics from the day of his arrival at Downing Street. On the timing of the general election, he recalled that,

---

27 Sir John Hunt, 'October 1978–April 1979 memorandum', 3 August 1978, TNA PREM 16/1621.

28 KRS [Ken Stowe], 'Personal: note for the record', 29 August 1978, TNA PREM 16/1621.

29 Interviews: Hattersley; Lord Bernard Donoughue, House of Lords, 6 July 2010; Worcester.

30 Callaghan recalled he marked 5 April 1979, the last day of the income tax year, based on a new electoral register in February (that would probably favour Labour) and British summer time starting on 18 March. Callaghan, *Time and Chance*, p. 516.

31 Bernard Donoughue, *The Heat of the Kitchen: An Autobiography* (London: Politico's, 2003), p. 258.

from the spring of 1978, 'we gave serious attention to when we should go to the country'. He also commented on the so-called *Daily Mirror* 'world exclusive' on 26 August 1978 that the anticipated election would be in October, based on a briefing by Tom McNally, the Prime Minister's chief political adviser. The Lipsey memoirs also reveal that Callaghan *did* tell McNally, in strict confidence, that the election was to be postponed.[32] In 1978 Matthew Oakeshott, who believed that the likely outcome of an autumn election would have been a hung parliament, recalled the fate of Harold Wilson in 1970 in calling an early election, when he was defeated by Ted Heath.[33]

Donoughue has provided a number of probable reasons for Callaghan's surprising decision. Above all was the Prime Minister's belief that he would not secure a clear overall majority at the polls in an autumn 1978 election. Donoughue wrote: 'He believed, perfectly sensibly, that a Prime Minister should dissolve for an early election only if he was confident of winning. Otherwise, he should soldier on and hope for a better opportunity.' Donoughue recalled that in September 1977 Callaghan had confided that he did 'not want an election next year [1978] if I can help it'.[34]

As we have seen, McNally believed that the Prime Minister (at the age of 66) wished to complete three years, rather than two, in office. He had consulted Cabinet ministers, particularly Michael Foot, Harold Lever and Merlyn Rees – his closest allies in his Cabinet – who were among the older members.[35] Callaghan was by nature a cautious person. Furthermore, he believed that the scourge of inflation could be eradicated by his counter-inflationary strategy based on the 5 per cent pay norm. Donoughue also commented:

> I think he wanted to go on another year. 'Three years sounds so much more than two', he once said. Jim Callaghan thought he could talk to the unions (and he could – to the union leaders), but what he didn't realise was that the trade union leaders he talked to could not deliver.[36]

In December 1977, Donoughue had sent Callaghan a paper reviewing the election strategy for 1978–79, including the timing of the general election. At the time, the government had an overall minority of 14 and was dependent on the Lib–Lab pact. If the pact was dissolved, Donoughue

---

32 David Lipsey, *In the Corridors of Power: An Autobiography* (London: Biteback Publishing, 2012), pp. 122–5.
33 Interview: Lord Matthew Oakeshott, OLIM Ltd, London, 28 September 2011. Matthew Oakeshott was special adviser to Roy Jenkins MP, 1972–76, and a Labour member of Oxford city council, 1972–76. He left the Labour Party and joined the Social Democratic Party. He was created Lord Oakeshott (a life peer) in 2000 and was Treasury and pensions spokesman for the Liberal Democrats from 2001.
34 Donoughue, *The Heat of the Kitchen*, pp. 260–1.
35 Interview: McNally.
36 Interview: Donoughue. See also pp. 125–9.

believed that the minority Labour government could continue surviving at Westminster, even if all the nationalists voted against it, provided two Northern Ireland MPs, Gerry Fitt (of the Social Democratic and Labour Party) and Frank Maguire (an Independent Republican), continued to back the government and the Ulster Unionists abstained. He also noted 'though it would be tempting fate to bank on our surviving the year, the common assumption that a 1978 election is now inevitable is not right either.' The economic outlook for 1978 and 1979 was generally good, with the prospect of growth based on increasing personal consumption.

> This should create a favourable economic background for an election in 1978. However, by 1979, familiar economic problems could be re-emerging – rising inflation; the balance of payments moving into deficit; sterling weakening and the economic expansion may prove unsustainable. In addition, there is the crucial (and unanswerable) question of how pay settlements will go next Autumn.[37]

This was a remarkable survey of likely trends a year ahead.

The *Daily Mirror* dealt uncritically with Callaghan's decision to defer the anticipated general election. The paper noted: 'His broadcast decision to soldier on into 1979 stunned the nation, amazed his closest colleagues and infuriated the Tories'. In a sympathetic editorial, the newspaper commented: 'He is gambling, but he is gambling bravely'.[38] The same edition of the paper featured an exclusive interview with the Prime Minister, in which he revealed that he had decided back on 17 August that there would be no autumn election. Only Chancellor Denis Healey and Commons leader Michael Foot knew of this decision. In answer to the question 'Why not go to the country now?' Callaghan replied: 'Because we believe that the policies we are following are leading to lower inflation, a better balance of payments, more growth and improved standards of living. We want to carry on with these and pursue them with determination.'[39] The *Daily Telegraph* reported that the Prime Minister's survival rested on 'wooing the Nationalists' and that Margaret Thatcher, the Conservative Party leader since 1975, had declared that he 'had made a mistake'.[40] The *Guardian* focused on the Prime Minister's 'two-fingered salute to the vast majority of politicians and journalists who believed he was about to call an autumn general election', as well as speculating on Callaghan's gamble on finding allies at Westminster to sustain his administration in office. However, the paper had missed a sensational scoop the previous day by relegating Peter

---

37 Bernard Donoughue to Prime Minister, 'Pre-election strategy – prospects, policies and options for 1978/9', 22 December 1977, TNA PREM 1667.
38 *Daily Mirror*, 8 September 1978, p. 2.
39 Terence Lancaster, 'Jim: why I'll carry on', *Daily Mirror*, 8 September 1978, p. 5.
40 *Daily Telegraph*, 8 September 1978, p. 18.

Jenkins's election commentary – on the likelihood that the Prime Minister would *not* be calling the election, as expected – to page 11.[41]

As Malcolm Rutherford wrote in the cold light of Callaghan's decision to defer the general election in 1978: 'it seems to me that by far the most unlikely result of a general election in the near future would be an overall majority for the Labour Party. Mr Callaghan must have thought so too.' Rutherford's evidence included an analysis of the most recent opinion polls, which showed little discernible improvement in the government's popularity. Three weeks before, Gallop, in the *Daily Telegraph*, gave Labour a 4 per cent margin over the opposition, with a Tory lead two months before. This, however, was the best lead for Labour since MORI (Labour's pollsters), in the *Daily Express*, had predicted a 2 per cent Conservative lead. On the available polling evidence, Labour and Conservatives seemed more or less level. According to a National Opinion Poll (NOP), Labour had had a lead of about 4–5 per cent but had slipped by September 1978.[42]

In the end, Callaghan's decision to postpone the election in the autumn 1978 had devastating repercussions that were milestones on the way to Labour's election defeat in May 1979. His government was forced into a new parliamentary term without the support of the Trades Union Congress (TUC) and was beset by industrial troubles that winter. Significantly, it put the timing of the general election, when it came unexpectedly, beyond his control. Government–union relations were placed in jeopardy and led to the collapse of Labour's social contract, which by then had become little more than out and out stringent wage restraint. The Labour government lost its biggest asset of being able to work harmoniously with the unions.[43]

Only two days before his television broadcast to tell the nation that he was not going to call for a general election, Callaghan had been introduced at the 1978 TUC congress in Brighton as 'the only Prime Minister in the country who has been a trade union official', at what was widely seen as a platform for the start of Labour's general election campaign. Callaghan did not wish to take his personal staff to the TUC congress. In London, Donoughue noted that he 'saw the draft of the PM's speech. Pretty heavy stuff on incomes policy.'[44] In his address to the TUC in Brighton that year, Callaghan referred directly to the government's unpopular 5 per cent pay norm: 'I come here today once more to ask for your support for this policy [for winning the battle against inflation] … although pay is by no means the only element in inflation, it is a vital factor and – just as important it is a factor that lies within our control … [in keeping] inflation under

---

41 *Guardian*, 8 September 1978, p. 1, and 7 September 1978, p. 11. Interview: Michael White, Westminster, London, 11 April 2011.
42 Malcolm Rutherford, 'Why Mr Callaghan had cold feet', *Financial Times*, 8 September 1978, p. 17.
43 For the origins and early history of the social contract, see chapter 1.
44 Donoughue, *Downing Street Diary, Volume Two*, p. 356 (diary entry: 5 September 1978).

control'. He also focused on the growing chasm between the unions and the government on pay.

> You have replied that you cannot accept a fixed figure of five per cent because what you want is free collective bargaining … but I must say also that free collective bargaining only serves the interests of your members if it produces real increases in their pay packets that will last and keep their value. That is going to be the test of the policies that you will follow during the next twelve months.[45]

However, with the expectation of a general election around the corner, most people in the trade unions took the unrealistic and inflexible 5 per cent norm, about which they had not been consulted, as little more than 'window dressing' until the election. If Labour was returned to power, a new round of wage negotiations was expected.

Brendan Barber, who was a departmental head at the TUC in 1978, recalled the mood at the Brighton TUC congress: 'I was standing right in front of the stage when he [the Prime Minister] was speaking – trying to keep the photographers in order…. He was not going to be rushed into an election.'[46] The 1978 TUC congress is often remembered because the Prime Minister towards the end of his address tantalised his audience about the election by singing a music hall ditty (wrongly attributed to Marie Lloyd) without revealing the election date.[47]

Callaghan went on to say at the congress:

> I understand the reasons for the present speculation about the prospects of a General Election. It was inevitable once the Liberals had withdrawn [from the Lib–Lab pact].… I had done nothing myself to fan that speculation.… I begin to wonder whether I need to do so if I am to believe all I read in the newspapers. The commentators had fixed the month … the date and the day. Well … remember what happened to Marie Lloyd. She fixed the day … she told us what happened … it went like this: 'There was I – waiting at the church … he sent me round a note … can't get away to marry you today – my wife won't let me.' Let me make it clear that I have promised nobody that I shall be at the altar in October. Nobody at all.… I certainly intend to indicate my intentions very shortly on this matter.[48]

45 TUC, *Report of the 110th Annual Trades Union Congress*, Brighton, 5 September 1978, p. 520.

46 Interview: Brendan Barber, Congress House, London, 4 August 2008.

47 Advised by Joe Haines, Bernard Donoughue told the Prime Minister that the song should be attributed to Vesta Victoria, not Marie Lloyd. Donoughue, *Downing Street Diary, Volume Two*, p. 356 (diary entries: 4–5 September 1978). However, Callaghan stuck to his script as he thought Marie Lloyd was the more well known performer. Possibly his reluctance to change was a small indication of his frame of mind about government pay policy. To the author's personal knowledge, Roy Hudd, comedian, television performer and historian of the music hall, wrote to the Prime Minister to point out his mistake.

48 TUC, *Report of the 110th Annual Trades Union Congress*, 5 September 1978, p. 522.

When, two days later, the Prime Minister did indicate his intentions, the trade union leaders felt misled, even betrayed. Larry Whitty, head of research at the General Municipal Boilermakers and Allied Trade Union (GMB) and later Labour Party General Secretary, commented that he 'wasn't convinced that we would have won it [the election]. So I didn't feel quite as betrayed as *some*, but the failure of Jim to talk honestly to the union leaders became a real problem'.[49] David Basnett, who was in his TUC presidential year, was reported as 'being furious'.[50] John Edmonds recalled: 'I couldn't believe it … an enormous unbelievable mistake … in that decision [were] hints of betrayal'. Later, Callaghan in conversation with Edmonds, then General Secretary of the GMB, remarked: 'It is very difficult to give up … you always think that it is going to get better … [and that later there will be] a better chance'.[51]

On the Friday evening before the TUC congress, the Prime Minister had entertained six senior TUC leaders at a 'secret dinner party' at his farm. Those present were Len Murray, TUC General Secretary, Moss Evans, who had succeeded Jack Jones at the Transport and General Workers' Union (TGWU), David Basnett, of the GMB, Alf Allen, of the Union of Shop, Distributive and Allied Workers (USDAW), Geoffrey Drain, of the National Association of Local Government Officers (NALGO), and Hugh Scanlon, of the Amalgamated Union of Engineering Workers (AUEW). When asked by Callaghan about the timing of the general election, each one (except Scanlon, who counselled the Prime Minister to wait until 1979) advised him to call the election rather than delay. Asked by Callaghan when he should 'go to the country', five senior TUC figures replied one by one: 'Go now. Don't wait until next year. We cannot guarantee industrial peace in the coming winter'. Yet they left sworn to secrecy that evening believing there would an election, probably in early October, as the Prime Minister had said nothing. In 1991 in conversation with the journalist Geoffrey Goodman, Murray expressed his astonishment that the Prime Minister had even raised the subject with them. At the 'farm summit', as the 'secret dinner party' became known, Murray revealed that he had told the Prime Minister:

> that we couldn't hold the situation that winter. We pointed to a yawning gap that was emerging in pay settlements between the public and private sectors. And I reminded him of what had happened to previous pay policies under

49 Interview: Lord Larry Whitty, House of Lords, 12 January 2011.
50 Paul Routledge told Tony Benn he had been with David Basnett 10 minutes before the television broadcast on 7 September. 'David Basnett had got all his statements drafted and the champagne was literally being brought in … Basnett had said it wasn't a question of if but when. He had recommended 28 September, but he thought Jim seemed to favour 5 October. Then Jim announced that there wouldn't be one.' Benn, *Conflicts of Interest*, pp. 358–9 (diary entry: 5 October 1978).
51 Interview: John Edmonds, Victoria, London, 17 November 2010.

a Labour government going back to Attlee's time … I told Jim that this is where the crunch would come again in the winter of 1979. But he wouldn't shift his basic view.[52]

This was nothing new to Geoffrey Goodman, with a lifetime in journalism, including 18 years at the *Daily Mirror*. In May 1978, he had lunch with the Prime Minister and fellow journalists and editorial executives for the *Mirror*.[53] Callaghan avoided the issue of the timing of the general election by focusing on the better economic news, such as the fall in the rate of inflation, improvements in the unemployment figures and better sterling balances. Instead, the Prime Minister wanted to know the views of the five journalists who formed the *Daily Mirror*'s five-man policy-making team on the government's pay restraint strategy.[54] In his memoirs, Goodman recalled:

> Callaghan turned to me and asked directly, 'Do you think the unions can deliver?' 'No, Prime Minister, I don't think they can … of course, the TUC certainly *wanted* to deliver … they were now under the lash of pressure from their members who were increasingly against the pay policy.… Then the Prime Minister waved an arm across the table.… 'Alright', he retorted, 'if that is the case then I will go over the heads of the trade union leadership and appeal directly to their members – and the voters. We have to hold the line on pay or the government will fall.'[55]

Callaghan's decision to defer the general election – and the way it was mishandled – has been described his 'greatest tactical mistake'.[56] It angered the trade union leadership at the time the government was trying to win support for its 5 per cent pay policy as the cornerstone of its anti-inflation strategy. The 1978 TUC congress demonstrated its opposition to this policy and at the same time displayed its support for a national minimum wage.

---

52 Geoffrey Goodman also recalls a dinner at Michael Foot's Hampstead home when Foot, in a telephone call, advised Callaghan 'to stand firm again an autumn election'. Afterwards, Foot told Goodman, who favoured an autumn election: 'No, it wouldn't be the right thing to do. We would be accused of lacking the courage to face the winter and that would go against us.' 'Brave words from a man of principle.' Geoffrey Goodman, *From Bevan to Blair: Fifty Years' Reporting From the Political Front Line* (London: Pluto Press, 2003), pp. 226–9. Interview: Geoffrey Goodman, Congress House, London, 22 July 2008.

53 Those present were: Geoffrey Goodman; Tony Miles, editorial director of the Mirror Group; Mike Molloy, editor of the *Daily Mirror*; Terry Lancaster, political editor of the *Daily Mirror*; and Joe Haines, chief leader-writer. *Ibid.*, p. 221.

54 *Ibid.*, pp. 221–2.

55 Goodman also recalled that he told the Prime Minister that Tom Jackson, General Secretary of the Post Office Workers' Union, had told him about the 'violent opposition' to the 5 per cent incomes policy among trade union officials and rank-and-file members he had encountered in the south Wales region, a Labour heartland, which included Callaghan's Cardiff constituency. *Ibid.*, pp. 223–4.

56 Robert Taylor, 'When the sun set on Labour the last time', *Tribune*, 19 September 2008, p. 28.

At the 1978 Labour Party conference in Blackpool, the government suffered another severe setback on pay policy, despite Callaghan making what Tony Benn described in a note to the Prime Minister as the best conference speech he had heard. The morning press had written the Labour Party off as finished, according to Bernard Donoughue, who noted in his diary: 'the PM this morning still had not written the central bit on pay policy and he told Roger Carroll that he was going to ad-lib it. And he did – brilliantly.... It was a brilliant performance and received a standing ovation.'[57]

However, the militant Liverpool Wavertree constituency resolution moved by Terry Duffy was passed overwhelmingly at the conference, by 4,017,000 votes to 1,924,000, demanding that the government must 'immediately cease intervening in wage negotiations and recognise the right of trade unions to negotiate freely on behalf of their members'. In addition, the resolution added 'the planning of wages would only be acceptable when prices, profits and investment were also planned', within the framework of a socialist economy.[58]

This was a body blow to the government, as noted by Benn:

Denis Healey breezed in and made an awful speech about how we must all support Jim and so on. After Michael Foot had wound up with a call for loyalty, to everyone's amazement the motion against the 5 per cent was not remitted but carried by about 4 million to 1 million and the alternative strategy motion was carried without a vote … the result was dazzling, and Jim's whole position now is endangered.[59]

Donoughue later reported that a great deal of unsuccessful arm twisting had taken place at the conference to bring the trade union leaders into line with the government's pay policy. He noted:

The PM had recovered a bit from yesterday's NEC [meeting of the party's National Executive Committee], which went on for five and a half hours in the afternoon! He persuaded them by 15 to 13 to support a motion to remit this afternoon's pay policy motion. Then afterwards Moss Evans told a press conference that he would still vote against it – and the PM began to talk about resigning. He stormed back to his room last night, sent for Healey and Varley and asked them to get to work on Boyd and others. Late last night he had Moss Evans, David Basnett and John Boyd in his room, but Evans was truculent and the PM was very rough with them.[60]

57 Donoughue, *Downing Street Diary, Volume Two*, p. 370 (diary entry: 3 October 1978).
58 *Report of the 77th Annual Conference of the Labour Party*, Blackpool, 2–6 October 1978, p. 314.
59 Benn, *Conflicts of Interest*, p. 355 (diary entry: Monday 20 October 1978).
60 Donoughue, *Downing Street Diary, Volume Two*, pp. 369–70 (diary entry: 20 October 1978).

In difficulty over reconciling wage demands with government incomes policy, like many previous Labour ministers since 1945, Callaghan spoke to the conference:

> We must find a better way to resolve the issue of pay levels. The power of the organised worker demands that we do. The power workers can shut off the lights. The sewage workers can stop work too with all the consequences. Yes, society today is so organised that every individual group almost has the power to disrupt it. How is that power to be channelled into constructive channels? That is the question for the government but it is a question for the trade union movement too.[61]

While in Blackpool, the Prime Minister convened an urgent meeting of his economic ministers to consider the future direction of the government's pay policy in preparation for meeting the TUC. Callaghan tried one formula: 'if some steps could be taken to help the lower paid, this could buy off some of the current political difficulties, though not difficulties on pay'. However, as the Chancellor of the Exchequer pointed out, public sector workers in the previous pay round (in 1977) had been restricted to a 10 per cent ceiling, whereas the wage agreements in private manufacturing industry had reached increases of 16 per cent. In particular, Alfred Booth did not think that an agreement with the TUC could be secured simply by assisting the low paid, since there were also strong sectional interests within the TUC advocating action on pay differentials. What, above all, emerged from this discussion in Blackpool was the Prime Minister's unchangeable determination 'not to desert the 5 per cent basic policy'.[62]

It was very clear at the Blackpool conference that there was now an unbridgeable impasse between the trade union leadership and the Callaghan government over pay policy. The left-wing Cabinet minister Stan Orme stated that he did 'not believe there is any other issue facing the Government which is anyway as important'. He warned that pressures that were building had finally come to a head. According to Orme, there were 'two immovable forces': the government's fixed 5 per cent pay policy and the trade union movement's swelling demand, after three years of wage restraint, for an immediate return to free collective bargaining.[63] Somehow a course had to be steered between Scylla and Charybdis.

At this time another perspective was provided by David Lipsey of the Policy Unit at Downing Street, in a paper in which he agreed that: 'Politically, abandoning 5% will be embarrassing. But could we win an election *after a winter of discontent* [emphasis added] in which a large chunk

---

61 *Report of the 77th Annual Conference of the Labour Party*, p. 214.
62 'Note of a discussion at lunch at the Imperial Hotel on Wednesday 4 October 1978', TNA PREM 16/1610.
63 Stanley Orme, 'Prime Minister: incomes policy', n.d. October 1978, TNA PREM 16/1610.

of the P.L.P. will be sympathising with the malcontents?' His adroit paper to the Prime Minister, which was circulated among the Downing Street Policy Unit, outlined possible economic difficulties, such as 'a run on sterling … or some immediate loss of production'. 'So long as we avoid an actual explosion, we live to fight another day', he believed. Lipsey also reviewed the likely outcomes of pay settlements in the private and public sectors. Five per cent was important in an election year. 'In other words we fight, but not to the death.' He finished on a very perceptive note:

> In the case of private sector negotiations with ill-organised workers, we should go for the lowest possible settlements. Such a policy will be unfair to the low paid, but sooner or later the British Trade Union movement will have to face the fact that it can have an incomes policy and social justice or it can have no social justice and no incomes policy; but what it cannot have is social justice with no policy.[64]

The Blackpool conference was followed by a meeting with trade union leaders in London on 10 October, which marked the start of six weeks of intensive but fruitless negotiations between the government and the TUC that did nothing to solve the gaping chasm between the two sides over the 5 per cent wages policy.[65] The meeting opened with the Prime Minister stating 'there was no point in having a re-run of the speeches at Blackpool'. Instead, his agenda was to reduce inflation to single figures during the next year, which all present approved.[66] He hoped for general agreement on pay policy – 'responsible settlements of a low order'. He revealed that settlements could be 7 or 8 per cent 'without the government having to change any of its policies'. He was also prepared to offer 'some flexibility' regarding the lower paid and possibly 'a greater emphasis on prices'. Michael Foot pointed out that if wage increases influenced price rises, the result 'inescapably' would be higher inflation. However, Moss Evans countered this possibility by proposing that wage negotiations would restrict price rises as part of the pay settlement. David Basnett proposed that the government publish a prices target as well as pay guidelines. However, the issue of the

---

64 Interestingly, this was the first contemporaneous use of the term 'winter of discontent' in a government source, although elsewhere this appellation pre-dates the winter industrial strife of 1978–79. See chapter 1, note 1, p. 1. David Lipsey, 'The pay prospect', 5 October 1978, TNA PREM 16/1610. Lord Lipsey earlier coined the memorable phrase 'The party's over' for Anthony Crosland, Foreign Secretary, when working as his research assistant, 1974–77. Interview: Lord David Lipsey, House of Lords, 9 February 2009.

65 Those present at the 10 October 1978 meeting were, on the government side: the Prime Minister, Lord President, Chancellor of the Exchequer and the Prime Minister's private secretary. On the trade union side were: David Basnett, Lord Allen, Geoffrey Drain, Moss Evans, Terry Duffy and Len Murray. TNA PREM 16/1611.

66 *Ibid.*

low paid and public services pay, which went hand in hand, still had to be solved.[67]

Callaghan had been appreciative of the significant support his government had received previously from the trade union movement for nearly three years. However, he did not appear to worry too much that relations with the TUC would be irreparably damaged by his inflexible stance on the 5 per cent pay policy. More important for the Prime Minister was the retirement of union leaders Jack Jones (TGWU), the principal architect of the social contract, in March 1978 and of Hugh Scanlon (AUEW) in May 1978 – who, in the 1960s, the media had dubbed the 'terrible twins' – which removed two leading actors from the political scene at a time of deteriorating government–union relations at the advent of the 'winter of discontent'. In the Prime Minister's view the trade unionist representation on the National Economic Development Council – the 'Neddy 6' – had been 'materially weakened'. Much to Callaghan's displeasure, Jones, a significant figure in industrial relations and a supporter of the Labour government, was replaced by Moss Evans as General Secretary of the TGWU and as one of the Neddy 6.[68]

Also, in October 1978 Eric Varley, Secretary of State for Industry, produced an 'apocalyptic paper' on four major public sector manufacturing companies – British Leyland (BL), Rolls-Royce, British Shipbuilders and the British Steel Corporation. He explained to the Chancellor of the Exchequer: 'I am very concerned that the trade unions did not appear to understand the realities of seeking wage settlements above the Government's guidelines'.[69] The Prime Minister took a keen interest and proposed that 'some of the material should be published in some form or other and mentioned, in particular the desirability of calling in the appropriate members of the TUC and going over it with them'.[70] In a memorandum, Varley commented on the union demand for a return to free collective bargaining to secure a level of wage settlement that manufacturers in the private sector could afford, which would probably mean increases of 10–15 per cent.[71] He also predicted that, in the current economic circumstances, 'the effect of the current attitude of the Trade Union movement must be to increase the number of companies going into receivership or liquidation in the foreseeable future and a substantial reduction in investment in an effort to stave off that fate'.[72]

In analysing the effect of excessive wage settlements, Varley considered the 'strike scenario' where, for example, Michael Edwardes, chief executive and

---

67 *Ibid.*
68 Callaghan, *Time and Chance*, pp. 520, 527.
69 Eric Varley to Denis Healey, 20 October 1978, TNA PREM 16/1611.
70 Kenneth Stowe to Eric Varley, 23 October 1978, TNA PREM 16/1611.
71 'Wage inflation: the consequences', October 1978, TNA PREM 16/1611, p. 1.
72 *Ibid.*, p. 2.

chairman of BL, had reported that the consequences of an eight-week strike would reduce total sales by 20 per cent in the first month, making it unlikely that the company would achieve a 20 per cent market share again. Loss of profits of £15 million a week, cash flow difficulties and loss of government funding 'would almost certainly lead the British Leyland Board to conclude that the volume car business was no longer viable'. There was a predictable loss of 90,000 jobs at BL – and this did not include the indirect employment loss. Varley pointed out: 'It has been traditional wisdom to assume that every job within the motor vehicle industry supports one job outside it … the loss of over 90,000 jobs as a result of the run-down of BL's volume car business would be a further 90,000 lost, mainly in the West Midlands'.[73]

However, this was another illustration of the gulf between the two sides of management and labour, where the captains of industry informed government ministers of the dire consequences, such as industrial closures, if their workforces exceeded the 5 per cent pay norm while at the same time the various chairmen of the nationalised industries were pressing the government for overly generous increases in their own remuneration packages.[74]

At the Cabinet meeting on 16 November, the Chancellor of the Exchequer reported on the outcome of the six-week negotiations between the government and the TUC, which had led to an agreement between the TUC Economic Committee and the ministers concerned on the text of a joint statement, to which would be attached advice by the TUC negotiators.[75] However, a tied vote 14–14 at the TUC General Council indicated the final breakdown of negotiations. It was not the last time that the government and the TUC failed to find an enduring agreement on the issue of pay policy. However, in November 1978, all that was left to the Prime Minister was to remind his Cabinet that: 'It was important not to let the present setback create the impression that the [5 per cent] policy approved by the Cabinet in the summer had been abandoned'.[76]

Addressing the TUC congress in October 1978, Callaghan had claimed living standards in Britain were improving and he provided a list of statistics:

> This year has been a year of success. Since Congress met 12 months ago there have been tax cuts amounting to £3½ billion, plus additional public expenditure amounting to £1 billion to pay for the higher child benefits, to aid the construction industry, to defer the increase in the price of school

---

73 *Ibid.*
74 For the Prime Minister's meetings with the chairmen of nationalised industries about pay policy on remuneration and recruitment, see 'Nationalised industries: May 1975–February 1978, TNA PREM 16/1770; 'Nationalised industries: top salaries review body', April 1977–February 1978, TNA PREM 1 6/1777; 'Nationalised industries: top salaries review body; salaries of nationalised industries review body members', 20 February 1978–April 1979, TNA PREM 12/2188.
75 'Statement by the government and the TUC: collective bargaining, costs and prices', TNA PREM 16/1613.
76 Cabinet conclusions, 16 November 1978, CAB 128/64.

meals, to provide free school milk, and to help with additional overseas aid. A lower rate of tax of 25p in the pound has been introduced for the first £750 of taxable income. Child benefit will be further increased to £3 a week for every child in November and to £4 per week in April. There are to be pension increases in November by £2 a week for a single person and £3.20 for married couples and inflation has declined from 17 per cent a year ago to between 7 per cent and 8 per cent. The living standards of your members have improved and are continuing to improve as a consequence of these policies.[77]

Yet this was a Prime Minister's speech in the run-up to a general election, albeit a few months later than his audience at Brighton were anticipating. Traditionally, the history of post-war Britain showed that increased social benefits and tax cuts invariably preceded an election day. Three years of wage restraint had contributed to a significant reduction in the inflation rate, from a peak of 27 per cent to around 8 per cent. However, the general perception of ordinary families was of a drastic fall in living standards, which affected the low paid and the squeezed differentials of skilled workers alike. Professor Chris Wrigley was chair of the Loughborough Constituency Labour Party 1977–79 and 1980–85. He recalled the deferred election and 'the missed opportunity of autumn 1978':

> We had held everybody together with difficulty and much effort, with unions notably unhappy by autumn of 1978. We had deployed our meagre finances and were ready to try and hold our marginal seat. The mining area remained strong, but Loughborough itself was wobbly or worse. Low paid workers were being pushed to the margins by pressure on real wages. Skilled workers were unhappy about wage restraint. When Callaghan did not call the election, I said I would not stand for re-election in January. Someone else could try to hold it all together. As I fully expected Loughborough was lost in 1979 … it was not just anger at garbage etc. that caused the debacle, but low paid people and skilled workers were not going to vote for squeezed wages, nor were many party activists going to work body and soul in electioneering after the crazy 5% figure.[78]

In 1976 the IMF crisis had been preceded and then was followed by cuts in public expenditure that reduced the wider social contract from 1974 to 1976 to a mechanism merely for wage restraint.[79] A fourth phase of the social contract with a 5 per cent pay increase norm was the Prime Minister's personal decision that famously 'popped out' in a 1978 New Year BBC radio interview with Gordon Clough on the *World This Weekend*.[80]

---

77 *Report of the 110th Annual Trades Union Congress*, p. 520.
78 Chris Wrigley to author, personal communication, 26 August 2012.
79 For discussion of the impact of public expenditure cuts and the social contract, see chapter 1.
80 Morgan, *Callaghan*, p. 663; Callaghan, *Time and Chance*, p. 519.

In a candid interview with John Cole about the 5 per cent policy, Len Murray, General Secretary of the TUC, said that, since becoming Prime Minister, Callaghan 'had reverted that summer to a bad habit from his Treasury days: he was too impressed by the Treasury's economic models and was too little prepared to rely on his own very sensitive political instincts'.[81] Shirley Williams later confirmed that the 5 per cent figure for phase 4 of the social contract was probably based on Treasury models.[82] Former Chief Secretary to the Treasury Joel Barnett readily declared that the Prime Minister

> was the kind of man who wouldn't waiver – he was not flexible. His fault was that he was very inflexible. Once he had got his figure [5 per cent], he thought it was *deliverable* – no doubt about that. The high degree of certainty about himself was always there. He never had any doubt about it. That's why we got stuck with it.[83]

As we have seen, Stan Orme had warned the Prime Minister that the 5 per cent wage agreement was not deliverable, a distinct difference from the previous year when the TUC was broadly supportive of the 10 per cent limit:

> This year the response initially has not come from the activists but from the rank and file as we saw from the explosion at the Ford Motor Company. In the Cabinet when we discussed the White Paper I anticipated that this might happen. I take no joy in reiterating this point because I realise the consequences. Whether this response will now be followed with the Local Government workers, health workers, tanker drivers etc, one does not really know, but the deep feeling which exists amongst the rank and file Trade Unionists rightly or wrongly is that they have made a sacrifice over the last two or three years, that they have been held back and they do not believe that their living standards are improving at the moment, irrespective of what we say. Therefore, the pressure which is building up has finally come to a head.[84]

These were discerning observations about the political and industrial volcano that was about to erupt. We must now turn to what Callaghan was later to call the 'bellwether of the flock', the Ford strike that had already started when Stan Orme MP was writing about his concerns to the Prime Minister at the 1978 Labour Party conference.

---

81 John Cole, *As It Seemed To Me: Political Memoirs* (London: Weidenfeld & Nicolson, 1995), pp. 181–2. In 1978, John Cole was deputy editor of the *Observer*; he was later to be a distinguished political editor at the BBC.

82 Interview: Baroness Shirley Williams, House of Lords, 12 October 2008.

83 Interview: Lord Joel Barnett, House of Lords, 22 June 2010.

84 Stan Orme to Jim Callaghan, 5 October 1978, TNA PREM 16/1610.

Chapter Three

The Ford strike, 1978

On the first day of the nine-week strike at the Ford Motor Company in late September 1978, the *Daily Mail* carried a typical banner headline: 'More than 3,000 Ford workers stormed out on strike against the pay limit'.[1] The *Financial Times* headlined a similar story on its front page: 'All-out strike call at Ford'.[2] From the beginning, media coverage portrayed the dispute as a major industrial stoppage, involving the 57,000 workforce at Britain's leading American-owned motor manufacturer, and mainly as an out and out challenge to the Callaghan administration. According to the *Guardian*, the strike was 'the first full battle against the pay policy in four years of Labour government'.[3] The *Daily Mail* declared in almost military tones: 'ALL-OUT WAR ON JIM'S 5%'.[4] In response to the unions' pay claim, estimated at around 30 per cent, the company's initial offer was within the government's 5 per cent pay norm. In 1977 Ford had settled at 12.3 per cent – above the government's 10 per cent guideline.[5] Left-wing support for the Ford workforce in 1978 came from the *Morning Star*, which proclaimed: 'all-out fight against government pay curbs: FORDS GRINDS TO A HALT'.[6] The front page of the *Socialist Worker* highlighted the '80% RISE FOR FORD CHIEF' next to its main headline: 'THEY CAN ALL AFFORD IT!'[7]

The initial walk-outs at the Halewood and Southampton Ford plants were quickly followed by walk-outs at Ford's Daventry, Swansea and Basildon plants, as well as the main Dagenham plant beside the River Thames in Essex. Within 24 hours, the strike had spread beyond these initial plants, with eventually a total of well over 50,000 workers downing

---

1   *Daily Mail*, 22 September 1978, pp. 1-2.
2   *Financial Times*, 23 September 1978, p. 1.
3   *Guardian*, 23 September 1978, p. 1.
4   *Daily Mail*, 23 September 1978, pp. 1-2.
5   *The Times*, 27 September 1978, p. 19; *Daily Telegraph*, 18 September 1978.
6   *Morning Star*, 23 September 1978.
7   *Socialist Worker*, 30 September 1978.

tools, at Dagenham (24,000 on strike), Halewood (12,000), Basildon (3,100), Daventry (1,280), Dunton (1,000), Swansea (2,100), Southampton (4,100) and Langley (2,000).[8] The two main unions at Ford, the Transport and General Workers' Union (TGWU) and the Amalgamated Engineering Workers' Union (AEWU), soon made the dispute official. The Ford Motor Company became the front line for the government's incomes policy in the private sector – as in 1969, 1971, 1974 and 1977.[9]

In the history of post-war British industrial conflict, the Ford strike from September to November 1978 represents a major dispute, but has received relatively little analysis.[10] The 'winter of discontent' is remembered primarily for industrial action by public sector workers, especially between January and March 1979, but the Ford strike in the private sector was the catalyst for the wave of industrial unrest that followed. Recently released Cabinet papers throw fresh light on the strike's political impact during the last crucial months of the Callaghan government. As we have seen, in September 1978, the Prime Minister, James Callaghan, after addressing the Trades Union Congress (TUC) at Brighton, had surprisingly deferred a widely anticipated autumn general election, which Labour might have won.[11] Instead, the minority Callaghan administration entered another parliamentary year with a stringent 5 per cent incomes policy without TUC support. The Ford strike therefore had highly significant consequences for the government's incomes policy, and the break-up of its social contract with the unions, which eventually culminated in Labour's 1979 election defeat.

After nine weeks, the Ford Motor Company settled the strike with a revised offer of 17 per cent, thereby driving a coach and horses through the government's pay guidelines and immediately raising the question of 'discretionary action' (or sanctions) against the Ford UK division of the American multinational. Callaghan remarked that the Ford pay claim was 'the bellwether of the flock'.[12] The figure for the pay increase that resolved the strike, which attracted intense media coverage, acted as a pace setter for groups of workers in both the private and public sectors in the annual pay round. The government suffered a calamitous defeat in failing to secure

---

8 *Daily Telegraph*, 23 September 1978, p. 1. The reported numbers of Ford strikers vary slightly. For instance, the *Morning Star* on 26 September 1978 gave a total of 52,180.

9 Peter J. S. Dunnett, *The Decline of the British Motor Industry: The Effects of Government Policy, 1945–1979* (London: Croom Helm, 1980), p. 173.

10 The most detailed account of the 1978 Ford strike is Henry Friedman and Sander Meredeen, *The Dynamics of Industrial Conflict: Lessons from Ford* (London: Croom Helm, 1980), pp. 269–79, 318–27. See also Kenneth O. Morgan, *Callaghan: A Life* (Oxford: Oxford University Press, 1997), pp. 655–6, 658–60; Huw Beynon, *Working for Ford* (Harmondsworth: Penguin, 1984), pp. 348–9, 357–60, 371–81.

11 For a discussion of why James Callaghan deferred the general election in September 1978, see chapter 2.

12 James Callaghan, *Time and Chance* (London: Politico's, 2006, first published 1987), pp. 534.

parliamentary support for its policy of sanctions against Ford, as well as
against other private companies that breached the 5 per cent guideline.
Following the Ford wage agreement, many other unions prepared claims
for 20 per cent pay rises and more – a pay explosion, supported by a range
of disruptive industrial action, that became famously dubbed Britain's
'winter of discontent'.

On 7 September 1978 H. A. Polling, chairman of the board of Ford
Europe Incorporated, wrote urgently to Callaghan requesting an immediate meeting at the highest level to discuss his company's response to the
trade unions' very substantial pay claim, despite the government's pay policy
in the White Paper *Winning the Battle Against Inflation* (July 1978), which
enshrined the 5 per cent pay norm. Otherwise, Polling feared the certainty
of a drawn-out dispute, with devastating effects on Ford's own prospects as
well as severe consequences for government policy and the British economy
as a whole.[13]

In 1987 Paul Roots, who had been director of industrial relations at Ford
at the time of the dispute, recalled that the claim advanced by the unions –
some of which wanted to negotiate separately – was more complex than
the simple issue of the ceiling imposed by the government's 5 per cent pay
policy. There had been a considerable press campaign, particularly for the
35-hour week and the restoration of the differential in earnings between
skilled workers, such as toolmakers, and other grades. Although the Ford
management had prepared to cope with the eight-point union claim, the
new union negotiator, Ron Todd, the chairman of the trade union side of
the National Joint Negotiating Committee (NJNC) at Ford, had raised the
issue of free collective bargaining at the outset. However, the Ford management would not go beyond the limit of the government pay norm. Roots
declared: 'The next day the plants starting walking. They started walking
on 22 September and by 26 September the company had totally gone.'[14]
In 1978, during discussions with the government, the Ford management
had claimed that only a minority of employees took part in demonstration
walk-outs. 'The strike itself was not spontaneous but orchestrated ... the
all-out strike ... was achieved by a calculated phone call to the company
on Friday 22 September, to confirm that it was only prepared to negotiate
within the [government] guidelines'.[15]

The 1978 TGWU wage claim, which had been meticulously prepared in
conjunction with the Industrial Relations Unit at Ruskin College, Oxford,

---

13 H. A. Polling to James Callaghan, 7 September 1978, The National Archives (hence-
    forth TNA) PREM 16/1708.
14 Institute of Contemporary British History, 'Symposium: the winter of discontent',
    Contemporary Record, vol. 1, no. 3, autumn 1987, p. 40.
15 EGV (Eric Varley) to Prime Minister (James Callaghan), 'Ford', 10 November 1978,
    and 'Memorandum: the seven-week strike at Ford of Britain', n.d. (probably c. 10
    November 1978), PREM 16/2123.

was published as a booklet. The claim had been well advertised as early as April 1978, with a union delegates' meeting in Coventry. It set out the workers' case in nine key points, which included a £20 per week pay rise, a reduction of the working week to 35 hours, sabbatical leave (three months for every ten years of service), increased holiday allowance and other improvements, such as a scheme to create 3,300 new jobs from the shorter working hours. In arguing for better pay, the Ford workers maintained that skilled workers' incomes had been depressed by the flat payment system and incomes policies. Moreover, Ford production workers had fared less well than comparable groups in the automobile industry, such as the employees at British Leyland, the car manufacturer nationalised by the government in 1975.[16] Also, basic pay for skilled Ford production workers was on a similar level to that of average manual labourers in Britain and, in some instances, only 85 per cent of the average earnings of all adult male workers.

According to the TGWU, the union claim was based on the Ford Motor Company's evident ability to pay, owing to boosted profits and cash surpluses. In 1976–77, the profit per individual vehicle produced by Ford had risen by £159, but increased labour costs amounted to only £26.[17] In April 1978 Ford announced that its pre-tax profits had grown from £121.6 million in 1976 to £264.1 million in 1977. However, while Ford offered only a 5 per cent award to its workforce, the company chairman and managing director, Sir Terence Beckett, received a colossal 80 per cent rise in his remuneration package, including a salary increase from £30,457 to £54,843. A familiar chant from Ford demonstrators accompanied the pay negotiations: 'We helped make the profits, now we want our fair share!'[18]

In response to the union claim, the initial Ford offer of 5 per cent was strictly within the government's guideline, though neither the company nor the union leaders believed this would be acceptable to the workforce. This offer, at about half the rate of inflation, brought spontaneous walk-outs by Ford workers. The day shift at the Halewood plant damaged the main gate in their rush to leave. The Ford (UK) Workers Combine – an unofficial grouping of Ford workers with members at the majority of the plants – printed a payslip for a single Ford worker of £46.94 for a week with no overtime as part of the demand for a £20 per week increase and a five-hour reduction to a 35-hour working week.[19]

Overall, as a detailed package, the union wage claim represented a 30 per cent pay rise – well in excess of the official guidelines. For the government it was imperative that Ford did not exceed the official 5 per cent ceiling

---

16 For British Leyland, see Stephen Wilks, *Industrial Policy and the Motor Industry* (Manchester: Manchester University Press, 1988); Michael Edwardes, *Back from the Brink: An Apocalyptic Experience* (London: Collins, 1983).
17 *The Record*, October 1978, p. 3.
18 *Ibid*. Anne Perkins, *The Archive Hour*, BBC Radio 4, 6 September 2008.
19 *Big Flame*, October 1978, p. 4.

that was the cornerstone of the administration's anti-inflation strategy. In these circumstances, the Ford Motor Company proposed to augment its wage package of 5 per cent by including an additional self-financing productivity scheme to increase the overall offer to 7.5 per cent. Additional money would be available to reward regular attendance (i.e. a reduction in absenteeism) and in the form of a holiday bonus.

Within a few days, many of the other 19 unions at Ford joined the action started by the TGWU and AUEW, and similarly declared the stoppage an official strike for a 30 per cent increase.[20] The TGWU General Secretary, Moss Evans, who had taken over after the retirement of Jack Jones, the main architect on the union side of the social contract, actively supported a return to free collective bargaining instead of an incomes policy. When Ford workers accepted the 12.3 per cent offer by the company the previous year, this had been against the advice of their union leaders. Subsequently, workers at other manufacturing companies had gained higher awards and, 12 months later, there was still considerable resentment about this among the Ford workforce. This was part of the reason for the spontaneous walk-outs in response to the company's 1978 offer.[21]

The 1978 Ford strike was the first major dispute at Britain's second-largest automobile manufacturer since an eight-week stoppage in 1971. The settlement became a significant point of comparison for other wage deals, for both unions and management. The dispute naturally caught the attention of Bernard Donoughue (now Lord Donoughue) and Tony Benn, the two diarists of the Wilson and Callaghan governments of 1974–79.[22] On 22 September, with the ominous news of the Ford workers' walk-out, Donoughue wondered if the Callaghan government would rue the Prime Minister's decision earlier in the month to defer a general election from autumn 1978. Yet, within a week, Donoughue thought the dispute might be resolved. He noted that the 'big Ford strike … still looks more promising'.[23] On 25 September 1978 Donoughue observed: 'the weather is beautiful, people feel better off … this would be the time to hold an election'. However, there was a dark cloud on the horizon. He soon added:

---

20 *The Record*, October 1978, p. 3; see also *Big Flame*, October 1978.
21 See John Bohanna, *Diary* (1979), cited in Beynon, *Working for Ford*, pp. 370–1.
22 Harold Wilson had recruited Donoughue from the London School of Economics, where he had taught from 1964 to 1973. He was then head of the Policy Unit at 10 Downing Street from 1974 to 1976, a position he continued to hold during the premiership of James Callaghan from 1976 to 1979. During these years, Tony Benn MP was Industry Secretary in the Wilson Cabinet 1974–76 and Energy Secretary in the Callaghan Cabinet. In the latter role he had special departmental responsibility for handling the dispute involving oil tanker drivers during the 'winter of discontent' (discussed in chapter 4).
23 Bernard Donoughue, *Downing Street Diary, Volume Two: With James Callaghan in No. 10* (London: Jonathan Cape, 2008), p. 366 (diary entry: 22 September 1978). For the 1971 Ford strike, see John Mathews, *Ford Strike: The Workers' Story* (London: Panther, 1972).

'Later may be difficult – the car workers are all going on strike against the 5% policy. It will be very difficult to hold it. I do not think that we should be too rigid in the private sector. For me it should be a public sector pay policy.' Within two days, lunch with the Prime Minister was constantly interrupted by the telephone with messages 'from the big Ford strike'.[24]

At the start of the Ford dispute, Tony Benn met with Moss Evans, who commented on the ill-timed 80 per cent pay increase awarded to Ford's chairman, Sir Terence Beckett, and the futility of the government's pay policy:

> 'It just isn't on; Ford have made great profits and our people have contributed to it. I cannot understand the government, because in the summer of 1977, when Jack Jones failed to carry the TGWU Biennial Conference behind a continuation of the Social Contract, it must have been obvious to everybody that it wasn't on for a fourth year.'[25]

In 1978, Beckett, in a circular for the Ford workforce, squarely blamed the government for the 5 per cent limit to his company's offer. He predicted the dispute would last three months. Evans showed his willingness to back even a lengthy dispute with TGWU funds: 'Oh well, we can take that; we've got £32 million in the bank.'[26]

From this point onwards, the Ford strike became a three-sided dispute involving the Ford Motor Company, the trade unions and the Callaghan Labour government. Within a few days, Britain's most profitable automobile manufacturer was suffering loss of vehicle production at a potential cost of £10 million per day. Two weeks after the start of the official strike, Beckett explained that the company had 'no alternative but to embark upon negotiations in an atmosphere of free collective bargaining'.

> We became involved in our current strike solely because of our defence of the Government's pay guidelines and for no other reason. The strike is now in its seventh week with grievous consequences to the Company because we are determined to reach a responsible settlement.[27]

On 12 September Denis Healey, Chancellor of the Exchequer, had met Beckett and Bob Ramsay of Ford to discuss the pay claim and made clear that 'discretionary action' would be taken by the government if Ford breached the pay policy; this could include stopping purchases of Ford cars under government contracts or future agreements. The Chancellor emphasised that, as there was to be no autumn general election, the Ford settlement 'would clearly be regarded as a test case in an area of policy to

---

24 *Ibid.*, pp. 366–8 (diary entries: 25, 28 September 1978).
25 Tony Benn, *Conflicts of Interest: Diaries 1977–80*, edited by Ruth Winstone (London: Arrow Books, 1991), pp. 347–8 (diary entry: 26 September 1978).
26 *Ibid.*
27 Sir Terence Beckett to Albert Booth, 6 November 1978, TNA PREM 16/2123.

which the Government attached prime importance'. At the outset there was certainly an impasse between the government, with its rigid pay policy of 5 per cent, the Ford Company, with recruitment difficulties, and the unions, pressing a well based pay claim that could not be met within the government's official pay guidelines.[28]

At first, Ford attempted to secure a settlement that exceeded the 5 per cent guideline by the inclusion of a 'self-financing productivity scheme' (SFPS). It included payments for attendance, reduction in absenteeism and no stoppages.[29] However, the SFPS, with an additional payment 2.5 per cent above the pay norm, attracted the Prime Minister's immediate dis-approval, as it was not in strict conformity with the 1978 White Paper.[30] This proposal was a microcosm of the government's intractable difficulties with its rigid and inflexible pay policy. In fact, after detailed discussions with Ford officials, the SFPS met with the approval of Denis Healey, Eric Varley (Secretary of State for Industry) and, particularly, Albert Booth (Secretary of State for Employment). At that stage it offered a possible way out of a major strike. Booth wrote to the Prime Minister:

> On balance therefore the three of us believe that the best way to promote a settlement within the guidelines is [to inform Ford] ... we have no objection to such a scheme in principle and for my officials to keep in close touch and to obtain from Fords firm assurances about regular monitoring and about revision of the scheme should the expected savings not accrue.

While Booth admitted there was no certainty the unions would accept this scheme, he concluded: 'if we object to them [Ford] following this produc-tivity path, they may well go for a straight breach to avoid a damaging strike. Discretionary action against Fords would probably only be margin-ally effective.'[31]

A hardworking, well respected and highly principled politician, Booth had been an active member of the left-wing Tribune Group and an opponent of incomes policies. Yet, in the 1974–79 Wilson–Callaghan governments, first as Minister for Employment (under Michael Foot as Secretary of State), successfully steering significant employment legislation through Parliament in 1974–76, and then in the key post of Secretary of State for Employment in the Callaghan Cabinet, Booth was a loyal supporter of the social contract

---

28 'Note of a meeting held in the Chancellor of the Exchequer's room, HM Treasury at 3.30pm on Monday, 11 September 1978', TNA PREM 16/1708.

29 'Note of a meeting at 11 Downing Street at 2.00pm on Tuesday, 19 September 1978', TNA PREM 16/1708.

30 'Nigel Wicks (NLW) to Miss J. M Bacon, 20 September 1979', TNA PREM 16/1708.

31 'Note of points agreed between Ford management and government representatives on 20.9.78. Concerning the company's proposed productivity deal'; see also Alfred Booth to Prime Minister, 19 September 1978; also 'Prime Minister: Ford's pay claim', 19 September 1978, TNA PREM 16/1708.

and government economic policy.[32] In difficult times that ended in the 'winter of discontent', Booth – a Methodist lay preacher – was a voice of reason among a small inner group of ministers handling deteriorating relations with the unions. A former engineering draughtsman, Booth displayed a mastery of detail – evident in the Ford productivity proposal – that might have provided the way out of a difficult industrial relations situation.[33]

As early as 22 September, more than 16,000 Ford workers were on strike, including 11,000 at Halewood (with a loss of production already of over 1,000 cars, worth £3 million) and over 1,000 at Dagenham. According to the *Daily Mail*, these stoppages at the various Ford plants were the 'contemptuous reaction from union leaders to a pay offer which the Ford management had kept down to five per cent because of immense government pressure'. At the Henry Ford public house, union strike headquarters opposite the main Ford gates, one picket said defiantly: 'We'll stay out as long as it takes. In 1971 we were out for 10 weeks – this could be longer.'[34] In the opening exchanges in the press, Paul Roots, for Ford management, declared the industrial action to be in direct breach of an undertaking not to strike during negotiations, whereas Moss Evans was 'not in the least surprised'. Within a couple of days, Evans responded:

> If the Ford Motor company will sit down and reach a square deal not based on the government wage ceiling, but on their ability to pay, I will personally undertake to argue with the Government that no sanctions should be imposed [on Ford].[35]

However, the die was cast when Ron Todd, of the NJNC, learnt of the company's refusal to negotiate under free collective bargaining. During a crucial telephone conversation between Roots and Todd, Todd had asked Roots without success: 'Are you prepared to respond to our claim on its merits and not within the confines of government policy?' Todd told the press:

> We further recommend to the executives of the signatory unions that they fully support any industrial action taken against the Ford Motor Company because of the company's refusal to negotiate under free collective bargaining

---

32 For Albert Booth as Minister of State at the Department of Employment 1974–76, see Kenneth O. Morgan, *Michael Foot: A Life* (London: HarperCollins, 2007), pp. 286, 288, 290, 300.

33 Janine Booth (Albert Booth's niece), 'Albert Booth 1928–2010: an "Old Labour" man', *Worker's Liberty*, 18 February 2010; Julia Langdon, 'Albert Booth obituary: MP and Employment Secretary in James Callaghan's Cabinet', *Guardian*, 10 February 2010; Tam Dalyell, 'Albert Booth: principled Labour MP who served as Secretary of State under James Callaghan', *Independent*, 11 February 2010; 'Albert Booth', *Daily Telegraph*, 15 February 2010.

34 *Daily Mail*, 23 September 1978, pp. 1–2.

35 *Daily Mail*, 25 September 1978, p. 1.

... the response of Ford reflects Government policy, and we are reflecting trade union policy. It is getting to this stage when to mention free collective bargaining is to sound revolutionary.[36]

As a precautionary measure, the government reviewed the available sanctions against Ford in the event of a pay settlement in breach of the government's pay policy. From the beginning, the Callaghan government was adamant about enforcing its guidelines and any breach would result in 'discretionary action' against the Ford Motor Company. Joel Barnett, Labour's Chief Secretary to the Treasury, recalled that the government 'had exerted as much pressure as possible on the Ford management'.[37]

The dispute revealed divisions among the principal Conservative politicians. Margaret Thatcher indicated to union leaders at the Ford plant at Halewood that a future Conservative government would not interfere in private sector pay negotiations. However, the shadow Chancellor of the Exchequer, Sir Geoffrey Howe, appeared to contradict his party leader with his public statement that the £20 per week pay claim was 'in the wrong ball park'.[38] Howe, though, was not in line with the views of Conservative politicians such as Jim Prior, shadow Employment Minister, who had adopted a more cautious and conciliatory approach to the unions, in contrast to the hawkish 'Stepping Stones' programme advocated by John Hoskyns and Norman Strauss as a revolutionary blueprint for a future Conservative administration.[39] Nigel Lawson predicted that Ford would be prepared to exceed the government's pay limit and would not be deterred by the threat of government sanctions. He added that previous actions against private firms were 'in my view unconstitutional; and some illegal'.[40]

On 26 September, representatives of all three sides in the Ford dispute – company, unions and government – convened at an informal evening meeting. The private, off-the-record discussion reveals the differing stances being assumed at the start of the nine-week strike. For the government, Eric Varley and Albert Booth were highly anxious to distinguish the strike as an industrial dispute over wages rather than an overt attempt to

---

36 *Guardian*, 23 September 1978, pp. 1, 22.

37 Joel Barnett, *Inside the Treasury* (London: Andre Deutsch, 1982), p. 164. Interview: Lord Joel Barnett, House of Lords, 2 June 2010.

38 *Guardian*, 26 September 1978, pp. 1, 26.

39 A former professional soldier and businessman, John Hoskyns served as head of the Policy Unit during the Thatcher government. Norman Strauss's early career was at IBM. The Stepping Stones programme was produced at the Centre for Policy Studies, which had been set up by Sir Keith Joseph. See John Hoskyns, *Just In Time: Inside the Thatcher Revolution* (London: Aurum Press, 2000), pp. 39–96. The differing Conservative views on industrial relations are well summarised in 'Minutes, Leader's steering committee 51st meeting', 30 January 1978, Thatcher papers, Margaret Thatcher Foundation. Interview: Lord Jim Prior, Beccles, 11 November 2011; Jim Prior, *A Balance of Power* (London: Hamish Hamilton, 1986), pp. 154–5.

40 *Guardian,* 28 September 1978, p. 26. For more on the differing attitudes of the Conservative opposition to trade union power in the late 1970s, see chapter 7.

destroy the government's pay policy. They stressed the need 'to get the men back to work' so that negotiations might continue. For the unions, Moss Evans of the TGWU cited the long history of successful negotiations with the Ford Motor Company without the observance of a rigid pay policy. In support, Ron Todd pointed out that Ford management was not negotiating in 'a free collective bargaining situation'. Two other union representatives, Terry Duffy and Hugh Scanlon, urged a return to work to begin negotiations and to avoid a long dispute. In response, for the company, Sir Terence Beckett and Bob Ramsay argued that Ford could not negotiate a final offer while the strike continued. In fact, the previous wage contract still had four weeks to run. The management had only discussed the interpretation of the pay guidelines with the government. However, there was the danger that the dispute could become 'a crusade against the government's pay policy'. Both management and unions were prepared, if need be, for a long dispute at Fords; the government was equally determined to defend its pay strategy.[41]

The Ford strike was in progress at the time of the Labour Party annual conference, in Blackpool 2–6 October 1978, and threw a sharp light on the government's pay policy. Despite attempts at wheeling and dealing with trade union leaders, Callaghan and his ministers were unable to avoid an overwhelming defeat as the conference firmly rejected the government's 5 per cent pay policy by a card vote of 4,017,000 to 1,924,000 in support of the Wavertree resolution, with the TGWU and the AUEW – the two leading unions in the Ford strike – in the vanguard of the opposition.[42] The resolution had been opposed by a number of smaller right-wing unions, including the Railwaymen, the Post Office Workers, the Electricians and the Association of Professional, Executive, Clerical and Computer Staff (APEX).[43] At the Blackpool party conference, Donoughue noted: 'Certainly we have little power over Ford or British Oxygen. But it could still work out OK. If the profitable firms get 10%, other firms get 8% and public services get 5%, with public industries spread around, we could end up with single figures.'[44] Despite an impressive performance by the Prime Minister in the conference debate at Blackpool, Ian Aitkin, political editor of the *Guardian,* sounded a realistic note:

> Few people, on reflection, believe Mr Callaghan has any hope of halting the current round of astronomical pay claims, headed by the Ford workers.... [Ministers] appear to have written off the Ford case gloomily accepting that

---

41 'Note of a meeting held at 7.30pm on Monday 26 September 1978 at Ashdown House', TNA PREM 16/1708.

42 *Guardian,* 3 October 1978, pp. 1, 18. On the Wavertree resolution, see chapter 2.

43 Interview: Brendan Barber, Congress House, London, 4 August 2008.

44 Donoughue, *Downing Street Diary, Volume Two,* pp. 366, 368–70 (diary entry: 9 October 1978). For more Donoughue comments on the Labour Party conference, see pp. 366, 386–71 (diary entries: 22 September, 1, 2, 3 October 1978).

the company probably will be driven to settle the strike in spite of the threat of Government sanctions. They recognise privately that Ford cannot be relied on to stand firm.[45]

To back their wage claim, Cllr John Davis had led the Ford TGWU delegation to demonstrate at the Blackpool Labour Party conference. Their large banner exclaimed: 'MOSES – YOU SPLIT THE RED SEA. JIM – YOU CAN'T SPLIT FORD'S'.[46]

The nine-week dispute in 1978 affected not only the men on strike in the 23 Ford plants. In Dagenham, Halewood and other parts of Ford UK, support for the largely male workforce came from their families, though strike action caused real hardship.[47] Yet women defiantly formed the Ford Wives Strike Support Group to back the Ford workers' pay claim at a critical point in the strike, at the end of October 1978. This was a counter to the group of Southampton wives who attempted to lead a 'back to work' demonstration against the strike.[48]

Ford UK had a long history of strikes, stoppages and lay-offs. The British company bore the imprint of its parent American multinational, created by Henry Ford and based at Detroit in the United States. For many years, Ford was infamous for being a paternalistic company and singularly anti-union. In Britain, Ford had been first established at Trafford Park, Manchester, in 1911, but became synonymous with Dagenham, east London, where its vast new plant built on Thames marshland commenced car manufacture in the late 1930s. In 1944 Ford UK reluctantly conceded union recognition, but maintained the 'Fordist strategy' in industrial relations: tight supervision, uniform work standards and negotiating only with national trade unions, particularly the two largest, the TGWU and the AUEW. By early

---

45 *Guardian*, 4 October 1978, pp. 1, 22. Interview: Lord Bernard Donoughue, House of Lords, 6 July 2010.

46 Interview: Cllr Johnny Davis, Dagenham, 2 April 2012; photograph of Ford delegation in Cllr Davis's papers (see illustration no. 1, opposite p. 58).

47 Florence Stubberfield and her husband, Mike, who worked in the Ford press shop at Dagenham, had four children. Florence said: 'When Mike came out on strike I was really dismayed. We just couldn't afford a strike … the cost of living doesn't allow us to manage on what Mike brings home…. It's come to a point where if you have any chance of winning you just have to make a stand … if they accept 5%, what will they get next year? [They] say inflation isn't rising. Well, I know about that and every other woman [does] … every time you go shopping.' *Socialist Worker*, 28 October 1978, p. 4.

48 Eileen, the wife of a worker at Halewood, commented on: 'the "wonderful" wages that we're told car workers get. We just about manage. If he doesn't work overtime and Saturday and Sunday, he'll pick up about £40 and that just about gets us over, but if he's on overtime and weekends we have enough to go out…. The rent has just gone up to £13 – so the original offer [5 per cent] … wouldn't help.' Ford wives (from Dagenham, Langley and Southampton) joined together to challenge the anti-strike Southampton women's group. 'Mind you we got a shock when we saw the news … they only told the side of the anti-strike "ladies" – you wouldn't have thought there were 200 of us there backing the strike. You can't believe the media.' Unnamed author, 'Ford wives say: let's make Fords pay', *Big Flame*, November 1978, p. 6.

1949 there had been 38 strikes and go-slows. In 1953 Ford took over the nearby Briggs body plant, which had a reputation for industrial militancy. In these post-war years Ford's wage structure triggered repeated disputes, stoppages and overtime bans.[49]

In September 1967 a new five-grade wage structure resulted in various stoppages and overtime bans. Most famously, the women sewing machinists' strike for equal pay, led by the redoubtable shop steward Rose Boland, in June 1968 brought the Dagenham and Halewood plants to a virtual standstill.[50] As Chris Wrigley has written, the women's defiant industrial action in a male-dominated world gained the attention of the combative Barbara Castle, Secretary of State for Employment and Productivity. She had the ear of Prime Minister Harold Wilson and was determined to prioritise women's equal pay. The sewing machinists' dispute was settled locally, with women receiving 92 per cent of the men's wage rate instead of 85 per cent. Eventually, Castle's Equal Pay Act was passed in 1970 and implemented in 1975.[51]

According to Cllr Johnny Davis, the memorable 1968 Ford sewing machinists' strike made a definite impact on the development of trade unionism at the Ford Motor Company in the late 1960s and 1970s.[52] The dispute escalated from a genuine grading grievance into a political issue of national significance, involving Cabinet ministers, and culminated in not only the Equal Pay Act, but indirectly other significant legislation to eliminate discrimination in the 1970s in Britain. As a landmark in women's history, that dispute was comparable to the strike of the Bryant and May match women at Bow, which, in raising the banner of women's rights in the workplace, inspired the London dock strike and 'New Unionism' in London's East End in the late nineteenth century.[53]

During the 1960s and 1970s there were significant developments in the composition of the Ford workforce and how it was recruited. In joining

---

49 Dave Lyddon, 'The car industry, 1945–79: shop stewards and workplace unionism', in Chris Wrigley (ed.), *A History of British Industrial Relations, 1939–1979: Industrial Relations in a Declining Economy* (Cheltenham: Edward Elgar, 1996), pp. 198–202.

50 In 2010 the 1968 Ford sewing machinists' strike reached a worldwide audience in the film dramatisation *Made in Dagenham*.

51 Chris Wrigley, 'Women in the labour market and in the unions', in John McIlroy, Nina Fishman and Alan Campbell (eds), *The High Tide of British Trade Unionism: Trade Unions and Industrial Politics, 1964–79* (Monmouth: Merlin Press, second edition 2007), pp. 55–7.

52 Johnny Davis was from a Labour family in Battersea. He started work in the Ford foundry at Dagenham in 1956 and in the next 38 years served as a TGWU shop steward and convenor, as well as a Dagenham Labour councillor and mayor. In 1969 he accompanied the delegation of women sewing machinists to see Barbara Castle. Interview: Davis.

53 Friedman and Meredeen, *The Dynamics of Industrial Conflict*, p. 339. For the Bryant and May match women, see Louise Raw, *Striking a Light: The Bryant and May Matchwomen and Their Place in History* (London: Continuum, 2011). Interview: Rt Hon. Patricia Hewitt, Holloway, London, 23 June 2010.

Ford in 1956, Davis recalled that the vast majority of his fellow workers in the Ford foundry were Irish Catholics, many from Cork. This common bond produced a strong camaraderie on the shop floor and in industrial disputes. While Ford at Dagenham largely recruited from east London and Essex, the company had also moved many of its workers from the Trafford Park plant in Manchester down to the new Dagenham industrial complex. As the Halewood plant in Liverpool was developed in the 1960s the company used volunteers from Dagenham to assist in training the Merseyside workforce.[54]

On his first day, Johnny Davis had become a lifetime member of the TGWU after immediate approaches from two different unions. Although there were 21 unions at Ford, the TGWU and AUEW, under their General Secretaries Jack Jones and Hugh Scanlon, were well organised, with strong links to the Labour Party. In particular, the Dagenham and Halewood plants were based in strong Labour constituencies. By the 1960s and 1970s, Ford recruited black and Asian workers from a diversity of ethnic and cultural backgrounds.[55]

In 1979 Dan Connor, convenor of Ford's Dagenham body plant, Communist Party parliamentary candidate for Dagenham and activist in the 1978 Ford strike, calculated that there were 26,000 Ford workers on the local Dagenham estate, though the company increasingly recruited its workforce from up to 25–30 miles away. He estimated that nearly two-thirds of those working in his body plant were from a minority ethnic background. Ford was a labour-intensive firm with a high level of productivity among its workforce. Traditionally, the Dagenham workforce had consisted of Irish labourers, miners from south Wales and workers from the north of England and Scotland. Women, mostly employed on trim work, comprised only a very small proportion of the workforce.[56]

In the late 1960s and 1970s, the recruitment of younger workers from a variety of minority ethnic backgrounds formed the basis of a different political culture from that founded on traditional union–Labour Party links.[57] Among the workforce were representatives of the International Socialist Group, the International Marxist Group and other left-wing organisations. These new groupings at Fords were part of a growing shop-floor militancy, to be seen in the 1969 wage dispute and the 1971 and 1978 strikes. In April

---

54 Telephone interview: Frank Bland, Ford worker and shop steward, Romford, 29 August 2012.
55 Interview: Davis.
56 Martin Jacques, 'The Ford strike: where does it take us? An interview with Dan Connor', *Marxism Today*, February 1979, p. 34.
57 For an example in the 1978 strike of campaigning on improving pay, poor working conditions that affected home life and the under-representation of black Ford workers in foremen grades, see Black Socialist Alliance, *Why Black People Should Support the Ford Strike* (London: Black Socialist Alliance, 1978).

1978, an independent shop steward movement, the 'Ford Combine', had been formed by various Ford workers in left-wing groups to counteract existing shop stewards. The Ford management had endeavoured to bring 23 convenors onto the NJNC to incorporate shop-floor representatives into national wage negotiations.[58]

In the early years after the Second World War, Ford's mass production techniques, pioneered in the United States and known as 'Fordism', revolutionised the automobile industries of Europe. In 1950, Britain, second only to the United States in motor manufacture, became the world's main exporter of cars, selling three times the number of vehicles as American companies.[59] However, by the 1970s, the British economy, including automobile manufacture, was hit by the world recession triggered by an oil embargo and oil price hike of late 1973.[60] Between 1972 and 1983, with the closure of over a third of 13 main car assembly plants, British car production declined dramatically, by around 50 per cent, with the loss of sales in both the domestic and the export markets.[61]

In the 1970s about 90 per cent of motor manufacturing in the UK was located within four main groupings: the British-owned British Leyland Motor Corporation, which produced half of the vehicles, and three subsidiary companies of the American-owned firms Vauxhall (General Motors), Rootes (Chrysler) and Ford UK (Ford). Compared with its main competitors, Ford UK held a commanding position as a highly successful British car manufacturer in terms of profits, sales and market share. From 1911 to 2002 the giant American motor company established in Detroit by Henry Ford produced over 24 million vehicles in Britain, including 18 million cars.

The late 1960s and 1970s were a key period in the history of industrial relations in Britain. Public and government uneasiness about poor economic performance and industrial unrest was often directly associated with the growth of unbridled trade union power, especially in various key industries, such as coal mining, transport and docks. In particular, automobile manufacturing increasingly symbolised the state of British industrial

---

58 Tara Martin, '"End of an era?" Class politics, memory and Britain's winter of discontent', PhD thesis, University of Manchester, 2008, pp. 92–96. Frank Bland, Ford worker and shop steward, claimed that there was little cooperation between workers who were members of the Labour Party and those who belonged to 'politically motivated Far Left groups'. 'We didn't want any of that…. [The 1978] strike was a trade dispute.' Telephone interview: Bland.

59 Geoffrey Tweedale. 'Industry and de-industrialisation', in Richard Coopey and Nicholas Woodward (eds), *Britain in the 1970s: The Troubled Economy* (London: University College London Press, 1996), pp. 258–9.

60 Niall Ferguson, 'Introduction. Crisis? What crisis? The 1970s and the shock of the global', in Niall Ferguson, Charles S. Maier, Erez Manela and Danile J. Sargent (eds), *The Shock of the Global: The 1970s in Perspective* (Cambridge, MA: The Belknap Press of Harvard University Press, 2010), pp. 1–24.

61 Christopher M. Law, 'The geography of industrial rationalisation: the British motor car assembly industry, 1972–1982', *Geography*, vol. 70, no. 1, January 1985, pp. 1–6.

relations in terms of the influence of shop stewards in disputes and the growth of workplace unionism in motor assembly plants.

Probably disputes in the automobile industry were largely responsible for the common belief that Britain, compared with its international competitors, was inherently strike-prone. The sacking of Derek Robinson – one of the foremost shop stewards in the British automobile industry, a member of the British Communist Party and known in the British popular press as 'Red Robbo' – by Michael Edwardes in November 1979 was symbolic. Edwardes claimed that Robinson, who had started work at Longbridge in 1941, had been at the head of the opposition to his 'recovery plan' for British Leyland. At the main plant at Longbridge there had been 523 industrial disputes, involving 'the loss of 62,000 cars and 113,000 engines, worth £200 million'.[62]

The case of Robinson typified the state of industrial relations in the British car industry, as disorder and the potential for disorder became a major focus of concern, particularly in the media, in the 1960s and 1970s. Particular attention was given to the rising incidence of unofficial strikes. Industrial conflict in the motor manufacturing industry became part of a wider picture of the industrial anarchy during these years, particularly the role played by shop stewards in British industrial relations.[63]

The Ford Motor Company had a long-standing association with the Callaghan Labour government. In 1977 the Prime Minister, whose son Michael was an executive director at Ford, had been instrumental in persuading the company to locate its new £180 million engine manufacturing plant at the Waterton Industrial Estate at Bridgend in south Wales (on the edge of the South Wales Development Area and close to Callaghan's Cardiff constituency), rather than in the Republic of Ireland or Spain. A key part in securing Ford's 'Erika programme' investment were the negotiations involving the Prime Minister and Henry Ford II, head of the American car giant.[64] The total cost of the Erika programme was of the order of £600 million, with the new engine plant at Bridgend providing, at full capacity, 2,500 new jobs.[65] The programme also formed the basis for additional US investment, plus British government grants, to create further employment. During 1978 nearly £25 million had been given to Ford under the Erika programme, alongside several other financial awards; these could not have

62 Edwardes, *Back from the Brink*, pp. 117, 119.
63 For more on Derek Robinson, see Nigel Fountain, 'A long, hot winter', *Guardian*, 25 September 1993, pp. 18–19, 22.
64 C. L. Mayhew to Philip Wood, 24 August 1977, TNA PREM 16/1702; 'Brief for the Prime Minister's meeting with Mr Henry Ford on 25 August, 1977', TNA PREM 16/1702.
65 For the Ford Erika programme negotiations, see H. J. Mitchell (private secretary, Industry Minister) to Nigel Wicks (private secretary, Prime Minister), 11 July 1977; J. J. Davies (Welsh Office) to Nigel Wicks, 12 July 1977; Philip Wood (Prime Minister's private office) to J. Mitchell, 13 August 1977, PREM 16/1702.

been withdrawn as part of the 'discretionary action' against the company when the 1978 Ford settlement breached the government's pay policy.[66]

There was a turning point in the 1978 Ford strike on 9 October, when the company management decided to consider negotiating in a free collective bargaining atmosphere. Up to this point, Fords had refused to negotiate until there had been a return to work. This change of attitude was caused primarily by developments in Ford Europe, with production halts in Belgium and delays to the design of an engine.[67] Ford UK was a multinational company and since 1967 an integral part of Ford Europe. A prolonged halt to production in Britain affected Ford's European operations in Germany, Spain and elsewhere. Ford also pointed to the enormous damage done by the long strike in 1971 to Ford's relations with the rest of the Ford world. Since then, the company had built up £1 billion of investments in Europe.[68]

The industrial action secured an unprecedented degree of external support in Britain and in Europe. During the third week of the strike, on 13 October, union negotiators turned down the company's improved offer of 8 per cent without any reference to the union membership. The International Metal Workers' Federation (IMWF) held a conference of trade unionists from Ford European plants in London on 19 October, which pledged financial backing for the strikers. Other examples of international support for the Ford workers included the refusal of Bosch workers in Germany to produce instrument panels and electrical components for Ford. At the IMWF conference it was agreed that work normally done at Ford's British plants would not be undertaken by workers at Ford's plants in mainland Europe, or at any subcontractors.

On 31 October 1978 Ford made a 'final' offer of 16.6 per cent (5.15 per cent to be paid as a weekly flat-rate attendance allowance, conditional on a code of practice with 13 grounds for disqualification). In reaching a settlement Ford was faced with the problem of whether 23 chief convenors, each addressing a mass meeting of several thousand workers, would recommend a return to work. The breakdown in negotiations had demonstrated that the 1978 strike was the most acrimonious dispute the company had experienced, as revealed by the great gap between the government and the NJNC at Fords.[69]

On 21 November 1978, the Ford workforce voted to accept the management's revised offer of 17 per cent at mass meetings at the various Ford plants and to return to work. The stoppage had lasted nine weeks. At the Halewood plant, shop stewards had failed to persuade workers to reject

---

66 'Ford Motor Company: government assistance', n.d., PREM 16/1702.
67 H. A. Polling to James Callaghan, 27 September 1978, TNA PREM 16/1708.
68 'Note for the record: Fords', 28 September 1978, TNA PREM 16/1708.
69 'Note of a meeting in the Chancellor of Exchequer's room, H.M. Treasury at 9.00am on Friday 29 September 1978', TNA PREM 16/1708.

the offer. The 17 per cent settlement broke the government's pay guidelines and raised the question of sanctions against the Ford Motor Company.
In the Commons, the Chancellor of the Exchequer defended taking discretionary action against Ford as the company had negotiated for seven
weeks during the strike outside the government's official pay policy, while
more than 500,000 workers in various industries had already settled fully
within the guidelines.[70]

In Cabinet on 7 December 1978 the Chancellor of the Exchequer re-
iterated that around 500,000 people had been covered by settlements in the
annual pay round so far. Only 2 per cent were outside the government's
guidelines, which was a smaller proportion than in the previous year. The
two major breaches were by the Ford Motor Company and the British
Oxygen Company settlement. There was also a comprehensive discussion
of the 'discretionary action' against companies that broke the pay guidelines,
which reveals that the government's sanction policy was to 'create a moral
climate in which the main penalty on such a company was loss of reputation'. The government also had 'discretionary powers' to determine how
public funds were allocated and in what circumstances financial support
would be made available – in similar ways to the French and American
administrations. The significant difference was that the British government's sanctions policy was the solitary plank of an anti-inflation strategy,
rather than a broader range of policies which could be enforced by law.
The Prime Minister summarised the government's difficulty in maintaining
public support for its pay policy and suggested that all ministers should
make the policy 'a regular theme in speeches and public statements'.[71] In
particular, the sanctions policy needed clarification, so that it appeared as an
'indication of public disfavour and a warning to others' rather than primarily a penalty on companies in breach of pay policy.[72]

By 1978 Ford was the beneficiary of different forms of government
financial assistance, and government contracts, including a three-year
Ministry of Defence contract for spare parts, cars and light trucks, as well as
a Home Office contract for the supply of tractors. The Labour government
had also awarded various grants and other financial assistance. The various
options for discretionary action were part of a wider-ranging discussion
between the Prime Minister and his colleagues well in advance of any Ford
strike settlement.[73]

---

70 *Parliamentary Debates* (House of Commons), fifth series, 28 November 1978, vol. 959,
      cols 217–21.
71 Cabinet conclusion, 7 December 1978, TNA CAB 128/64.
72 *Ibid*, p. 12.
73 For examples, see Roy Hattersley to James Callaghan, and Eric Varley to James
      Callaghan, both 'Prime Minister: discretionary action against Ford', 9 November 1978
      and 14 November 1978, TNA PREM 16/2123.

On 21 November, Ford's final offer of 17 per cent was eventually agreed as a package with the unions. This settlement devastated the government's efforts to sustain its 5 per cent guideline. 'If you have tears to shed, join the queue', declared the *Daily Mail*. 'Seventeen per cent without productivity strings. Three-and-a-half times the Government's norm. This can't be good. Who benefits…? Ford workers?'[74]

Yet the Ford settlement had far wider implications for the minority Callaghan administration's embattled pay policy, as the government had prepared throughout the course of the dispute to implement 'discretionary action' against Ford or any other private employer in breach of its pay policy. As a result of the award, Ford was in danger of incurring financial sanctions – including cancellation of orders for vehicles and other products. On 28 November the Chancellor of the Exchequer made a statement in the House of Commons on the government's position on the pay settlement reached at Ford:

> In the government's view, the settlement cannot be reconciled with the pay guidelines contained in the White Paper 'Winning the Battle Against Inflation' Cmnd. 7293.… After considering the settlement in the light of all the relevant circumstances, the government have reluctantly reached the conclusion that such discretionary action should be taken and the company have been informed accordingly.[75]

On 7 December the main item on the Cabinet agenda was the government's pay policy after the Ford settlement, with the prospect of an adjournment debate forced by the Conservative opposition that evening on 'the unjust and arbitrary use of sanctions on industry'.[76] The Prime Minister was unyielding on the pay policy as the central plank in the fight against any return to double-figure inflation in Britain. In this respect, as we have seen, he considered it imperative that all government ministers, not just those directly concerned with pay negotiations, highlight the government's pay policy in their speeches and public statements.

More encouraging news for the government was that a large number of workers had already made moderate wage agreements in 1978, and only 2 per cent of settlements in phase 4 of the social contract had exceeded the government's guidelines on pay policy – notably the Ford Motor Company and the British Oxygen Company. According to Tony Benn, Bill Rodgers queried whether it was wise to have a pay policy of 5 per cent if it was liable to be broken frequently. 'The PM slapped him down and said (1) we stick to 5% and (2) we openly admit it if particular settlements are in breach'. Moreover, there were a large number of wage claims by public sector

---

74 *Daily Mail*, 22 November 1978, p. 6.
75 *Parliamentary Debates* (House of Commons), fifth series, 28 November 1978, vol. 959, col. 217.
76 Benn, *Conflicts of Interest*, pp. 411–12 (diary entry: 7 December 1978).

workers in the pipeline after the New Year. As Callaghan emphasised, the government response to a major breach of the 5 per cent norm, such as the Ford settlement, had direct implications for maintaining an effective pay policy in the public sector, where the government was a major employer.[77]

The Cabinet was determined to maintain a full array of sanctions that could be imposed against private companies in breach of the pay policy, even for pay settlements deemed non-inflationary on prices. Discretionary action against companies appeared to have significant public backing, including among Labour Party supporters and trade unionists. According to Tony Benn, Denis Healey said that sanctions could act as a deterrent for other firms.[78] Callaghan added: 'it's in the public sector that we shall have the most trouble'.[79]

At the meeting of the Parliamentary Labour Party also on 7 December the Prime Minister spoke about the forthcoming vote in Parliament:

> The motion tonight on the adjournment debate is not a technical motion but a political one. If we lose it will be a body blow to the Government. The Tories expect to win and Saatchi & Saatchi [the then relatively unknown advertising agency used by the Conservative Party to design its campaigns] would be very quick to exploit it.... Personally I don't like sanctions, but the private sector must be checked to help with the public sector.

However, owing to the confusion caused by several points of order and a disturbance in the Strangers' Gallery, the adjournment debate was postponed for one week.[80]

As the Lib–Lab pact, agreed in 1977 and which guaranteed Liberal votes to support the minority Callaghan administration on votes of confidence at Westminster, had ended in the summer 1978, the government was now even more dependent on temporary alliances and deals with the various minority parties – Plaid Cymru, the Scottish National Party and the Northern Ireland MPs – as well as on maintaining party discipline within its own ranks.

---

77 Cabinet conclusions, 7 December 1978, TNA CAB 128/64; Callaghan, *Time and Chance*, pp. 633–4; Benn, *Conflicts of Interest*, pp. 411–12 (diary entry: 7 December 1978); Donoughue, *Downing Street Diary, Volume Two*, p. 398 (diary entry: 7 December 1978).
78 The Callaghan government had imposed sanctions before the 1978 Ford strike, including 'discretionary action' against three firms in breach of the 1976–77 pay guidelines. On 23 September 1977 the Belfast firm J. Mackie & Sons was not granted export credit guarantees after it granted a 20 per cent pay award. Also, when Holliday Hall failed to implement a national pay award (owing to government pay policy), the Electrical, Electronic, Telecommunications and Plumbing Union took strike action. 'Discretionary action' was taken against various firms in 1978 (74 in August; 65 in September; 55 in October; 65 in November). See Andrew Taylor, *The Trade Unions and the Labour Party* (Beckenham: Croom Helm, 1987), p. 113, n. 76.
79 Cabinet conclusions, 7 December 1978, TNA CAB 128/64.
80 Benn, *Conflicts of Interest*, pp. 411–12 (diary entry: 7 December 1978).

On 12 December 1978 a meeting at 10.45 a.m. with the Prime Minister, Denis Healey, Fred Mulley and David Owen on nuclear strategy in the Cabinet room at Downing Street was unexpectedly interrupted by Michael Foot and Michael Cocks (chief whip) with news that threatened the survival of the minority Callaghan government. The Tribune Group of left-wing Labour MPs were unlikely to support the government in the parliamentary vote on sanctions against the Ford Motor Company.[81] Lord Owen later recalled the incident 'in some detail because it is a vignette of how that Labour government, without sufficient votes, constantly had to cobble together a majority. It was a daily part of the government's life which I rarely saw at close quarters. With the benefit of hindsight, *I have no doubt that this was the moment the Labour Party lost the 1979 general election*' (emphasis added).[82] With a delegation of Labour MPs away in Europe, the whips were unable to guarantee a majority on the Ford sanctions division. In the end, Callaghan and Foot decided not to make the pay policy a vote of confidence, although that would probably have brought the Tribune Group MPs into line.[83]

In the debate that evening, the government was defeated by 285 to 279 votes by a combination of Conservatives, Liberals, Scottish Nationalists and Ulster Unionists. Crucially, a number of the Tribune Group MPs decided to abstain. The Prime Minister accepted that the financial penalties on the Ford Motor Company had to be withdrawn. While the government won a vote of confidence the next day by a majority of 10 votes (300 to 290), it had lost the power to impose sanctions against firms in breach of the government pay policy.

According to Lord Owen, if they had lost the vote of confidence, Labour could have won a general election in January 1979. 'Even more important,

---

81 David Owen, 'Stick to your principles and damn your party', *New Statesman*, 24 January 2011.
82 Interview: Lord David Owen, House of Lords, 16 November 2011.
83 Lord Owen, who did not keep a diary, thought the occasion so significant for the future of the Labour government that he recorded a special note about the 12 December meeting (which had resumed at 12.45 p.m.). Michael Cocks 'reported marginal chance of winning if we made it a vote of confidence – uncertain about delgation [*sic*] at European Parliament.... Issue complex with differing viewpoints. It was finally decided in the Prime Minister's Room in the House at 3.00pm.' Present were Denis Healey, Roy Hattersley, Joel Barnett and Jack Diamond, one of the whips who confirmed that the Labour delegation was 'stranded in Luxembourg'. Owen noted: 'Jim [Callaghan] wavered ... Roy backed Denis [in favour of a confidence vote]. Joel yes to confidence if we could win but could we win? I kept quiet watching Jim. Suddenly he moved decisively to Michael's viewpoint [i.e. certain he could win a vote of confidence, if necessary, the following day] and in doing it put strong psychological pressure on Michael to deliver the Left. Very critical was I think his wish to go on as a duo – to separate now after all these months was wisely thought ot [*sic*] be too damaging. Gamble to make it confidence option to call an election in January, February, March or April'. Handwritten note, 12 December 1978, Lord David Owen papers, Sydney Jones Library, University of Liverpool, D 709 3/1/14.

if we had not lost the Ford vote Jim Callaghan's morale would have been much higher. He would have confronted any trouble that winter with more confidence and we might even have won a September 1979 General Election.'[84] Moreover, as Lord Owen has written: 'sanctions were like a finger in the dyke; once removed the whole edifice of restraint collapsed. Before we knew where we were the Winter of Discontent descended on us, dooming us to lose the general election.'[85]

Ten years after his resignation as Prime Minister, Callaghan reflected on his years at 10 Downing Street with Geoffrey Goodman.[86] Goodman had been present at the news conference in a West End hotel when Sir Terence Beckett announced the settlement of the union pay claim and defended the Ford pay rise as being 'within the intentions of the Government White Paper'. The Ford chairman declared it was cheaper to settle at £48 million than incur over double that amount in a prolonged official stoppage. Beckett claimed that there had been over 600 unofficial strikes at Ford in 1977–78.

After his 1979 election defeat Callaghan admitted: 'I went back to the farm that weekend and wrote in my diary an expression of relief and also a strong desire to hand over the party leadership … I had had enough. I came to the job too late and I was weary.' He later added: 'and if by a miracle we had won [a general election in the autumn of 1978] we would still have faced a 17% wage rise by Fords'.

Goodman observed: 'How bitterly that Ford deal still rankles. No one in the Callaghan government will ever forget it. It was the final nail in the coffin.'[87]

---

84 David Owen, *Time to Declare* (London: Penguin, 1992), p. 385.
85 *Ibid.*, pp. 384–5.
86 Geoffrey Goodman, a distinguished industrial correspondent, was deputy editor of the *Daily Mirror* and former head of the Anti-Inflation Unit during Harold Wilson's government 1974–76. Interview with Geoffrey Goodman, Congress House, London, 22 July 2008.
87 Geoffrey Goodman, *From Bevan to Blair: Fifty Year's Reporting from the Political Front Line* (London: Pluto Press, 2003), pp. 230–1, 242.

Illustrations

1. Delegation of Ford strikers led by Cllr Johnny Davis at the Labour Party conference, Blackpool, 1978

2. Public service workers demonstrating during the National Day of Action, London, 22 January 1979

3. Merseyside gravediggers and crematorium workers on strike, Liverpool, February 1979

4. Surrey shoppers at almost empty supermarket shelves during the road hauliers' strike, January 1979

5. 'Labour Still Isn't Working': Conservative Party poster, 1979 general election

6. Prime Minister James Callaghan leaves 10 Downing Street after 1979 election defeat

Chapter Four

The oil tanker drivers' dispute and the road hauliers' strike

On 19 January 1979 Bernard Donoughue, head of the Policy Unit at Downing Street, wrote: 'The end of the worst week – worst, politically, that is – since I came to No. 10.' The day before, after a difficult Cabinet meeting, the Prime Minister had said in all seriousness to his press secretary, Tom McCaffrey: 'How do you announce that the government's pay policy has completely collapsed?' During a bitter 'winter of discontent', the Callaghan administration had to cope with an avalanche of unremitting wage demands from both the private and public sectors. As Ken Stowe, James Callaghan's principal private secretary, observed, the convergence of different pay claims was also a cause of considerable problems. 'That bloody elaborate machinery in the Cabinet Office delays everything while it monitors every 10p. We should just set out broad guidelines and let the negotiators get on with it.'[1]

In the pipeline were a string of claims by employees at British Oxygen, bakery workers and manual workers in the water industry, all threatening major strikes to back their wage demands. At the same time, the four major unions representing public sector workers – the Confederation of Health Service Employees (COHSE), the General Municipal Workers' Union (GMWU), the National Union of Public Employees (NUPE) and the Transport and General Workers' Union (TGWU) – already had well laid plans for a National Day of Action on 22 January 1979 in their campaign for a national minimum wage for the low paid.[2] Yet what provoked

---

1   Bernard Donoughue, *Downing Street Diary, Volume Two: With James Callaghan in No. 10* (London: Jonathan Cape, 2008), pp. 425, 427 (diary entries: 18, 19 January 1979).
2   Addressing a large rally at Newcastle upon Tyne, four months before (at the time of the 1978 Ford strike), the General Secretary of the 710,000-strong National Union of Public Employees, Alan Fisher, declared: 'We are prepared to fight for the policy of the TUC in seeking our objective of a £60 per week minimum rate of pay. The government's pay policy comes nowhere near that objective … it may lead to a major confrontation in the public sector.' *Daily Telegraph*, 18 September 1979, p. 1. See also *Sun*, 18 September

Donoughue's gloom and doom was the major industrial unrest between late December 1978 and January 1979, concerning the oil tanker drivers and road hauliers, that threatened to bring Britain to a halt at the time when the Prime Minister was abroad at an international summit of world leaders.

This chapter explores the causes, character and impact of this large-scale industrial action by lorry drivers and the interplay of forces between government, unions and employers at the centre of the 'winter of discontent' that swept Britain. These two industrial disputes also throw significant light on the state's contingency plans for crisis management in industrial relations. A divided Callaghan Cabinet was brought to the brink of declaring a state of emergency, in case troops had to be deployed and vehicles requisitioned to maintain essential services.

This account also draws on the testimony of various participants at the centre of the crisis. The Energy Secretary, Tony Benn, recorded in his diary the day-to-day handling of the overtime ban, leading to a possible full-blown strike, by the oil tanker drivers.[3] Also in the Callaghan Cabinet, the hawkish Minister of Transport, William Rodgers, had departmental responsibility for the national road haulage strike. He remained an unyielding stalwart of the 5 per cent government pay norm. Before the recent release of official 1979 Cabinet papers, his writings on the action in the road haulage industry were one the few detailed first-hand accounts of a specific strike during the 'winter of discontent'. The Cabinet papers also reveal the part played by the Secretary of State for Employment, Albert Booth, during the negotiations in the oil tanker drivers' dispute and the role of the deputy secretary in the Cabinet Office, Sir Clive Rose, at the Civil Contingencies Unit (CCU) in the government's response to the industrial disputes.[4]

At the end of 1978 the government's incomes policy had suffered two major contraventions. First, the Ford workers received a 17 per cent wage increase, which shattered the official 5 per cent pay norm; this was followed by the parliamentary defeat of sanctions against firms in breach of the government's pay policy, which effectively rendered the government powerless against private employers who exceeded the government's pay

---

1979. For the planning of a National Day of Action by the major public sector unions and its results, see chapter 5.

3   The most detailed day-to-day account of the oil tanker drivers' dispute (which lasted from 11 December 1978 to 8 January 1979) is in Tony Benn, *Conflicts of Interest: Diaries 1977–80*, edited by Ruth Winstone (London: Arrow Books, 1991), pp. 407, 413–14, 417, 418, 419–20, 421, 422, 423, 424, 431, 433.

4   William Rodgers, 'A winter's tale of discontent', *Guardian*, 7 January 1984, p. 11; William Rodgers, 'Government under stress, Britain's winter of discontent', *Political Quarterly*, vol. 55, no. 2, 1984, pp. 171–9. For important accounts of the 1979 road haulage strike, see Paul Smith, *Unionization and Union Leadership: The Road Haulage Industry* (London: Continuum, 2001); Chris Wrigley, 'The winter of discontent: the lorry drivers' strike, January 1979', in Andrew Charlesworth, David Gilbert, Adrian Randall, Humphrey Southall and Chris Wrigley, *An Atlas of Industrial Protest in Britain 1750–1990* (Basingstoke: Macmillan, 1996), pp. 210–16.

ceiling. Then, second, immediately before the Christmas holiday, a 12 per cent wage agreement was fixed with striking BBC staff to prevent a television blackout during the holiday period.[5]

Most serious, however, was the industrial news on 30 November of an overtime ban by oil tanker drivers, with the strong likelihood that the dispute would develop into a full-blown national strike in the New Year as 8,500 tanker drivers – employed by the five main oil companies (Mobil, Shell, BP, Esso and Texaco) – submitted a pay claim comprising a new basic rate of £90, a 35-hour week and other concessions. Altogether, this would represent at least a 40 per cent increase on the oil companies' pay bill. In response, the companies put forward offers based on their ability to pay – to the order of 5 per cent (while negotiations were conducted separately with each oil company, their different offers were normally coordinated). The union immediately rejected this offer, as well as the possibility of productivity deals, until a satisfactory increase on basic pay rates had been successfully bartered.

All the drivers were members of the TGWU, led by Moss Evans, an avowed advocate of free collective bargaining. After the Ford settlement, as the government was well aware, the General Secretary was determined to maintain the TGWU wages policy, and to reinforce his new position by inflicting another defeat on the government's 5 per cent pay policy.[6] To add to the government's concerns, at the peak of the 'winter of discontent' it was also faced with a national strike in the road haulage industry, which started as unofficial industrial action in Scotland on 3 January. Two days later the Prime Minister left Britain for six days to attend an international summit on the Caribbean island of Guadeloupe, followed by a visit to Barbados. During this time the road hauliers' strike spread rapidly to other parts of Britain, accompanied by reports of shoppers panic buying, shortages of food and animal supplies, as well as predictions of large-scale lay-offs of workers.

Both industrial disputes threatened to bring the country to a grinding halt and raised the crucial question of a declaration of a state of emergency. Haunted in part by memories of five states of emergency during the Heath government's 'three-day week' and the miners' strikes in 1972 and 1973–74, no state of emergency was declared in mainland Britain. Although the social contract was in shreds, the Callaghan administration continued to claim it was able to work with the unions at least better than its Conservative opponents.

---

5 *Financial Times*, 22 December 1978, p. 1; *Financial Times*, 23 December 1978, p. 1.
6 At the outset of the 1978 Ford strike, the Prime Minister, in conversation with Albert Booth, commented that 'Moss Evans was not yet firmly in the saddle and had to prove himself'. 'Note of a telephone conversation between the Prime Minister and Albert Booth on 24 September 1978', The National Archives (henceforth TNA) PREM 16/1708.

However, the events of the 'winter of discontent' in January and February 1979 were a major turning point for Callaghan and his ministers that carried serious political implications. On 10 January a sun-tanned Prime Minister famously arrived back in snow-bound Britain to an arctic blast of escalating industrial unrest and a hostile British press. A narrow Labour lead in the previous autumn had turned into a 19 per cent margin in the polls for the Conservatives by February 1979. The minority Callaghan administration on 28 March lost a vital vote of no confidence, the first time a government had been dismissed in this way since Ramsay MacDonald's first Labour government, in 1924. On 3 May 1979 the general election returned Margaret Thatcher to 10 Downing Street with a Conservative overall majority of 43. Labour then spent the next 18 years in opposition.

The legacy of the previous oil tanker drivers' dispute, with an overtime ban in 1977, still hung over the November 1978 negotiations. The oil companies had settled the 1977 claim by agreeing to calculate overtime and shift payments from November 1978 on a new '£75 basic' rule, subject to various other considerations. To accommodate this proviso, the companies would have had to offer 8.5 per cent, significantly above the current government pay norm. In addition, the TGWU was adamant that productivity deals were possible only if an improvement in basic rates was settled first. Negotiations continued between the various shop stewards and their oil companies, from Shell meeting on 20 November to Mobil on 28 November, against a bleak background of pending industrial action. At this stage of the dispute, Albert Booth, Secretary of State for Employment, was the government minister responsible. He reported that 'the shop stewards at BP are meeting tomorrow and may possibly decide then on some form of industrial action. Otherwise the companies are generally convinced that unless they increase their offers next week industrial action will follow.'[7] Booth also observed that 'Shell were in the van this year and the others were the followers ... but they also had the most militant shop stewards and if ... the company did not move beyond the 5% then industrial action would be virtually certain'.[8] At the same time, Booth made clear to the union representatives – including Jack Ashwell, the national officer of the TGWU handling the dispute – that the eventual settlement had to be within the 5 per cent government guideline. Surprisingly, in these negotiations, Booth was instructed by the Prime Minister's private office to 'stick to the line that basic rate increases must be limited to 5%. But he (the PM) feels that in this case, if at the end of the day, the employers offer 8.5% and this is accepted, the government would have to go along with it.'[9]

---

7   Albert Booth to Roy Hattersley, 15 November 1978, TNA PREM 16/1707.
8   Albert Booth to Roy Hattersley, 16 November 1978, TNA PREM 16/1707.
9   T. P. Lankester to I. A. Fair, 17 November 1978, TNA PREM 16/1707. On 5 December, Booth reported: 'My officials again stressed to the companies that the eventual settlement must be capable of justification under the 5% guidelines on the one hand and the

On 11 December the Prime Minister received a detailed assessment of the effects of a national strike by oil tanker drivers; these would be 'severe and quickly felt', as around 60 per cent of oil products were moved by road, with the remainder supplied by pipeline or coastal shipping, and, further, most of the tanker drivers were members of the TGWU. While the government had contingency plans for using troops to move oil, at best this would amount to about 30 per cent of normal supplies and would cover only essential services. The strike would bite quickly as most consumers held minimal supplies. Filling stations normally had only two to three days' supply of petrol and industrial users of fuel oil probably stocked supplies for one to two weeks. On the other hand, the Prime Minister was informed that the heaviest oil users, such as power stations, were not supplied by oil tankers but by rail or pipeline or boat.

However, the most far-reaching effect of a national strike by oil tanker drivers would be felt in the road haulage industry, which would quickly come to a virtual standstill, with serious repercussions for the British economy. It was a chilling observation. Industrial action over a period of time by the tanker drivers raised questions about the industry's capacity to get by without national road haulage. Advice on the matter was requested by the Prime Minister. The confidential memorandum he received in response concluded with a reference to the Heath government:

> A strike lasting any length of time would seem to be potentially very serious. On the other hand, ex-ante analyses of the three day week tended to underestimate industry's ability to cope, and it is always possible that industry would cope without road transport better than might be expected.[10]

The advice to the Prime Minister also noted that the oil tanker drivers' dispute in 1977 had involved an overtime ban by drivers employed by Shell, BP, Esso and Texaco, causing an overall reduction in supplies of 75–78 per cent of normal. One of the most significant results then was the effect on users of industrial gases, as only limited stocks were held by manufacturers. Areas affected by the overtime ban on oil distribution included bus services in west Scotland, Manchester and London (especially the capital's General Taxi Company).[11]

According to Tony Benn, government policy became a damage-limitation exercise after the Ford strike. As Energy Secretary, Benn became directly involved in mid-December 1978, as the threat of this kind of industrial action raised the critical issue of a proclamation of an energy emergency,

---

productivity criteria on the other. They rejected any suggestion that a settlement at 8.5% plus productivity might be acceptable to Ministers.' For reports of further negotiations, see Albert Booth to Roy Hattersley, 1, 5, 14 December 1978, TNA PREM 16/1707.

10　A. M. W Battishall to T. L. Lankester, confidential memorandum, 'Effects of industrial action by oil tanker drivers', 11 December 1978, TNA PREM 16/1707.

11　*Ibid.*

to avert fears of a national crisis in essential supplies of oil and petrol across Britain.[12] On 11 December 1978, Benn's under-secretary, Robert Priddle, forwarded him the Civil Contingency Unit's plan, 'Operation Drumstick', in connection with a strike by oil tanker drivers. It included a timetable with two options for the mobilisation of troops: either before Christmas 1978, or after the holiday period, to move essential supplies of fuel. However, Benn was against using troops to transport supplies of fuel to maintain essential services. He favoured what he described as 'the slower option' so that agreement might be made with the unions to maintain essential services and thereby avoid the political difficulty of openly employing troops on the streets of British cities.[13] As in 1977, where a similar situation had arisen with an oil tanker drivers' overtime ban, he argued in Cabinet, again without success, that an agreement should be secured with the TGWU to guarantee supplies for essential services should a strike occur.[14] According to Sir Clive Rose, under the 1976 Energy Act a declaration of a state of emergency would in fact comprise four orders: to release the oil companies from their legal requirement to supply fuel; to restrict the opening hours of petrol stations; to arrange for the closure of some petrol stations; and to prohibit cans being filled at petrol stations.[15]

In this situation, the government was in close touch with union leaders about the oil tanker drivers' dispute. On 18 December, Tony Benn met Len Murray, General Secretary of the Trades Union Congress (TUC), together with Merlyn Rees (Home Secretary) and Albert Booth, at the Department of Employment to discuss the dispute, which was followed by a further meeting with Booth, Moss Evans and Jack Ashwell in view of the likelihood of a declaration of a state of emergency in the New Year.

On 19 December Benn gave Evans a paper called 'Essential services', which detailed the various government actions should an oil emergency occur. In addition, the Energy Secretary suggested future types of co-operation between government and unions. According to Benn he appealed to Evans:

> Look Moss, we are in a hell of a jam because the timetable for the use of troops is such that I will have to make a move this week if I can't get the TGWU's agreement. We have got to find a way through…. I can't give a

---

12 Benn, *Conflicts of Interest*, pp. 407, 413–14, 417, 418, 419–20, 421, 422, 423, 424, 431, 433.

13 *Ibid.*, pp. 413–14 (diary entry: 11 December 1978).

14 The senior civil servants were completely against the Benn's proposal. Sir Ken Stowe, Callaghan's principal private secretary, wrote to the Prime Minister 'under strong pressure from Mr Benn (who has at last woken up as to the fact that he is now in the hot seat when petrol supplies dry up)'. Stowe to Callaghan, 15 December 1978, TNA PREM 16/1707.

15 Benn, *Conflicts of Interest*, p. 418 (diary entry: 18 December 1978). See also Sir Clive Rose's contribution to 'Symposium: the winter of discontent', *Contemporary Review*, vol. 1, no. 3, autumn 1987, p. 41.

nod and a wink to the oil companies: the Government can't now push the companies to settle – that's asking too much.[16]

Discussion of a possible state of emergency was not restricted to strikes by oil tanker drivers, as the government anticipated other industrial action – by water and sewage workers, local authority manual employees and other groups who could halt essential public services. There were many examples that might involve the army and other military personnel. It was clear that the growing industrial unrest could bring the nation to a standstill and provoke possible public confrontations if troops were deployed in different parts of Britain.[17] The government was well briefed on states of emergency and the use of troops under the 1920 Emergency Powers Act (EPA) or the more flexible 1964 Act of the same name (table 4.1).[18]

Table 4.1 *Use of troops in industrial disputes, 1970–79, under the Emergency Powers Acts of 1920 and 1964*

Year	1920 Act (state of emergency declared)	1964 Act
1970	Dock strike Electricity overtime ban	Local council workers' strike
1972	Dock strike Miners' strike	
1973		Glasgow firemen's strike
1973/74	Miners' strike	
1975		Local council workers' strike
1977		Air traffic control dispute
1977/78		National firemen's strike
1978		Naval dockyard workers' action
1979		Ambulance crews dispute

By late December, the government was planning the announcement of a state of emergency, though the news that the unions at the Esso company unions had recommended a settlement indicated a possible breakthrough. However, concerning the plans for the training of troops to operate heavy goods vehicles (HGVs), Donoughue noted in his diary:

16 Benn, *Conflicts of Interest*, p. 419 (diary entry: 19 December 1978).
17 Donoughue, *Downing Street Diary, Volume Two*, pp. 399–400, 404–5 (diary entries: 11, 19 December 1978).
18 Between 1970 and 1978 troops directly intervened in seven industrial disputes. During the 'winter of discontent' soldiers were involved only in the 1979 ambulance crews dispute, by providing front-line cover with volunteer services. Cabinet: Civil Contingencies Unit, 'Legality of the use of servicemen to aid the civil ministries', April 1979, TNA DEFE 24/1780; Steve Peak, *Troops in Strikes: Military Intervention in Industrial Disputes* (London: Cobden Trust, 1984).

But we are still planning to announce a state of emergency on 29 December –
which will mean *no* petrol for private driving, just for emergency purposes.
Hundreds of troops are being specially trained to move in early in the New
Year. This will be quite dramatic. Having troops on the street strike breaking
will take us beyond Ted Heath in 1974! It will also look bad and is not a
good way to prepare for a general election. Also it won't work, distributing
petrol is a complicated matter.[19]

In the case of the industrial disputes involving the oil tanker drivers and
the road hauliers (discussed later in this chapter), which carried a direct
threat to the life of local communities, the government was relatively well
prepared in terms of civil contingency planning. Where necessary, as noted,
the armed services could be deployed to maintain essential services. In
the nine-week 1977–78 firemen's strike, the Callaghan government had
used 20,750 soldiers (supported by fire officers and part-time firemen) to
provide an alternative fire-fighting service numbering 32,000. In that industrial dispute authorisation to use troops came from the Defence Council
(comprising 13 members, including Fred Mulley, Secretary of State for
Defence, senior military personnel and civil servants) under section 2 of the
1964 Emergency Powers Act, without any direct reference to Parliament.[20]

The deployment of troops in strikes could also be authorised under the
main 1920 Emergency Powers Act, which was passed to deal with widespread industrial unrest during the Lloyd George coalition government. It
allowed a government to declare a state of emergency if industrial action
threatened 'the supply and distribution of food, water, fuel or light, or the
means of locomotion' such as to deprive the community of the 'essentials
of life'.[21] Since 1945 there had been at least 23 industrial disputes in which
the military were deployed and since the 1920 Emergency Powers Act
there had been 11 occasions when there had been a declaration of a state
of emergency.[22]

---

19 Donoughue, *Downing Street Diary, Volume Two*, p. 406 (diary entry: 22 December 1978).
    In this diary entry, Donoughue appears to have forgotten how the Callaghan govern-
    ment used troops against the firemen during their nine-week strike in 1977–78.
20 The author's brother, Bob Shepherd, a fireman in the London Fire Brigade, took part
    in the 1977–78 national firemen's strike. Interview: Robert Shepherd, Gravesend, 20
    August 2012. *State Research Bulletin*, no. 4, February–March 1978; Gillian S. Morris,
    Strikes in Essential Services (London: Mansell, 1986), pp. 99, 101, 131–5. For more dis-
    cussion of the Callaghan government and the 1977–78 national firemen's strike, see
    'Firemen's strike 1977–78', TNA DEFE 23/789; Victor Bailey, *Forged in Fire: The
    History of the Fire Brigades Union* (London: Lawrence & Wishart, 1992).
21 *State Research Bulletin*, no. 4, February–March 1978, pp. 55–6.
22 Christopher J. Whelan, 'Military intervention in industrial disputes', *Industrial Law
    Journal*, vol. 8, no. 4, December 1979, pp. 222–3, 226. There was no proclamation
    of a state of emergency under the 1920 Emergency Powers Act in mainland Britain
    during the Callaghan government (there was a brief one in Northern Ireland). However,
    Whelan includes the ambulance drivers' dispute (1979) as one of the five proclamations
    of emergency under the 1920 Act since 1970 (p. 222 n. 3) (see table 4.1) and also
    includes this dispute in his tabulation of military interventions since 1945 (p. 233).

Government contingency planning has a long history, reaching back to the early twentieth century, and even earlier for the use of the military in industrial disputes.[23] Following the miners' strike in 1972, the Heath government established a full review of central civil planning procedures, which culminated in the establishment of the CCU under its secretary, Brigadier R. J. 'Dick' Bishop from 1972 to his death in 1981, in which post he was assisted by Sir Clive Rose, at the time the deputy secretary in the Cabinet Office and a former member of HM Diplomatic Service.[24] Bishop was the longest-serving member of the CCU during the industrial unrest of the 1970s. On joining the civil service after an army career, he was put in charge of planning and developing the Cabinet Office emergencies organisation. In particular, his main role was in connection with COBRA (Cabinet Office Briefing Rooms), known as the Cabinet Office's 'doomsday' operations centre. Bishop was at the centre of the government response to various winter crises, natural disasters, hijackings and terrorist threats.[25] The CCU was chaired by the Home Secretary, Merlyn Rees, when it met as a committee of ministers, civil servants and military advisers. In 1976 Rose joined the CCU and chaired its meetings when just the civil servants sat. By 1978–79 was Rose was heavily involved in dealing with the civil emergencies during the 'winter of discontent'. In 1978, he reviewed the state of readiness of contingency plans in the event of industrial action involving oil tanker drivers. He predicted that if the meetings between the oil companies and the unions were abortive, industrial action at first might comprise a ban on the use of contractors' vehicles (used by oil companies at peak times during winter), calculated to carry about 15 per cent of industrial supplies, which could then be followed by an overtime ban. The previous year, industrial action involving a ban on overtime and rest-day working and working to rule resulted in a loss of around 30 per cent in supplies within three weeks. A repeat of this kind of industrial action was anticipated, possibly involving all five main companies.

Under Operation Drumstick, the government would not be directly involved until oil supplies fell below 65 per cent. Until then, the oil companies, through the Oil Industry Emergencies Committee (OEIC), would handle supplies in terms of contractual obligations. With supplies below 65 per cent of normal, government intervention under the 1976 Energy Act would authorise the oil suppliers to ignore their contractual

---

23 For the use of troops in the 1893 national coal strike (the 'Coal War'), see John Shepherd, 'James Bryce and the recruitment of working-class magistrates, 1892–1894', *Bulletin of the Institute of Historical Research*, vol. 52, no. 126, November 1979, pp. 155–69.
24 Keith Jeffery and Peter Hennessy, *States of Emergency: British Governments and Strike Breaking Since 1919* (London: Routledge & Kegan Paul, 1983), pp. 237–8.
25 *Ibid.*

obligations and would include control of opening times at filling stations and other measures.[26]

The key operational strategy of Operation Drumstick was the deployment of troops if supplies then fell below 30 per cent. The CCU readily acknowledged that involving members of the armed services 'would be a very difficult exercise both operationally and presentationally'. Operation Drumstick would require the declaration of a state of emergency and statutory restrictions on the use of oil. How it was to be implemented in late December/early January was especially problematical as this would involve the Christmas and New Year holiday period. It would take a minimum of 17 days for military drivers to be fully engaged in oil deliveries, or a minimum of seven days from the date of the declaration of a state of emergency. Confidential talks had to be scheduled between district army commanders, chief constables, chief executives and the Department of Energy's regional representatives. Operation Drumstick also required the requisitioning of around 4,000 tankers from the different oil companies, as well as the assistance of the supervisory and management staff. In addition, the possibility of industrial sabotage to vehicles arose, if their drivers suspected the deployment of troops in a strike-breaking capacity.[27]

There would be extremely difficult logistics of timing in implementing Operation Drumstick. Troops would have to be brought back from different parts of Britain and West Germany. Having some 9,000 soldiers driving requisitioned HGVs on British roads, in order to maintain essential fuel supplies, was a serious matter in terms of road safety. Sir John Hunt, the Cabinet secretary, warned Callaghan that the full implementation of Operation Drumstick would require the declaration of a state of emergency by 4 January, the date of his departure for Guadeloupe summit in the Caribbean.[28]

On that day, Callaghan did indeed fly out of Heathrow airport bound for an international summit on the Strategic Arms Limitation Talks (SALT II) on the sun-drenched Caribbean island of Guadeloupe with world leaders President Valery Giscard D'Estaing, President Jimmy Carter and Chancellor Helmut Schmidt. However, before take-off, Callaghan's VC10 plane was held up for an hour as it had to be dug out of the impacted frozen snow on the airport tarmac.[29]

As Ian Aitken of the *Guardian*, who covered the Guadeloupe summit, acknowledged, international summits usually were meticulously planned well in advance and took place with extensive media coverage. World leaders leaving the comfort of their home country are always accompanied

---

26 'Home Secretary: oil tankers' drivers dispute: contingency plans', 21 November 1978, TNA PREM 16/1707.

27 *Ibid.*; 'Note by the Ministry of Defence', 13 December 1978, TNA DEFE 24/1781.

28 Merlyn Rees to Denis Healey, 22 November 1978, TNA PREM 16/1707.

29 Donoughue, *Downing Street Diary, Volume Two*, p. 415 (diary entry: 4 January 1979).

by a full retinue of advisers, permanent staff, officials and security personnel. However, Guadeloupe was different. The secluded resort in the West Indies had been chosen for a two-day meeting for a relaxed atmosphere for the political leaders, with only a few staff and no formal agenda.[30] However, in an almost last-minute decision at Christmas, President Carter planned instead to arrive with a press corps numbering 150 reporters. Among the Prime Minister's entourage in Guadeloupe were the Cabinet secretary, Sir John Hunt, Tom McNally, Callaghan's chief political adviser, Tom McCaffrey, Callaghan's political secretary, Philip Wood and Sir Clive Rose, also from the Cabinet Office. He was also accompanied by a press contingent numbering nearly 30.

However, back in Downing Street, Bernard Donoughue became increasingly concerned about the Prime Minister' 'image' problem as the British media, camped out in Guadeloupe, did their best to portray the world leaders on a junket with their wives in the sun.[31] On his return on 10 January a disastrous press conference at Heathrow in which the Prime Minister appeared casual and insouciant led to a famous banner press headline: 'Crisis? What crisis? Rail, lorry, job chaos – and Jim blames the Press.'[32]

In particular, his critics censured him for being out of touch with the escalating industrial unrest in Britain despite his ill-judged endeavours at Heathrow to demonstrate otherwise.[33] Yet the press verdict on the Prime Minister was unfair. It is now clear that, while out of the country, Callaghan kept closely in touch with the industrial unrest at home, especially the oil tanker drivers' dispute and the likelihood of a national strike by road hauliers. In Guadeloupe, Rose was responsible for keeping the Prime Minister informed and handling the many communications with his private office at No. 10 Downing Street.[34]

In Downing Street Donoughue was also fully aware of developments in the Caribbean:

30 For the Guadeloupe summit, see James Callaghan, *Time and Chance* (London: Politico's, 2006), pp. 530, 541–2, 544–53, 557–8. See also Ian Aitken, 'The island summit in the full glare of privacy', *Guardian*, 4 January 1979. Interview: Lord Tom McNally, House of Lords, 23 July 2007.

31 Donoughue, *Downing Street Diary, Volume Two*, p. 416 (diary entry: 5 January 1979).

32 *Sun*, 11 January 1979. See also: 'He's back from the beaches but his head is still in the sand: THE OSTRICH PRIME MINISTER', *Daily Mail*, 11 January 1979.

33 At Heathrow, Callaghan said: 'Thanks to the miracle of modern communications I was able to lift a telephone and press a button and I was through to No 10 before you could say "Jack Robinson".' With which one leader writer chided the Prime Minister on his good fortune – no cross-lines, misdirected calls, strikes or pickets to obstruct him. 'Is it any wonder, from this comfortable cocoon of office, Mr Callaghan took a rosy view?', *Daily Telegraph*, 11 January 1979, p. 12. For more discussion of the Guadeloupe summit and the press coverage, see chapter 6.

34 Interview: Sir Clive Rose, Lavenham, 24 June 2011.

The PM phoned Private Office just before lunch. [Tim] Lankester took
it but I was there *and listened in* [emphasis added]. He was very concerned
with the industrial front and was reacting to our telegram last night. He
wanted us to continue to keep an eye on it. We also told him about Bill
Rodgers's tough speech last night, in which he took a firm stand on the five
per cent policy.[35]

On 8 January, Donoughue arrived at Downing Street to find Tim Lankester
already arranging for different departments to prepare answers to the Prime
Minister's 20 or so detailed questions about the strikes.[36]

By the end of 1978, the oil tanker drivers' dispute had not been resolved.
Esso's pay offer was rejected in a ballot. Offers by other companies were in
the balance: 'All this means that the situation remains extremely uncertain',
Lankester informed the Prime Minister. He also noted that Jack Ashwell at
the TGWU had not been very good at forecasting the outcome of developments in the oil tanker drivers' dispute.[37]

On 5 January, the Guadeloupe communications had concentrated on
the oil tanker drivers employed by Texaco, who had voted 520–420 against
the latest company pay offer. That offer was very similar, at 15 per cent,
without any productivity deal, to other company pay offers. The Texaco
drivers' industrial action, including picketing of terminals operated by other
oil companies, meant that the Texaco decision would affect the outcome of
voting on other companies' offers by their drivers. The report for Downing
Street canvassed the possibility of sympathetic strike action by Shell and
Esso drivers. The Prime Minister was reassured that decisions on emergency action would not be needed until the votes by the Shell and Esso
drivers became known.[38]

In Guadeloupe, the Prime Minister (via Sir Clive Rose) received further
news of the escalation of the Texaco strike, especially in Northern Ireland,
where in Belfast the only oil deliveries being made were to essential services
selected by the unions. There was also a threat from oil refinery workers of a
strike if troops were used to deliver oil. The supply situation in Manchester
was also assessed as severe.[39]

---

35 It was normal practice for the members of the Policy Unit to listen in on calls. On 8
    January Donoughue listened in to the Prime Minister's delayed call to Denis Healey at
    9.30pm (5.30pm in the Caribbean). 'The Chancellor reported at great length … they
    both agreed that something tough would have to be done about the unions.' Donoughue,
    Downing Street Diary, Volume Two, p. 417 (diary entry: 8 January 1979). Interview: Lord
    Bernard Donoughue, House of Lords, 6 July 2010.
36 Interview: Sir Tim Lankester, Dry Drayton, 30 May 2011.
37 Tim Lankester to Prime Minister: 'Oil tanker drivers', 29 December 1978, TNA
    PREM 16/2124.
38 Tim Lankester to Philip Wood, 5 January 1979, Telegram no. 31 for Prime Minister's
    party, TNA PREM 16/2124.
39 I. A. W. Fair to Sir Clive Rose, 5 January 1979, Telegram no. 43 for Prime Minister's
    party, TNA PREM 16/2124.

As a result of these communications, the Prime Minister's private office in Downing Street received, on 7 January, a detailed telegram from Guadeloupe asking for replies to 11 specific queries – by 4.00 pm Barbados time (20.00 GMT) on Monday 8 January. Particular attention was asked to be given to: the outcomes of each ballot of the oil tanker drivers; the effect on industrial costs of a 20 per cent pay increase for drivers; the declared intentions of union representatives after the outcome of the ballots; and possible numbers of people thrown out of work if a state of emergency were to be declared and oil supplies reduced to 30 per cent. The Prime Minister also requested a report on the discussion between the Chancellor of the Exchequer and the General Secretary of the TUC about pay. Philip Wood, secretary in the Prime Minister's private office, also pointedly noted: 'The Prime Minister is particularly concerned that Moss Evans should be persuaded not to make the road haulage strike official: We suggest it should be left to Mr Booth to consider the best way of proceeding privately with Moss Evans on this.'[40]

On 9 January Callaghan was sent a report on the oil tanker drivers' and the road haulage disputes following a meeting in Whitehall of GEN 158 (the Cabinet committee handling industrial disputes, under which the CCU came). The BP drivers had voted 1,024–699 in favour of the company's offer. Pickets were being withdrawn in some areas and around 50 per cent of oil supplies were getting through, though in the north-west of England only 5–10 per cent of deliveries had been achieved. In Northern Ireland the industrial situation was described as 'severe', though Esso drivers had voted to resume work. A crucial mass meeting of all company drivers was taking place the next day. The oil tanker drivers' action and the associated picketing were having an effect on the road haulage industry, which faced its own strike (this had started in Scotland on 3 January). The report emphasised that 'picketing is becoming increasingly effective ... a major one [of the targets] is the operation of own-account firms whose drivers are not involved in the dispute'. Moss Evans, described as 'evasive', was asked by Albert Booth to try to stop this form of picketing.[41]

In Downing Street an anxious Donoughue wanted the Prime Minister to make an early return to Britain in view of the developing industrial situation. Yet, after the Guadeloupe summit had closed, the Callaghan party continued on to Barbados, ostensibly for an official visit. In view of the criticism in the British press, it was a most unfortunate decision.

However, on 2 January, before he left Britain, the Prime Minister had been informed that a meeting of GEN 158 'took the view that the unions and the companies were now getting near agreement'. As a result, troops

---

40 Philip Wood to Tim Lankester, 7 January 1979, Telegram no. 12, TNA PREM 16/2124.
41 *Ibid*. The 'own-account' sector comprised companies that had their own fleets of vehicles as part of their production or distribution systems.

on standby could be taken off their alert until the following Monday.
Also, no state of emergency could be considered until the Prime Minister
returned from Barbados.[42] This decision was confirmed the following day
when GEN 158 met again: 'barring any extraordinary developments, no
further action is needed until next Tuesday ... in other words, if they *were*
to recommend any action, this would be for you to consider on your return
from Guadeloupe'.[43]

One welcome sign of improvement in the oil tanker drivers' dispute
was the decision of the Energy Secretary, Tony Benn, to leave Britain for
Brussels to attend an international European conference with the approval
of Merlyn Rees and Denis Healey.[44]

In a Cabinet meeting on 11 January, after his return from Guadeloupe,
the Prime Minister said he had received a letter from Margaret Thatcher
asking for a statement about the industrial situation on Monday 15 January.
Callaghan would decide which minister would make the statement, depend-
ing on the circumstances. The main threat had shifted from the oil tanker
drivers' dispute to the industrial action in the road haulage industry. Also
to be considered was the possible need still to declare a state of emergency.

The Cabinet also heard from Roy Mason, the Secretary of State for
Northern Ireland, where a full-scale strike by the oil tanker drivers on 5
January had culminated in 10,000 workers being laid off, with possibly
another 10,000 to follow. The tanker drivers in the province had voted
against the employers' pay offer and this could also be seen as an expression
of right-wing Protestant reaction against the Labour Party and British influence. Appeals to the drivers were being made by John Freeman, chairman
of the Northern Ireland Board of the TGWU and General Secretary Moss
Evans – with little effect. Troops were being deployed to get supplies to
64 filling stations for priority users. Under Northern Ireland legislation,
the Privy Council did not have to meet if GEN 158 considered a state of
emergency should be declared.[45]

While the oil tanker drivers' dispute had been settled at around 15 per
cent by the second week in January, the government still faced a series of
related problems on pay policy. The road haulage strike had now been made
official by the TGWU. Moss Evans believed that the employers would soon
surrender in excess of the government's guideline, which would make it
very difficult for the government to maintain its 5 per cent policy in the
public sector. Even so, the Prime Minister thought the decision to fix the
pay guideline at 5 per cent 'had been the right choice at the time'. As he

---

42 'Prime Minister: oil tanker drivers', 3 January 1979, TNA PREM 16/2124.
43 *Ibid.*
44 Tim Lankester to Philip Wood, 9 January 1979, Telegram no. 63 for Prime Minister's
   party, TNA PREM 16/2124.
45 Cabinet conclusions, 11 January 1979, TNA CAB 128/65.

told his Cabinet colleagues 'he did not need to remind the Cabinet of the consequences of the wage and price explosion of 1974–75'.[46]

With oil supplies returning to normal, there was no longer a case for declaring a state of emergency. Troops would have transported at most about 30 per cent of the oil supplies to maintain essential services, but not sufficient for industrial employment or output.[47] The Cabinet also discussed requesting the TUC to issue a code of conduct concerning secondary picketing.[48]

As Minister of Transport in the Callaghan Cabinet, William Rodgers provides a valuable interpretation of the 'winter of discontent' as the departmental minister with responsibility for handling the 1979 road haulage dispute.[49] However, by the time of publication he had already broken away from Labour as one of the four founding members of the Social Democratic Party (SDP). Rodgers described the unofficial strike of oil tanker drivers in December 1978 as 'a dress rehearsal for the industrial disputes that followed'.[50] Rodgers' view was that 'if the tanker drivers' dispute was a warning to the government, the road haulage strike was the battle fully joined'. This industrial dispute is particularly remembered for its militancy, seen in the robust secondary picketing of blockaded ports and industrial estates. Thatcher famously declared in Parliament that 'the place is practically being run by strike committees'. Rodgers later acknowledged that public perceptions of the hauliers' dispute were shaped as much by its regular coverage in the popular press and on the nation's television screens as by direct personal experience.

The road haulage industry, which formed an important part of the British economy, had a fragmented regional structure, a variety of sectors and a complex system of wage negotiation. The 1979 dispute was primarily centred on the 'hire and reward' sector (sometimes described as 'professional' or 'public haulage' carriers), comprising hauliers who delivered goods for other firms, which amounted to around 63 per cent of goods transported by road in Britain. The economic importance of the industry can be seen from the various goods and materials carried by road transport: bulk liquids, car transportation, express delivery for mail-order companies, international services and special heavy-haulage operations. In addition, firms represented by the Road Haulage Association (RHA) were responsible for moving large quantities of food items, mill flour and animal foods, as well as delivering livestock for the domestic market and transporting live animals for export to the continent. The industry included companies with

---

46 *Ibid.*
47 *Ibid.*
48 *Ibid.*
49 Rodgers, 'Government under stress'.
50 *Ibid.*, pp. 174–5. Rodgers was wrong in describing the oil tanker drivers' dispute as a strike. It was mainly an overtime ban with the threat of a strike which largely did not materialise.

vehicles to carry refrigorated meat. High-volume industrial waste was also handled by the road haulage industry. Road transport was used for the distribution of items over relatively short distances once the main journey had been completed on the long-haul routes. The other main sector of the road haulage industry comprised 'own-account' carriers, comprising companies with their own fleet of vehicles for moving manufactured goods, different retail supplies and similar items for supermarkets, stores and shops.

In August 1978, the TGWU Road Transport Commercial (RTC) trade group, at its annual road haulage conference, put together a pay claim amounting to a total pay increase of around 50 per cent. In an industry with a history of poor basic wages, the union sought £65 for a 35-hour week (the 35-hour week was later dropped in order to press for the increase in basic rates). The pay claim also included increases in the overnight subsistence allowances (from £6.50 to £8.50), as well as improved rates for late-evening and night work.

In response, the RHA established a working party (consisting of members of its Labour Relations Committee and the chairman of the Regional Negotiating Committee). Its recommendations included support for the government's 5 per cent pay norm and a guaranteed 40-hour week (but no reduction as such in the working week). It also added the proviso that 'no area would be permitted to make offers in excess of the limits until the situation had been carefully examined by the working party'.

In an early endeavour to reach a settlement, the RHA in December 1978 had increased its pay offer to 15 per cent. However, the TGWU made an immediate response. A recalled road haulage conference voted for strike action starting on 3 January 1979 if the employers continued to turn down the union's claim of £65 (now for a 40-hour working week).[51]

The 1979 road haulage strike soon became an inflamed dispute between a weak and ineffective employers' association and highly determined groups of aggrieved lorry drivers in various parts of Britain. As Minister of Transport, Rodgers observed that the leadership of the fragmented RHA did not measure up to the TGWU in industrial bargaining.[52] In some regions, such as Scotland and south Wales, strikers voted in large majorities to take industrial action, even though the strike at first was unofficial. In turn, the RHA complained that some shop stewards at the outset of the industrial action tried to dupe drivers into believing that the union had already declared the stoppage official. According to Paul Smith, in many localities the lay membership was in effective control of the strike but union officers were more dominant where, ironically, union organisation was weaker.[53]

51 Wrigley, 'The winter of discontent', pp. 211–12.
52 Bill Rodgers, *Fourth Among Equals* (London: Politico's, 2000), p. 181.
53 Paul Smith, 'The winter of discontent: the hire and reward road haulage dispute, 1979', *Historical Studies in Industrial Relations*, vol. 7, spring 1999, pp. 38, 41, 44; Paul Smith, 'The road haulage industry, 1945–79: from statutory regulation to contested terrain', in

By the 1970s workers in the road haulage industry had become a more militant grouping within the TGWU, which was not prepared to settle the strike, even at 15 per cent, particularly when, in their view, their employers could afford to pay 20–25 per cent. They were encouraged by previous, localised industrial action in 1978 that had resulted in a 15 per cent settlement outside the third round of the government's pay policy. At the same time, it was significant that the 1979 road haulage strike started on 3 January with the unofficial action by Scottish drivers, one of the groups most likely to be adversely affected by the new regulations from the European Economic Community (EEC), particularly the reduction in working hours affecting overtime payments.[54]

In declaring the road haulage strike official (except for in the Birmingham area), despite pressure from the Prime Minister not to do so, Moss Evans disregarded the government's pay policy. Instead, he justified his action in support of what he said was a wholly reasonable pay claim and declared: 'I'm not bothered by percentages. It is not my responsibility to manage the economy. We are concerned about getting the rate for the job.'[55] Some of his TGWU members were employed by the firm Runcorn Transport Services, which delivered materials throughout Britain for ICI. At the outset of the road hauliers' strike, the *Guardian* interviewed two pickets. Jim Peters, a lorry driver with 26 years' experience, had take-home pay of £53 for a basic working week of 40 hours (he could gross £80 based on overtime up to a total of 57 hours a week). However, he received no sick pay or pension. His fellow lorry driver, John Lowden, declared: 'All we want is a decent basic wage, so that we can live without being dependent on bonuses and being away from home five nights a week'.[56]

Like many other workers who participated in the 'winter of discontent' (often for the first time in the public sector), industrial action was a direct response to the government's rigid 5 per cent pay norm at a time of inflation, falling living standards or squeezed differentials in earnings. In the case of the road hauliers, this was only one of a number of grievances fuelling their dispute.

Road hauliers enjoyed 'the freedom of the road', largely distant from the usual day-to-day managerial controls and discipline associated with factory- and office-based employment. Driving was a skilled occupation, particularly with the advent of HGVs, but could be poorly paid, especially in terms of basic earnings. In the 'hire and reward' sector there were considerable disparities between different groups of lorry drivers. Those working in car transportation, for example, might earn up to £150 per week, compared

---

Chris Wrigley (ed.), *A History of Industrial Relations 1939–1979: Industrial Relations in a Declining Economy* (Cheltenham: Edward Elgar, 1996), p. 227.
54 *Financial Times*, 11 January 1979, p. 20.
55 *Daily Telegraph*, 8 January 1979, cited by Wrigley, 'The winter of discontent', p. 212.
56 *Guardian*, 4 January 1979, p. 11.

with oil company drivers on a basic £75 per week (possibly up to £100 per week with overtime). In the road haulage industry the basic rate for drivers was £50 for a 40-hour week and total earnings were dependent on the size of the firm. Generally, those driving smaller vehicles had their wages downgraded. In addition, the subsistence allowances for drivers on the long trunk routes were considered inadequate by the late 1970s. While some long-distance drivers could earn £90 or more a week, the likely wage for the more numerous drivers of the smaller commercial vehicles was nearer £48 per week, with fewer possibilities of overtime. These pay differentials, the threat of EEC regulations, long, arduous, antisocial hours, increasing regulation and police monitoring were all sources of discontent and concern in the British road haulage industry.

The forthcoming EEC regulations threatened overtime earnings by cutting the number of working hours from 10 hours per day (established by the 1968 Transport Act) to 8 hours. The working week would be reduced by stages from the maximum of 57 hours to 48 hours, thereby seriously curtailing overtime earnings. In addition, another common concern among lorry drivers was the introduction of the notorious tachograph (despised initially by drivers as 'the spy in the cab') that recorded the haulier's driving performance. It led to a widespread unease among drivers that their traditional 'freedom of the road' would be increasingly subjected to managerial intrusion and control.[57] Similarly, at a time of worsening traffic conditions, the road hauliers increasingly resented what they felt to be harassment from both the police and the Department of Employment in the heavily regulated haulage industry.[58]

The 1979 road haulage dispute brought increased public attention to the RHA's role and functions as the main employers' organisation for 15,500 operators out of an estimated total of 46,000 British hauliers. The RHA had played a primary role in wage agreements since the Road Haulage Wages Council (RHWC) had been abolished in 1978. Yet, in terms of size and financial income (about £782,000 in 1978) the RHA was a relatively small trade association compared with the importance of the haulage industry in Britain.[59]

With the abolition of the RHWC, wage negotiations had passed to 18 separate regional committees composed of union and RHA members. In the 1976 reorganisation of the pay bargaining structure, the Advisory Conciliation and Arbitration Service (ACAS) had sided more with the unions than with the employers. Both sides fixed annual wage claims and offers in the road haulage industry at their different national headquarters. While the TGWU favoured regional regulations, ostensibly to give

---

57 Smith, *Unionization and Union Leadership*, pp. 143–5.
58 *Financial Times*, 20 January 1979, p. 17.
59 *Financial Times*, 17 January 1979, p. 8.

attention to local issues, the union's wages claim was fixed in London at the annual meeting of senior shop stewards. Similarly, the employers' offer, decided at the RHA's headquarters, generally became the norm for most of the different regions. In the 1979 road haulage dispute, the TGWU national strike coordinator declared: 'There's no loyalty among road hauliers. It's a cut-throat game. The haulage association has no control whatsoever over its members.'[60] Road haulage companies were under pressure on the wages front, which in the 1970s averaged 45 per cent of total costs in the 'hire and reward' sector and 54 per cent in the 'own-account' sector.[61] Of the estimated 46,000 hauliers, many were owner-drivers or small companies with fleets of two to five vehicles.

The 1979 road hauliers' strike began on 3 January, when 5,000 drivers stopped work in snowbound Scotland. Within 24 hours they were joined by truckers in Cumbria, Bradford, Leeds, Birmingham and Oxford. As Paul Smith has observed, there were distinctive features to this industrial dispute. It rapidly spread to most parts of Britain, involving drivers mainly in the 'hire and reward' sector. It also spread to other sectors, including the own-account drivers. As noted, a relatively novel feature of the strike was the amount of control exercised by the lay membership from the start of the dispute.[62] However, at the outset, the road hauliers' strike attracted relatively little media attention, owing to the simultaneous oil tanker drivers' dispute.[63]

By 15 January, secondary picketing by road hauliers at the docks was in strong evidence, according to the Freight Transport Association. More than 18,000 people had been laid off work in Northern Ireland, where around two-thirds of goods were transported by sea. In Ulster, a state of emergency was declared owing to the fuel shortage but it was relatively short-lived as the 900 tanker drivers soon called off their unofficial strike.

In 1973–44, a three-week strike by Scottish hauliers had made a considerable impact on British industry. By the time the dispute was settled, there were concerns that up to 30,000 workers could have been laid off. In the 1979 road haulage strike, the fierce winter conditions in Scotland seriously affected road transport, particularly the delivery of fuel. Don Brothers, a textile manufacturer in Angus, Scotland, predicted a shorter working week owing to industrial action. Similarly, in north-west England, 50,000 workers had been laid off, with few parts of industry unaffected. In Wales and the south-west of England shortages were reported of basic food items such as flour, butter, frozen foods and fresh fruit. At Halewood, Merseyside, the Ford Motor Company cancelled a full Sunday overtime production shift – the first Sunday working for two months – at the cost of

---

60 *Ibid.*
61 Smith, *Unionization and Union Leadership*, pp. 143–5.
62 Wrigley, 'The winter of discontent', p. 212.
63 Smith, 'The winter of discontent', p. 38.

employment for 4,000 men in the assembly and body-stamping plant and the loss of production of 400 Escort cars, valued at £1 million.[64]

Various parts of British industry were particularly vulnerable to a road hauliers' strike, such as food and retail distribution. As a result, supermarkets and manufacturers warned against panic buying as package stocks would last only for a few days. While there were several large haulage companies – such as SPD (a subsidiary of Unilever), which handled the distribution of Birds Eye, Van De Berghs, Batchelors and other Unilever products throughout Britain – they were not typical of the industry as a whole. Most of the distribution trade was undertaken by local hauliers and small regional groups. Other products, such as coal and coke, were, in the main, delivered by rail transport, but chemicals and fertilisers were largely carried by road transport.[65]

As Minister of Transport, Rodgers called for daily situation reports from the regional traffic commissioners. As the dispute became an official strike on 11 January, the regional emergency committees, which had not been used for several years, were put into operation.

As Paul Smith has written, the TGWU supported the road haulage drivers' strike in 1979, but union activists in many areas had already seized the initiative by organising local strike committees. Lay control of the dispute was particularly apparent in areas such as central Scotland, Hull, Liverpool, Birmingham, south-east London and Southampton, where the power of union local branches in effect restricted union officers to the margins. In many cases, various strike committees were not willing to give up control (even where union loyalists comprised part of the committee membership). It was, thus, essentially an official strike run on an unofficial basis.

There was a considerable difference between Transport House (TGWU headquarters) and Whitehall in London and the various areas where the road hauliers' strike took a strong hold through the lay membership rather than union officials. The TGWU soon made the strike official in an attempt by its leadership to secure control over the dispute. Particular centres of rank-and-file resistance included industrial estates of north-west England, where uncompromising secondary picketing by lorry drivers culminated in around 30,000 lay-offs of workers in various industries in the region.

In the port of Hull in January 1979, Fred Beach, a local truck driver and TGWU shop steward, together with other Hull union officials, organised a highly effective blockade of the east Yorkshire city that earned it the name of 'Stalingrad' or 'siege city' in the press. Certain foodstuffs became rationed in the shops and cargoes remained on board ships in the docks. Thirty years later, Fred Beach told the *Guardian* journalist Andy Beckett, who visited the city to investigate the nature of the industrial action:

---

64 *Financial Times*, 15 January 1979.
65 *Financial Times*, 4 January 1979, p. 16.

> Normally in the seventies, you could not get lorry drivers to go on strike …
> to lorry drivers low pay and long hours was just a way of life. Drivers were
> ten a penny. Ex-army men with heavy goods licences. Easy sacking, easy
> hiring … sixty, seventy, eighty hours a week was normal.

Beach's first-hand testimony admirably captures the rumbling discontent
of the local lorry drivers concerning three years of wage restraint and poor
working conditions. Beach recalled that 'pickets were on the docks and the
main roads in and out of Hull'. Bevin House in Hull, the TGWU's local
headquarters, became the centre for local employers and others who wanted
dispensations to move essential goods or deliveries to hospitals, nursing
homes and pensioners. Thirty years later Andy Beckett discovered that this
period of industrial action in Hull – which he termed a 'peasants' revolt' –
was still remembered with as much passion as was evident in 1979.[66]

In nearby Grimsby, where there was a combination of rank-and-file
activism and official union organisation, the local paper declared 'IT'S
CHAOS IN THE GRIMSBY AREA' as around 1,000 drivers voted almost
to a man to join the strikes. Pickets took place on the docks and elsewhere.
Four Icelandic trawlers due to land had to be diverted to Germany. The
10/31 branch of the TGWU in Grimsby, with over 500 members present,
unanimously agreed 'to take strike action to support local negotiations and
the £65 wages policy per week'.[67]

Birmingham, normally the personal fiefdom of local union boss Alan
Law, was another example of grassroots strength, where nearly 1,000 lorry
drivers started strike action at midnight on 3 January, hours before union
shop stewards held their meeting. Within two days striking lorry drivers
had taken over the local union office in Broad Street to coordinate their
strike activities.[68]

Rodgers' assessment of the impact of the strike was that it produced more
warnings of shortage and more signs of damage than actual disruption. In
his autobiography, while the Transport Minister condemned picketing by
drivers as 'ugly and arbitrary', he readily acknowledged there were hardly
any severe food shortages and that fewer jobs were lost than anticipated.[69]
Predictions by employers that up to 2 million men and women would
be laid off work were far from accurate. In particular, the chemical con-
glomerate ICI had stated that if the road haulage strike continued, all of its
plants would be shut down within a fortnight. According to the Transport
Minister, the Labour-voting deputy chairman of the company announced

---

66 Andy Beckett, *When the Lights Went Out: What Really Happened to Britain in the Seventies*
(London: Faber & Faber, 2009), pp. 484–91.
67 *Grimsby Evening Telegraph*, 8 January 1979. Minutes of the 10/31 branch meeting held at
the Winter Gardens, Sunday, 7 January 1979. Interview: Jim Clark (of TGWU/Unite),
Grimsby, 28 August 2012.
68 Chris Wrigley, 'The winter of discontent', p. 212.
69 Rodgers, *Fourth Among Equals*, p. 181.

that no one had stopped work at ICI as a result of the strike.[70] Within a short time the *Economist* exploded some of the myths surrounding the impact of road hauliers' strike:

> On January 10th the CBI predicted that 1m workers would be laid off 'by the end of the next week'. Lay-offs were still only 200,000 four weeks later. Sir John Methven, the CBI's director-general, was in even more apocalyptic mood at the start of the strike; he talked of it bringing Britain to a halt within 10 days. ICI, also on January 10th, threatened to shut up shop within 10 days. It didn't. On January 16th Mr Derrick Hornby, president of the Food Manufacturers Federation ... predicted '600,000 lay-offs will be a reality ... I'm talking of days'. But the supermarket shelves stayed well stocked (apart for a few items) and Mr Hornby's lay-offs turned out to be as illusory as the CBI's.[71]

The strike was limited as it covered only about 40 per cent of hauliers – that is, those who were members of the TGWU. Many of the small firms were non-union and so were not affected. Also, many non-haulage companies had their own fleet of vehicles. Together, this meant that the dispute involved about 35 per cent of HGVs in the haulage industry.[72]

In January 1979 pay policy dominated Cabinet discussions. In Parliament, Thatcher called for a declaration of a state of emergency to deal with the road hauliers' strike.[73] However, none was declared, partly owing to divisions within the Cabinet and to the logistical difficulties of troops replacing road hauliers. Rodgers declared: 'Although a hawk in other respects, I was amongst those doubtful about the advantages of a state of emergency. Troops could be used quite legitimately without one.'[74]

Five years after the 1979 road haulage dispute, in a newspaper article, Rodgers criticised Callaghan for being absent in Guadeloupe during a crucial stage of the 'winter of discontent'. Moreover, he felt that the Prime Minister had failed to take direct action on his return from abroad, such as appearing on television to reassure the nation.[75] The central strategy of the Labour government of 1974–79 was cooperation with the trade unions, as seen in the social contract. Labour's main claim was that it was the party, as opposed to its Conservative opponents, that could get on with the unions. In Rodgers' view, the Prime Minister's failure to challenge the unions head on in the road haulage strike revealed that Callaghan 'was a prisoner of his own trade union past'.

---

70 Rodgers, 'Government under stress', p. 187.
71 *Economist*, 3 February 1979, p. 68.
72 Morris, *Strikes in Essential Services*, p. 70.
73 *Parliamentary Debates* (House of Commons), fifth series, 18 January 1979, vol. 960, col. 1959.
74 William Rodgers, 'A winter's tale of discontent', *Guardian*, 7 January 1984, p. 11.
75 *Guardian*, 7 January 1984, p. 11.

At the time, Rodgers was convinced that the government had to stand firm on the 5 per cent pay policy. While Callaghan was in the Caribbean, he had made a public keynote speech to this effect in north Yorkshire.[76] Five years later, Rodgers later recalled the TGWU's 'holy war against 5 per cent': 'Only one practical course was available: an open attack on the irresponsibility of the TGWU and the spinelessness of the TUC coupled with an unqualified determination to keep supplies moving.'[77]

The road hauliers' strike was settled after arbitration in the Bristol area resulted in an award of about 20 per cent, which was adopted by other regions in haulage industry. By this stage, the Callaghan Cabinet was mostly in favour of settling the dispute as speedily as possible. However, the Minister of Transport stood firm. Rodgers wrote directly to the Prime Minister in blunt terms:

> I am gravely concerned with the view you expressed in Cabinet that we should tip the wink to the RHA to settle as soon as possible and presumably on any terms. I think you misjudge the situation in the Country and, more to the point, the mood of the people … tipping the wink would be widely seen as giving in to the TGWU and more particularly to Strike Committees and pickets.[78]

After a sterling performance on 16 January in the House of Commons debate on the industrial unrest, the next day Thatcher was making a seminal television appeal to the nation for a joint approach with the government to the trade unions. She advocated banning secondary picketing and amending the law on the closed shop, the state-funding of secret ballots for union members and a no-strike rule for vital public services. The leader of the opposition declared: 'These are three concrete proposals for a common effort to meet a common danger. I hope Mr Callaghan and his colleagues will give them a fair wind.'[79] The previously cautious Thatcher appeared for the first time like a Prime Minister in waiting. Her television broadcast marked a turning point in Conservative fortunes. It was probably the most significant political outcome of the 1979 road hauliers' strike.

---

76 Rodgers was snowbound and unable to travel to deliver the speech. Nevertheless, the press published it prominently. *Guardian,* 5 January 1979.
77 *Guardian,* 7 January 1984, p. 11.
78 Rodgers to Callaghan, 18 January 1979, TNA PREM 16/2128.
79 *Guardian,* 18 January 1979. See also chapter 7, pp. 130–2.

Chapter Five

Public sector strikes

On 22 January 1979, an arctic winter's day, 1.5 million workers stopped work as part of a 'National Day of Action' in Britain. This was the largest turn-out since the 1926 General Strike. The *Daily Telegraph* called it the biggest rally since the large-scale demonstration against the Heath government's Industrial Relations Act in 1971.[1] About 60,000 people had journeyed to London to gather in Hyde Park and march to Parliament. Jeff Baker, from Port Talbot, a young hospital porter and shop steward in the National Union of Public Employees (NUPE), recalled a strong feeling of solidarity travelling up to London for the 'National Day of Action' by one of the special trains that collected trade unionists en route. At the Hyde Park rally he heard for the first time Alan Fisher, NUPE General Secretary.[2] Also at the rally, Albert Spanswick, General Secretary of the Confederation of Health Service Employees (COHSE), declared: 'this is the first time ever that the public service manual unions with the nurses have come together to fight the shame and indignity of low pay'.[3] There were similar large demonstrations of public sector workers in Glasgow, Manchester, Liverpool, Belfast and other cities on the same day.

The *Sun* pursued a familiar theme – first used on James Callaghan's return from Guadeloupe almost two weeks before – of the Prime Minister's incompetence in the face of escalating industrial mayhem. On its front

---

1   *Daily Telegraph*, 22 January 1979. The following day the newspaper changed its description to 'the biggest since 1926'.

2   Jeff Baker recalled that the occasion 'drove home to me the bias of the tabloid press and [it] upset me personally being described as "one of Alan Fisher's storm troopers".… This was me … [and] the men and women I worked with … my colleagues, genuine people, on strike for the first time.… I was proud to have taken part in the "winter of discontent"… I defend it. I always thought it was good political and industrial grounding.' He remembered the women's enthusiastic participation at branch meetings. Encouraged by branch secretary Olwyn Davies, later NUPE's first woman President, he became very active in NUPE and UNISON. Telephone interview: Jeff Baker, Swansea, 1 May 2012.

3   *Morning Star*, 23 January 1979.

page the newspaper proclaimed: 'CRISIS BRITAIN: CHAOS ON ALL SIDES', supported by stories of troops replacing striking ambulance personnel, of 4 million children forced to stay away from school and of the threat of another national rail strike. For good measure, *Sun* readers were also given a two-page spread of strike news – entitled 'YOUR MISERY MONDAY'.[4] For the *Daily Mail* 'BLACK MONDAY' had 'just a chink or two of light', owing to the change of mind by the London ambulance staff to answer emergency calls. Nonetheless, the paper spelt out the extent of the national industrial action in no uncertain terms:

> Today's stoppage is by dustmen, school caretakers, meals staff and crossing patrols, sewer men, street lighting maintenance men, grave diggers, rat catchers, drain cleaners, road repairers, estate caretakers and office heating and canteen staff. Hospitals will have no domestic staff, caretakers, porters, ward or theatre orderlies, laundry or kitchen staff. Airports hit will include Manchester, Birmingham, Newcastle and Leeds … ground staff, baggage handlers, catering staff and cleaners.[5]

In backing the public sector manual workers' low-pay campaign, the *Socialist Worker* designed its final page to be pinned up in workplaces as an illustrated poster advertising the National Day of Action: 'All Out on January 22nd! Fight Low Pay: 11.30am. Monday, Speakers Corner, Hyde Park. March to Parliament.'[6] The weekly paper's next issue carried a banner headline: 'The only way low-paid can win: ALL-OUT STRIKE!'[7]

The *Daily Mirror*, usually a Labour-supporting paper, revealed its hostility to the unions during the 'winter of discontent' by choosing a similar headline to the rest of the popular press: 'DAY OF THE REBELS – warning of further industrial action: As yesterday's industrial stoppage came to an end, the workers threatened guerrilla action throughout the country.'[8]

Characteristically, the *Morning Star* gave up most of its front page to Alan Fisher. He made the case for industrial action by public service workers in pursuit of a wage claim of £60 a week and a 35-hour working week. The main objectives were to oppose the government's attempt to impose its 5 per cent pay policy on the public sector and to abolish low pay for public service workers. According to Fisher, the earnings of public sector workers had declined between 1975 and 1978. Weekly earnings of male ancillary workers in the National Health Service (NHS) had fallen from 84 per cent

---

4 *Sun*, 23 January 1979.
5 *Daily Mail*, 22 January 1979.
6 *Socialist Worker*, 20 January 1979.
7 *Socialist Worker*, 27 January 1979.
8 *Daily Mirror*, 23 January 1979, p. 1. Despite the appalling January weather that affected sport, Arsenal defeated third division Sheffield Wednesday in the third round of the FA Cup after 4 games, 9 hours and 16 goals, watched by 143,000 fans. *Daily Mirror*, 23 January 1979, p. 24. (In the Wembley final in May, Arsenal beat Manchester United 3–2 – including three goals in the last five minutes.)

to 76 per cent of the national average for all male industrial workers. In consequence, the extensive national stoppage of work by public service employees on 22 January would close schools, colleges and universities; only emergency treatment would be provided in hospitals or by ambulance men and women. Local authority services, such as the gritting of roads, would also be withdrawn.[9]

In January 1979, the Callaghan government faced major difficulties in terms of industrial relations and pay policy. For Callaghan and his ministers, the first three months of 1979 witnessed the most significant union challenge since Labour had returned to power in 1974.[10] In a general election year – with time running out – the government had to tackle not only the oil tanker drivers' dispute and a national road hauliers' strike, but also industrial action by over a million public service workers, during the most bitter weather since the winter of 1947 – endured by the beleaguered post-war Attlee Labour government.

Facing the Callaghan government from November 1978 to spring 1979 was an enormous range of wage claims by public sector workers, including a sizeable contingent of white-collar and local authority staff, as well as those in the nationalised industries (see pp. xii–xiii for union abbreviations):

- 24,000 university staff (represented by NUPE, TGWU, GMWU)
- 1.1 million local authority workers (NUPE, GMWU, TGWU)
- 250,000 hospital ancillaries (NUPE, COHSE, TGWU, GMWU)
- 30,000 in the water industry (GMWU, NUPE, TGWU)
- 18,000 ambulance crew (TGWU, NUPE, COHSE)
- 42,000 gas workers (GMWU)
- 200,000 post office staff (UPW)
- 230,000 miners (NUM)
- 90,000 electricity supply workers (EPTU, GMWU, AUEW, TGWU)
- 420,000 nurses and midwives (Royal College of Nursing, COHSE, NUPE, NALGO)
- 280,000 railway workers (NUR, TSSA, ASLEF)
- 600,000 civil servants (CPSA, SCPS, IPCS, CSU)
- 520,000 teachers (NUT, NASUWT)

Above all, the Callaghan government was in jeopardy of losing its main electoral card: its claim that it could get on with the unions better than the Tories could. Maintaining good government–union relations was the primary reason Callaghan did not declare a state of emergency in mainland Britain in 1979. The Heath government had introduced five

---

9 *Morning Star*, 22 January 1979.
10 *Financial Times*, 13 January 1979.

states of emergency in four years, which had led to its defeat at the polls in February 1974.[11]

The National Day of Action, a French-style one-day strike, had been organised jointly for the first time by four of the major unions for public service employees.[12] The wave of industrial stoppages that followed for over two months was also characterised by out-and-out displays of militancy by public service workers, many of whom were involved in disputes for the first time. Militancy and strikes in public sector unionism – relatively rare in until the late 1960s – increased in the 1970s as unions became affiliated to the Trades Union Congress (TUC) to defend standards of living in the wake of government incomes policies.[13]

On 22 January in London, at a packed meeting of 3,000 public service workers at the Central Hall in Westminster, platform speakers from the unions – including general secretaries – were shouted down in a rebellious demonstration in favour of further extended strike action.[14]

Tony Ventham, a London ambulance man, described the scene:

> Union officials were visibly shaken by the aggressive demands for *all out strike action* [emphasis in original] and nothing less. Waves of strikes have paralysed hospitals, schools and great chunks of the public sector.... It's amazing that so many people saw through the empty rhetoric of the officials. I've never seen union leaders so unable to deal with the rank and file.[15]

The four unions responsible for the National Day of Action – NUPE, COHSE, the Transport and General Workers' Union (TGWU) and the General Municipal Workers' Union (GMWU) – had a common purpose,

---

11 The Callaghan government declared a short state of emergency in Northern Ireland in early January 1979. In reviewing the industrial situation, a well briefed Margaret Thatcher took a close interest in the parallels with the Heath administration, in which she had served as Education Secretary. For her marginalia on the states of emergency, see Margaret Thatcher papers, Churchill Archives, 'State of emergency' list. Interview: Lord Giles Radice, House of Lords, 26 January 2011.

12 Industrial action by the four public sector unions in January 1979 might have been prevented. On Christmas Eve, Larry Whitty, head of the GMWU Research Department, and Derek Gladwin, GMWU southern regional secretary, presented a proposition (written by Whitty) for a settlement to 10 Downing Street. The proposal had the agreement of David Basnett, GMWU General Secretary, and the other unions, including Alan Fisher of NUPE. Lord Whitty recalled: 'Derek Gladwin wanted a deal ... he had had some discussions with Tom McNally and Tom McCaffrey [Callaghan's chief political adviser and press secretary] and thought it might be a runner ... all that public sector stuff would have at least been deferred. We would have called off the strike.' Interview: Lord Larry Whitty, House of Lords, 12 January 2011.

13 Chris Wrigley, *British Trade Unions Since 1933* (Cambridge: Cambridge University Press, 2002), pp. 45–6, 60–1; Robert H. Fryer, 'Public service trade unionism in the twentieth century', in R. Mailly, S. J. Dimmock and A. S. Sethi (eds), *Industrial Relations in the Public Services* (London: Routledge, 1989), pp. 47–8.

14 Wrigley, *British Trade Unions Since 1933*, pp. 45–6, 60–1; Fryer, 'Public service trade unionism in the twentieth century', pp. 47–8.

15 *Socialist Worker*, 27 January 1979.

despite some significant differences over policy and rivalries in the recruitment of new members. In the autumn of 1978 NUPE, the main driving
force behind the National Day of Action, had launched its low-pay
campaign for a basic £60 minimum a week (two-thirds of the national
average wage) and a 35-hour week (a policy adopted at the NUPE national
conference in Margate). This was subsequently adopted by the TGWU,
GMWU and COHSE as the basis for a joint campaign.

As General Secretary since 1968 of one of the fastest-growing unions,
Fisher was an articulate and flamboyant figure, highly admired within
NUPE, which he had joined in 1939 as a junior clerk. As Assistant General
Secretary, Fisher had seen that NUPE needed a new sense of direction in
the world of trade union politics, including new relations with the 'general
unions' at the TUC and alliances to combat public sector employees and
unfriendly governments. As General Secretary, Fisher was responsible for
commissioning and carrying out the University of Warwick research report
Organisation and Change in NUPE (1974), a radical strategy of constitutional
change in union organisation to promote participation and democracy.
A fundamental part of the root-and-branch reform was the institution of
work-based union stewards and special provision for women on important decision-making NUPE committees, including reserved places on the
union's executive council.[16]

Fisher was an energetic General Secretary, who could articulate and
proselytise. His union was often envied for its militancy. He claimed to be
able to mobilise 60,000 NUPE members on the street: 'We are a thrusting,
campaigning union. NUPE's militancy is often the envy of others who lack
the drive and aggression to copy its methods', he declared.[17] He formed a
formidable partnership with Bernard Dix, Assistant General Secretary of
NUPE, who provided the intellectual drive in terms of policy and strategy.
Together they drove policy developments, including promoting grassroots
socialism, planned by Dix and publicly presented with eloquence by Fisher,
particularly at the Labour Party conferences in 1978 and 1979 in support of
the low-pay claim.[18] Under their leadership, NUPE campaigned to make a

---

16 The Warwick report was prepared by a team of university academics led by Bob
Fryer. For more on this important period, see Stephen Williams and Robert H. Fryer,
*Leadership and Democracy: The History of the National Union of Public Employees: Volume
Two, 1928–1993* (London: Lawrence & Wishart, 2011), pp. 234–6.

17 Robert Taylor, 'NUPE: the four letter word', *Observer*, 4 February 1979.

18 During the 'winter of discontent', Dix was ill. Reg Race, NUPE's senior research
officer, played a key role in organising strike action. Interview: Lord Tom Sawyer, House
of Lords, 12 January 2011. At this time, Fisher and Dix had been divided over settling
the pay claim advanced by NUPE and the other three main unions representing public
service works. Fisher was prepared to be 'flexible' in accepting a lower (single-figure)
rise linked to measures other than the current 'going rate' of 15–16 per cent, to avoid a
complete government defeat in a difficult dispute, whereas Dix argued successfully for
rejecting the local authorities' offer of 9 per cent (£3.50 pus consolidation of supple-
ments) and a comparability study offering improvements in August 1979 and April 1980.

statutory minimum wage part of the social contract between the TUC and the Labour government.[19]

The union had more women members than any other British trade union. While the number of male NUPE members increased 53.4 per cent in the 1970s, the union's female membership had increased by almost twice the number. Tom Sawyer had joined NUPE in 1971 and became a shop steward at 22 and northern regional officer in 1975. He recalled that the union successfully recruited many women members, particularly in part-time and casual work, whereas other unions wrongly believed these groups of working women were difficult to organise.[20]

By 1980 the National Association of Local Government Officers (NALGO) had 391,000 women members, COHSE 167,080, the Civil and Public Services Association (CPSA) 103,140 and the National Union of Teachers (NUT) 148,260, but NUPE had been the most successful in recruitment and retention of members, with a peak total of 466,100. At the same time, NUPE's militant public image received considerable media coverage, difficult to dispel, of a public sector union with a 'callous, un-thinking leadership, oblivious to the helplessness of the sick and needy'.[21]

For a detailed discussion of the various public service workers' disputes, including the industrial action in the NHS, which continued virtually up to the fall of the Labour government, see Williams and Fryer, *Leadership and Democracy*, pp. 335–47.

19 At the 1974 TUC conference Fisher and Dix had launched their book *Low Pay and How To End It*, written specifically for a readership of trade unionists and Labour Party members. Interview: Rodney Bickerstaffe, Russell Square, London, 23 June 2009. William McCarthy and C. S. Nicholls, 'Fisher, Alan Wainwright (1922–1988)', in H. C. G. Matthew and Brian Harrison (eds), *Oxford Dictionary of National Biography* (Oxford: Oxford University Press, 2004), pp. 658–9. Robert H. Fryer and Stephen Williams, 'Dix, Bernard Hubert (1925–1995)', in Keith Gildart and David Howell (eds), *Dictionary of Labour Biography* (Basingstoke: Palgrave Macmillan, 2010), vol. 13, pp. 88–108.

20 Tom Sawyer said in interview that 'the big manual unions had not woken up to the potential of part-time women workers.... [Other union officials] believed they wouldn't join, wouldn't stay or couldn't be shop stewards. In NUPE, in places like Newcastle and Sunderland, we challenged this view – went round schools and hospitals. In a school we would recruit NUPE women members and include a shop steward, but the male care-taker would be in the GMWU – "we don't want them". The women were enthusiastic, did a marvellous job – organising, on picket lines ... a very liberating experience for them'. Interview: Sawyer. For examples of women activists in the 'winter of discontent', see National Union of Public Employees, Northern Division, *Together We Can Win: The Story of Two NUPE Branches Involved in the Council and Hospital Workers Pay Dispute Winter 1978/79* (Newcastle upon Tyne: NUPE, 1979); Tara Martin, 'The beginning of Labor's end? Britain's "winter of discontent" and working-class women's activism', *International Labor and Working-Class History*, no. 75, spring 2009, pp. 49–67.

21 *Guardian*, 2 January 1979. NUPE realised the difficulties of prosecuting a strike in the public services which would adversely affect the general public, particularly the sick, the old and the vulnerable. Tom Sawyer commented that in his north-east region emergency cover was provided during strikes. His NUPE members on picket lines often received sympathy from members of the public, although he 'was on television in Newcastle virtually every night trying to explain the union's position'. Interview: Sawyer.

With the establishment of the NHS by the post-war Attlee Labour government, COHSE had been founded in 1946 by a merger of the Mental Hospital and Institutional Workers' Union and the Hospital and Welfare Services Union. The new union provided health service trade unionism and recruited from workers principally in the NHS. Though COHSE campaigned publicly for nursing students' pay (1948) and nurses' pay (1962) in its early years, the union had a reputation for caution and conservatism. In fact, in 1971 COHSE registered under the Heath government's Industrial Relations Act (which attempted to put industrial relations on a comprehensive legal basis, but which was opposed by most of the union movement) and consequently in the following year was expelled from the TUC. However, there were key changes in the union leadership and significant developments in trade union politics in the 1970s. In 1974, COHSE's new General Secretary, Alfred Spanswick, brought a fresh and more militant tone to his union's affairs. Among his first initiatives was to de-register COHSE from the Industrial Relations Act and to rejoin the TUC. He also gained election to the TUC General Council. At the same time, significant changes in the NHS in the 1970s provided COHSE with a different political platform and orientation in public service trade unionism.[22]

By contrast, the GMWU had been a conservative 'middle of the road' union, loyal to the TUC and Labour Party leadership. From 1973, under the leadership of David Basnett, a key figure on the TUC General Council and a member of the TUC 'Neddy 6', the union's organisation was reformed and its finances strengthened. In 1979 Basnett also founded Trade Unionists for a Labour Victory (TULV). The union expanded its membership, particularly in local government, and broadly retained its membership numbers in public services (gas, water, electricity) as well as other industries. The research department under Larry Whitty, later a Labour Party General Secretary, was highly effective and influential. Yet whereas NUPE requested its water workers to demonstrate on 22 January, the GMWU was in favour of keeping its water industry members out of the campaign.[23]

The TGWU had already been directly involved in the oil tanker drivers' and road hauliers' disputes, as well as the Ford Motor Company strike in 1978. With strongholds in Scotland, Northern Ireland, the West Midlands and various large cities, the TGWU was ready for indefinite and continuous strike action in the public sector.

The first three months of 1979 witnessed the most extensive strikes and further forms of industrial action by public sector workers, often attributed

---

22 Mick Carpenter, *Working for Health: The History of the Confederation of Health Service Employees* (London: Lawrence & Wishart, 1988), pp. 365–7; Robert Taylor, *The Fifth Estate: Britain's Unions in the Modern World* (London: Pan, 1980), pp. 353–5.

23 Interview: John Edmonds (GMWU national industrial officer from 1973, General Secretary of the GMB previously the GMWU, 1986–2003), Victoria, London, 17 November 2010. Interview: Whitty.

to the influence communist and Trotskyite shop stewards. According to Christopher Andrew, the MI5 archives do not reveal 'either a Communist or a Troskyist masterplan', but bewilderment on the part of the far left about how to exploit the industrial unrest. Within the unions involved in the public sector strikes, the 39 members of the TGWU general executive council included nine Communists, two Communist sympathisers and two Trotskyist sympathisers, whereas there was only one Trotskyist on the GMWU executive council. Similarly, the militant NUPE had only one Communist sympathiser on its 26-member executive council, one more than COHSE. Andrew has also observed that MI5 probably 'had a more realistic view ... and was less likely than successive governments to see subversion as a key element in industrial disruption'. After the 'winter of discontent' the Communist Party realised it had to make up lost ground in its workplace activities.[24]

The principal cause of these public sector strikes was in fact chronic low pay: public sector workers' wages were typically between £49 and £54 a week before tax (between £35 and £42 after tax), while the average industrial wage was in the region of £90 a week. Moreover, those working in the NHS led a national campaign for a national basic weekly minimum wage in 1978–79 of £60 and a 35-hour week. Nurses from COHSE had joined the campaign.[25] NUPE's strategy of selective action was appropriate for a union representing some of the lowest-paid workers, the majority of whom were part-time women employees. Selective industrial action avoided bringing emergency services to a halt and prevented the laying off of other workers, which would have affected different public services at different times.[26]

As Tara Martin has shown, women played a significant role in the 'winter of discontent' in the largely male world of trade union politics, particularly in the strikes in the service sector industries. Their activism helped to promote women's issues and to destroy the myth of the male breadwinner. At the same time as the development of the women's movement in the 1970s, experience gained by female trade unionists was a vital 'rite of passage' for later activism, particularly in NUPE and the Labour Party politics in the Thatcher years.[27]

After 22 January, there was further strike action in the second phase of the campaign for a minimum wage of £60 per week. In the London borough of Southwark, 3,000 manual staff received instructions to remain

24 Christopher Andrew, *The Defence of the Realm: The Authorised History of MI5* (London: Allen Lane, 2009), pp. 665–7.
25 *Financial Times*, 19 January 1979.
26 *Ibid.*
27 Martin, 'The beginning of Labor's end?' Interview: Baroness Joyce Gould, House of Lords, 12 September 2011.

out on indefinite official strike. Similar industrial action was taken in several other London boroughs and also at municipal airports.[28]

David Ennals, Social Services Secretary, warned ambulance workers in different regions who were refusing to answer emergency calls that their case would 'not be strengthened by some of them adopting what will be seen as a callous attitude to the lives and health of their fellow-men'.[29] Emergency cover in the hard-hit areas, such as London and the West Midlands, was provided by the police, army and voluntary organisations.[30]

On 1 February 1979, the *Daily Mail* ran the front-page banner headline 'THEY WON'T LET US BURY OUR DEAD'. It became one of the iconic images of the British 'winter of discontent' and has resonated in popular memory over the decades.[31] During a bitter winter of strikes, industrial stoppages and go-slows, the strike by the Merseyside grave-diggers and crematorium workers struck a deep emotional chord. They received little sympathy from the Labour government. In his memoirs, Jim Callaghan wrote:

> Even with the passage of time I find it painful to talk about some of the excesses that took place. One of the most notorious was the refusal of the Liverpool gravediggers to bury the dead, accounts of which appalled the country when they saw pictures of mourners turned away from the cemetery. Such heartlessness and cold-blooded indifference to the feelings of families at moments of intense grief rightly aroused deep revulsion and did further untold harm to the cause of trade unionism that I, like many others, have been proud to defend throughout my life.[32]

National media coverage of the Merseyside dispute, by 60 gravediggers and crematorium staff, focused on the postponement of funerals and even the likelihood of bodies being buried at sea. This warning was put forward by Liverpool's Medical Officer of Health, Dr Duncan Dolton, who said that it might have to be seriously considered as a last resort if the strike was not settled quickly. He advised: 'We hope that Government will take some immediate action. We are faced with this awful problem of the disposal of a number of bodies due to the state of putrefaction.'[33]

During the dispute, about 300 unburied bodies were stored in a temporary mortuary established in a disused Plessey electronics factory in Speke, Liverpool, after being embalmed and placed in polythene bags by local funeral directors.[34] The provincial paper asked: 'What can be done … search continues for a solution … the worst industrial crisis since 1926 …

---

28 *Financial Times*, 23 January 1979, p. 1.
29 *Ibid.*
30 *Ibid.*, p. 9.
31 *Daily Mail*, 1 February 1979, p. 1.
32 James Callaghan, *Time and Chance* (London: Politico's, 2006), p. 537.
33 *Guardian*, 1 February 1979.
34 *Liverpool Echo*, 26 January 1979.

the government's election prospects are being severely damaged by inaction in the face of the continuing crisis'.[35]

Yet minimal coverage was given by the national media to the grievances that underpinned the strike or to the working and living conditions, which resulted in similar industrial action elsewhere in the north-west and in other parts of Britain. Only the provincial press commented on the circumstances that drove the bitter gravediggers to take strike action. One Merseyside gravedigger confessed: 'We are emotionally disturbed. We know it is an emotional situation. We have been attacked by the press, the public and, in some cases, our own families.'[36] Grave-digging was filthy work, physically hard in winter and extremely low paid. It could also be dangerous, as graves might collapse at any moment and smother the gravediggers with mud.[37] Unlike miners, gravediggers had no workplace baths. One gravedigger told the local newspaper: 'You carry the smell of death to your house and it never goes away ... it doesn't bear thinking about what diseases we might catch or take home to our families'.[38] The Prime Minister later wondered: 'what would the men of Tolpuddle have said [about the gravediggers]? My own anger increased when I learned that the Home Secretary, Merlyn Rees, had called upon Alan Fisher, the General Secretary of NUPE, to use his influence to get the [Merseyside] gravediggers to go back to work, and Fisher refused.'[39]

In Parliament, Peter Shore's statement on this industrial dispute revealed that, by 2 February, the Liverpool cemetery workers had agreed on a return to work. The shadow Minister for the Environment, Michael Heseltine, however, raised the point that 'other disputes still had to be resolved; particularly in the North-West'.[40] For three days, the question of picketing in relation to the gravediggers' and crematorium workers' dispute was debated at Westminster. It produced a forthright contribution from one backbencher ready to defend striking trade unionists who were being pilloried for the impact of their industrial action on the more vulnerable members of society. Dennis Skinner, MP for Bolsover, interjected:

35 *Liverpool Echo*, 29 January 1979. See also *Daily Telegraph*, 25 January 1979.
36 *Liverpool Echo*, 2 February 1979.
37 Callaghan's biographer acknowledged 'that gravediggers were exceptionally badly paid'. Kenneth O. Morgan , *Callaghan: A Life* (Oxford: Oxford University Press, 1997), p. 664.
38 *Liverpool Echo*, 2 February 1979.
39 Callaghan, *Time and Chance*, p. 537. Callaghan was wrong about the Merseyside gravediggers, who were not in Alan Fisher's NUPE, but were members of the Liverpool Branch 5 of David Basnett's GMWU. Denis Healey made a similar mistake: 'In some cities the gravediggers refused to bury the dead. Their union leader, Alan Fisher, refused to ask them to go back to work.' Denis Healey, *The Time of My Life* (London: Penguin, 1990), p. 463. There were also gravediggers' strikes elsewhere in the north of England (including NUPE members in Tameside, Manchester) and in various London boroughs.
40 *Parliamentary Debates* (House of Commons), fifth series, 2 February 1979, vol. 961, cols 1839–45.

Is it not a fact that on this occasion we are witnessing, with a few exceptions, the whole House indulging in a bout of utter hypocrisy? Is it not also
a fact that the House of Commons and the Government could resolve this
matter, could get rid of these dead bodies, and could ensure that people
were buried properly if the Opposition would encourage the Government
to pay a decent wage to those concerned in the dispute? Is it not a fact that
no-one in this House – no-one – would do the job that these people are
doing for a take-home pay of about £40 a week?[41]

Lord Barnett, Chief Secretary to the Treasury at the time, later recalled:

We were going through probably the heaviest battering any Government
had experienced in a long time and on the whole, Ministers and officials
stood up to it well.... Peter Shore seemed to panic, even though he had
to deal with one of the most outrageous strikes of all ... that by the gravediggers. At one time, in Peter's native city of Liverpool, bodies awaiting
burial had to be stored in warehouses.[42]

His colleague Denis Howell took a similar view of the industrial troubles of
the 'winter of discontent':

Alan Fisher of NUPE would not intervene to get his gravediggers back
to work and David Basnett of the GMBW could not succeed either with
his graveyard members in Liverpool, although he tried. They preferred to
bury the Labour Government. Never has public opinion been so bitterly
expressed against the unions.[43]

After the National Day of Action, there was little effective cooperation between the different public sector unions. In NUPE's case, it was
often left to the local branches to decide on the conduct of further strike
action, including the organisation of emergency services. Take, for instance,
the London Borough of Camden, from where public sector workers had
turned out in large numbers on 22 January 1979.[44] Between 1974 and 1977
control of the NUPE Camden branch had been wrested from a right-wing
Labour branch secretary and a Tory branch chairman by left-wing activists.
According to John Suddaby, the local branch secretary, the branch, with a
membership of 2,200, drawn from most of the local public services, was
generally revitalised, particularly in terms of shop steward organisation and

---

41 *Parliamentary Debates* (House of Commons), fifth series, 31 January 1979, vol. 961,
   cols 1475–6.
42 Joel Barnett, *Inside the Treasury* (London: Andre Deutsch, 1982), p. 171.
43 Denis Howell, *Made in Birmingham: The Memoirs of Denis Howell* (London: Queen Anne
   Press, 1990), p. 282.
44 What follows draws mainly on one of the few contemporaneous accounts of a local
   strike during the 'winter of discontent': John Suddaby, 'The public sector strike in
   Camden: winter '79', *New Left Review*, no. 116, July–August 1979, pp. 83–93. See
   also Ken Livingstone, *You Can't Say That: Memoirs* (London: Faber & Faber, 2011),
   pp. 138–40.

resistance to cuts in Camden's public expenditure.[45] Also, from August 1978 the NUPE Camden branch lobbied the local council to support the union's national pay claim.[46]

In 1979 the London Borough of Camden included the well heeled residential suburb of Hampstead in the north, a large artisan area in the centre and to the south highly rated commercial properties, which provided the Labour-controlled council with a larger income than many other London boroughs. In 1978 Ken Livingstone, later leader of the Greater London Council (GLC) (1981–86), was elected to Camden Council and became chair of the powerful Housing Committee. He later recalled that, from the 1960s, 'services in Camden were of a higher standard and greater strides had been made in tackling the housing problem'. However, on his arrival in Camden there were also political divisions among the Labour councillors. 'The seeds were being sown for the inevitable collapse of the Labour Group's initial radical period. It was the aftermath of the winter of discontent dispute in February 1979 that finally forced a full retreat to rightwing policies', he added.[47]

After 22 January 1979 there were different views within the NUPE Camden branch on the type of industrial action to pursue locally. At first, the shop stewards committee elected a strike committee. This committee decided from 29 January to call out the plumbers and petrol attendants and to cut petrol supplies to council vehicles, which led to a dispute with management, followed by further strike action by dustmen and other council workers. This escalation culminated in a mass meeting of the NUPE branch, when there was a decision by over 1,000 workers, by a majority of only 100, for an all-out strike, while 1,000 members had not attended. There was considerable opposition among the council workers, notably by employees in social services, works department transport and housing caretakers. After a tense start to the strike, by week 2 the Camden Council Labour group at first decided to grant the NUPE claim in full. Effective picketing was conducted to prevent the Labour Group from backing down. Suddaby noted the difficulties of mobilising workers in the public

---

45 The following list of NUPE members in Camden illustrates GMWU General Secretary David Basnett's comment that public sector workers were the people 'who look after us from the cradle to the grave': dustmen, road sweepers, sewer workers, stores staff, road labourers, masons, public lighting workers, fitters, plumbers, gardeners, cemetery workers, drivers, cleaners, caretakers, catering staff, meals-on-wheels staff, care assistants in old people's homes and day centres, home-helps and pest control assistants. They were based throughout the borough (and some outside districts), in over 200 depots and centres. From the late 1960s NUPE had also recruited widely among NHS auxiliary staff (e.g. hospital porters, cleaners, laundry staff, technical assistants). Given the distribution of hospitals in the metropolis, possibly these occupations were represented more in other NUPE branches. Suddaby, 'The public sector strike in Camden', p. 84.

46 *Ibid.*, p. 87.

47 Ken Livingstone, *If Voting Changed Anything, They'd Abolish It* (London: Collins, 1987), pp. 94–9.

services: 'the problems we ran into here ... [included] the ways in which the issue of moral conscience could be used by the press and management to weaken action'.[48]

During the 'winter of discontent' the popular press gave partisan attention to the impact of any industrial action by public service workers on the local communities they served, irrespective of any emergency cover or voluntary code of conduct arranged by a union. The NUPE decision for an all-out strike in Camden included the staff employed in the home-helps section and in the old people's homes and meals-on-wheels section, which raised the urgent issue of emergency services cover. However, the meals-on-wheels and social services transport section decided to strike without emergency cover. Suddaby observed:

> Moral considerations aside, it was clear that we would not win our strike by risking, or appearing to risk, the lives of old people. With the Meals-on-Wheels section and the Social Services transport section refusing to provide emergency cover, the level of emergency cover required of the Home Helps was not very different from normal working. The necessity for this was clear enough but the question remained whether it was going to be under *our* control or that of management.[49]

The strike committee was faced with the dilemma that if the home-helps were allowed to return to work, other sections would follow. At a mass meeting, 300 home-helps had overwhelmingly voted to return to work. The so-called 'home-helps revolt' was assisted by political right-wingers and attracted a great deal of media attention. In the end, the strike committee found a judicious compromise of granting the home-helps exemption from the Camden strike and accepted their offer to pay £5 a week into the strike fund. Significantly, this did not undermine the strike by encouraging others to return to work, and there was even some favourable press coverage of 'the Union showing mercy on the old people'. As Suddaby explained:

> against the views of left sectarian members who wanted to brand the Home Helps publicly as scabs, we decided to act diplomatically. We made it clear that we disagreed with the Home Helps' refusal to organise emergency cover ... in the circumstance we had no alternative but to let them go back to work, so that the lives of the old people would not be jeopardised. The Home Helps left the meeting telling the waiting TV cameras that they were still backing the Union in its fight.[50]

A revolt by Labour councillors against the council leadership eventually brought the strike to an end, with the NUPE wages claim being settled almost in full. Among the various factors, electoral and political, surrounding the dispute was the key issue of low pay, which attracted considerable

---

48 Suddaby, 'The public sector strike in Camden', pp. 89–90.
49 *Ibid.*, p. 90.
50 *Ibid.*, pp. 90–1.

sympathy, even among Camden councillors of the centre. Nonetheless, characteristically, the right-wing London *Evening Standard* produced a censorious editorial:

> The London Borough of Camden is the most incorrigibly spendthrift local authority in this city, if not all Britain ... it is the first council in Britain to be won over by NUPE's campaign of spurious figures, emotional blackmail and physical disruption. Last night Camden's ruling Labour group voted to concede to its manual workers an effective minimum wage of £66.67 for a 35 hour week.... Nor are there prizes for guessing who proposed this largess: Ken Livingstone, the full-time housing committee chairman and ambitious young activist who moved into the borough.[51]

As Callaghan and his ministers often emphasised, there was significant support among trade unionists for the 5 per cent pay policy. During 1978–79, the Union of Post Office Workers (UPW), which had suffered an unsuccessful seven-week national strike in 1971, was one of the unions which supported the Labour government's social contract, accepting a settlement of 5 per cent in phase 2 of the government's incomes policy in December 1976. At the UPW annual conference in May 1977, rank-and-file attempts to repudiate the social contract were unsuccessful. However, the UPW's efforts on 1 November 1977 for threshold payments as part of a productivity deal, amounting to 7 per cent, did not succeed, either with the Post Office as employer or with the Secretary of State for Industry, Eric Varley. Nonetheless, in 1978 the UPW did win a pay award of 10 per cent. During the 'winter of discontent', the UPW continued to give general support to the social contract, but held a special conference on wages in Bournemouth in December 1978 that culminated in a claim that included an overall 8 per cent increase and a reduction in the working week by three hours. In a complicated set of negotiations with the UPW in early 1979, the Post Office would grant the 8 per cent wage rise but not the other elements of the claim. This exposed a significant gulf between the union leadership and the rank-and-file membership, notably when this deal was thrown out by a six-to-one vote by the union membership. The UPW was able to secure 1 per cent as an interim settlement and slightly more than 5 per cent later in 1979.[52]

After the National Day of Action, selective industrial action by various public sector unions affected a range of services in hospitals and local government. In particular, the popular press coverage presented a picture of union action adversely affecting the old, the sick, children and the bereaved. In 1987 Jack Jones observed:

---

51 *Evening Standard*, 14 February 1979, p. 15.
52 Alan Clinton, *Post Office Workers: A Trade Union and Social History* (London: George Allen & Unwin, 1984), pp. 594–5.

I think in retrospect it is interesting to reflect on whether the Government's firmness on the one hand, and the enormous press publicity on the other, fanned the flames on the public services strike. They really felt that they were on the attack and had to defend themselves. It became the macho thing of standing firm and demanding more. I agree with those who say they could have settled earlier and probably could have done without all that.[53]

For Barbara Castle, former Secretary of State for Health and Social Services (1974–76), the 5 per cent pay norm led directly to the industrial unrest of the 'winter of discontent', particularly after Callaghan had deferred the general election in the autumn of 1978.[54] Castle discovered to her horror at a meeting of the Labour and Trade Union Liaison Committee in early 1978 that Jim Callaghan had fixed a 5 per cent pay norm:

The trade unionists sitting opposite me listened in a state of bewildered shock, obviously believing that the government had gone out of its mind … whoever was responsible, the result was disastrous and predictable. The unions on the Liaison Committee listened sullenly as Jim propounded his determination to go into the next election with inflation still in single figures and that in order to keep inflation down to that level he was going to enforce the 5 per cent norm in the public services.[55]

At the end of a difficult discussion, the General Secretary of NALGO told her in a sombre mood, 'Barbara, we cannot deliver'.

During the 'winter of discontent', Castle was a patient in a London hospital. To avoid media criticism, she insisted on being on a public ward. She described her experience as follows: 'I know my British press: they would have been round to the side room like vultures, describing it in their write-ups as a "private" ward. My prognosis was proved right when not a single press man showed any interest in my presence in the hospital the moment they found I was in a public ward.'[56]

In her memoirs, Castle wrote about the close community of patients. For instance, they would, where possible, help with the hospital's domestic life, including washing-up. She added:

I know that people on the picket lines outside – many of them low-paid manual workers in the NHS – were caring members of caring unions who were stirred into action by a strong sense of injustice, but I felt, not for the first time, that these are the last people who should be driven to use

---

53 Institute of Contemporary British History, 'Symposium: the winter of discontent', *Contemporary Record*, vol. 1, no. 3, autumn 1987, p. 43.
54 *Ibid.*
55 Barbara Castle, *Fighting All The Way* (London: Macmillan, 1993), pp. 508–9.
56 *Ibid.* See also Anne Perkins, *Red Queen: The Authorised Biography of Barbara Castle* (Basingstoke: Macmillan, 2003), pp. 436–7.

the strike weapon, because it inevitably damages the very people that their professions are designed to help.[57]

Another politician in hospital during the 'winter of discontent' certainly did not escape the attention of either the media or, particularly, the NUPE strikers. David Ennals, Secretary of State for Health, was admitted to Westminster Hospital, only a stone's throw from Parliament and Whitehall as well as the Labour Party and Conservative Party headquarters. From 1974 Westminster Hospital, which had been founded in the eighteenth century, was the place of employment of 25-year-old Jamie Morris, who, by the 'winter of discontent', was the hospital's domestic supervisor. He managed low-paid cleaners and non-medical staff, who earned between £49 and £54 a week. Morris was also a Labour borough councillor, NUPE branch secretary and shop steward responsible from mid-January for organising any industrial action in support of the NUPE campaign for £60 a week and a 35-hour working week.[58]

During Ennals' hospital stay for two days of tests from 6 March, Morris declared the Cabinet minister 'a legitimate target for industrial action' by NUPE members and promised he 'would be as uncomfortable as possible'. The various goings-on at Westminster Hospital as NUPE industrial action took hold attracted considerable national media attention. Normal hospital services were curtailed – at one point culminating in no admissions of new patients, even in emergencies, as well as the army being called in to unload medical and food supplies. For a few weeks at least, Morris, who fitted the media stereotype of the British shop steward portrayed by Peter Sellers in the film *I'm Alright Jack* (1959), became as notorious in the right-wing press as the Communist convenor Derek 'Red Robbo' Robinson, dismissed by Michael Edwardes at British Leyland in 1979, or the demonised leader of the National Union of Mineworkers (NUM), Arthur Scargill in the 1980s. Yet Morris was instrumental in resolving some of the difficulties between NUPE and the Westminster Hospital authorities in a late-night clandestine meeting with Alan Fisher, Len Murray, Bob Jones (NUPE

---

57 Castle, *Fighting All The Way*, p. 509. Brenda Treadwell, a nursing auxiliary in a south Wales care home during the 'winter of discontent', said that, to protect vulnerable patients, the staff maintained essential services (such as meals and medication) while on strike, but might not take patients on occasional outside visits or provide other less essential help. Interview: People's History Museum, Manchester, 30 September 2012. See also Ray Marriott, *Limping and Waddling to Revolution: A Memoir of Colin Barnett* (Kirkby Stephen: Hayloft Publishing, 2007), pp. 9, 96–8. For other perspectives on hospital work, see Jonathan Neale, *Memoirs of a Callous Picket* (London: Pluto Press, 1983).

58 For a more detailed account of the NUPE industrial action at Westminster Hospital, see Andy Beckett, *When the Lights Went Out: What Really Happened in Britain in the Seventies* (London: Faber & Faber, 2009), pp. 469–79.

national negotiator) and David Ennals, which resulted in a 9 per cent pay award plus a comparability review between public and private sector pay.[59]

Among the pay claims awaiting settlement among the public sector workers in early 1979 was a claim by 30,000 employees in the water industry, represented by the GMWU, NUPE and TGWU, which led to industrial action. There had never been a national water strike, though there had been limited unofficial action by water workers in the Pennine division of the North West Authority in early January 1979.[60] Media coverage concentrated on the impact of any industrial action by water and sewerage workers, but gave little attention to the wages and working conditions in this essential industry. Journalist Tom Forrester was an exception in investigating at first hand the conditions at the Chadderton sewerage works on the outskirts of Oldham. As Eddie Foreshaw, a skilled fitter, and Pete, a 'waterman', explained to Forrester:

> The worst job is when you have to get right down into the primary tanks to clean them. 'Primary' means raw sewage. Sometimes you get two or three feet of fat in the channels. We all excrete fat. Then there's rat droppings everywhere. All sewerage works are rat infested. You can get Weil's disease from old rat's piss. Bloke died last year. We can get every disease that's going.[61]

Both employees took part in an unofficial strike by 600 workers following the water authority's offer of 9.3 per cent.[62]

The water authorities were very hesitant about calling in troops and had clandestine talks with the local military at a public house near their Warrington headquarters. Emergency measures to treat sewerage and maintain supplies of drinking water included diverting raw water direct from Pennine reservoirs to households. While the appearance of raw sewerage on British streets was a constant concern and would be an indication of a civil breakdown in government, managerial staff carried out night-time maintenance of sewerage plants and, in the north-west region, sewage was pumped into the local river.

In 1987, Sir Clive Rose (deputy secretary in the Cabinet Office and chair of the CCU) recalled:

---

59 *Ibid.*, p. 475. For examples of industrial unrest in London hospitals at the time, see the following from the *Evening Standard*, 22, 31 January, 1, 2, 5 February 1979 (respectively): 'Troops called in … army fills mercy gap'; 'Walkout threat to five hospitals: strike may shut wards'; 'Sabotage hospital calls army'; 'Total strike threat to hospitals … at breaking point'; 'Walkout threat to key hospitals lifted: back from the brink'.
60 Keith Jeffery and Peter Hennessy, *States of Emergency: British Governments and Strike Breaking Since 1919* (London: Routledge & Kegan Paul, 1983), p. 249. Interview: Sir Clive Rose, Lavenham, 24 June 2011.
61 Tom Forrester, 'The bottom of the heap', *New Society*, 18 January 1979, pp. 125–6.
62 *Ibid.*

We spent many fraught hours: thinking about what we would do in case of strikes in these two industries [water and electricity] than any of the strikes mentioned today, including the gravediggers. The one we hadn't got a plan for was the gravediggers strike. We did have plans for those things but we were woefully aware how very defective they would be if the case came up of a major strike in either industry.[63]

David Ennals agreed that 'fear existed throughout the Cabinet'.[64] As related by Bernard Donoughue, head of the Policy Unit at Downing Street, the declaration of a state of emergency was considered at an emergency Cabinet meeting on 17 January. However, the Prime Minister did not have full Cabinet support. According to Donoughue, the government had decided to buy off the water workers 'at any price'.[65] This can be seen in the complex negotiations over the water workers' claim, in which an initial offer of 9.3 per cent had been raised to 13.9, then to 15.9 by February 1979, and then reached 16.5 per cent, which the Environment Minister, Peter Shore, vetoed. In the end, after further negotiations, the claim was settled at 15.9 per cent, comprising 9 per cent on basic rates plus a further 6.9 per cent as an attendance allowance.[66] The settlement was endorsed by the NUPE executive council and a ballot of the union membership.

An important issue in these negotiations was that the influence of a high settlement by the employers for the water and sewerage workers could sway other wage claims by a million local authority employees and other public sector workers. It was widely acknowledged that the water workers were one of the most powerful industrial groups, and the NUPE National Water Committee used the water workers' industrial muscle to assist local authority manual workers and NHS ancillaries. In Manchester, unofficial industrial action resulted in 2,000 homes without water supplies, as was remembered 30 years later by Lord Lipsey, special adviser to the Prime Minister 1977–79, at the 2009 British Academy debate on the 'winter of discontent'.[67]

---

63 Institute of Contemporary British History, 'Symposium', p. 43. Interview: Rose.
64 *Ibid.*
65 Bernard Donoughue, *Downing Street Diary, Volume Two: With James Callaghan in No. 10* (London: Jonathan Cape, 2008), pp. 399–400, 424, 426, 427 (diary entries: 11 December 1978, 17, 18, 19 January 1979).
66 Williams and Fryer, *Leadership and Democracy*, pp. 333–4.
67 Lord Lipsey: 'I am not sure where you were [in 1979] Professor Hay [who presented the paper at the 2009 British Academy debate], but I can tell you some of the places you weren't. You weren't in Manchester where for ten days people were getting water out of stand pipes in the street. You weren't in Liverpool when the mortuaries were closed because the grave diggers wouldn't dig the graves, and serious consideration was being given to dumping bodies at sea ... and you certainly weren't in Downing Street ... where I was ... where hour by hour "the newest grief ... of an hour's age doth hiss the speaker" ... was not only morally wearing, it was positively terrifying ... I am sorry that [the' winter of discontent'] was *not* a constructed crisis. That was a real crisis.' Cited

With the Labour government's defeat in the May 1979 general election and the return of the Conservative leader, Margaret Thatcher, as Britain's first woman Prime Minister to 10 Downing Street, the Low Pay Unit reviewed the position of Britain's poorest workers – particularly in terms of its own achievements, the failures of the outgoing Labour government and prospects under the new Tory administration. The Unit identified tackling low pay as a significant failing of the 1974–79 Labour governments and as a major contributory factor underpinning the industrial troubles of the winter of 1978–79. As David Jordan of the Low Pay Unit put it: 'Indeed some would argue that poetic justice was done when the issue of low pay played such a prominent part in undermining the government during the 1978–79 "winter of discontent"'.[68]

Despite five years in office, the Labour government by and large did not possess a comprehensive strategy for remedying low pay in the British economy. Between 1974 and 1978, at best there was only a slight decline in the total number of low-paid workers, from 6.0 million (without overtime taken into consideration) to 4.4 million; the corresponding figures after taking overtime payments into consideration were still 4.7 million to 3.6 million. Moreover, these figures did not include part-time workers, male youths under 21 years or girls aged under 18.

Based on the latest available government data, the Low Pay Unit reported that the numbers of poor people in Britain had actually increased in the 1970s. As the Callaghan government was about to embark on a new parliamentary term with a 5 per cent pay norm (about half the rate of inflation), and just before the beginning of the 'winter of discontent', in the autumn of 1978 the Unit published some startling facts about the numbers of working poor, the effects of low pay and the extent of poverty in Britain. Since 1974 there had been an increase of 123 per cent in people in full-time work earning less than the poverty line (taken to be the level at which people qualified for supplementary benefit). Adding their dependants increased the figure to 147 per cent. In terms of numbers, the figures rose from 130,000 to 290,000 people in full-time work earning less than the dole (adding their dependants, the totals increased from 360,000 to 890,000). As Frank Field, of the Low Pay Unit, noted: 'We hear a great deal about the numbers who opt for unemployment because it is to their financial advantage to do so. These figures give lie to the great scrounger myth of the 1970s.'[69]

---

in Lawrence Black and Hugh Pemberton, 'The winter of discontent in British politics', *Political Quarterly*, vol. 80, no. 4, October–December 2009, p. 556.

68 David Jordan, 'Five year's hard labour', *Low Pay Bulletin*, April/June 1979, p. 2.

69 Frank Field, *Rising Tide of Poverty: A Challenge to the Political Parties*, Low Pay Paper No. 25 (London: Low Pay Unit, September 1978), p. 1. Field was also Director of the Child Poverty Action Group (1969–79) and became a Labour MP in 1979. See also, Chris Pond, 'The unacceptable face of Labour's pay policy', *New Statesman*, 17 November 1978, p. 565.

Between January and March 1979, great attention was given to the public sector strikes by the government, the media and the public in general. With the virtual collapse of its pay policy, after the 5 per cent norm had been broken by the Ford workers and the oil tanker drivers' industrial action in the private sector, the Cabinet devoted much time and energy to restoring the government's credibility by devising other pay norms for public service workers, as well as offers of help for the low paid and comparability studies of the private and public sector pay.

At the same time, while the disputes involving the oil tanker drivers and road hauliers were close to settlement at around 14–15 per cent, the government still tried to maintain its 5 per cent pay norm in the public sector – or as near to that as possible – rather than conceding a double-figure settlement. During this time, the Callaghan administration tried to reach an agreement with the unions on pay for the long term. Yet, as we have seen, after Callaghan had postponed the general election in early September 1978, he had fatally committed his government to a new parliamentary term in 1978 *without* TUC support for the 5 per cent pay policy. Overwhelming difficulties arose both at the Labour Party conference in October and at the TUC General Council in November.[70] While the majority of trade union leaders wished to see the return of a Labour government at the next general election, the Prime Minister's dilemma, particularly during the public sector strikes, was that the majority of trade unionists continued to reject a voluntary incomes policy – whether under a Labour or a Conservative administration.[71]

In early January, Callaghan and his colleagues also found themselves under increased pressure from the Tory opposition, led by Margaret Thatcher, which secured a new lease of life, particularly after Thatcher's television broadcast on 17 January.[72]

On 11 January, after his return from Guadeloupe, Callaghan announced in Cabinet that he had received a letter from the leader of the opposition requesting a parliamentary statement on the industrial situation. He also warned of the possible need to declare a state of emergency, particularly as a settlement had not been secured in the national road haulage strike.[73] At the same meeting, the Cabinet agreed on a basic offer for NHS ancillaries, ambulance personnel and local authority manual workers, of 5 per cent plus the promise of a comparability exercise to be implemented over two years, as well as an 'underpinning' for the lowest paid, to be decided by the Ministerial Committee on Economic Strategy, Sub-Committee on Pay Negotiations (EY(P)). By this arrangement, the Prime Minister announced

---

70 For a detailed analysis of these events, see chapter 2.
71 *Financial Times*, 13 January 1979.
72 For more on this point, see chapter 7, pp. 130–2.
73 Cabinet conclusions, 11 January 1979, The National Archives (henceforth TNA) CAB 128/65(1).

the government should be able to maintain its 5 per cent pay policy, despite a slight modification with the 'underpinning'.

On 15 January, the Chancellor of the Exchequer outlined the proposal from the EY(P) on the development of permanent pay comparability machinery for establishing comparisons between public sector pay and suitable outside analogues, such as direct job comparisons. As a first step, a feasibility study was proposed for local authority manual workers, NHS ancillaries, ambulance workers and university technicians. It was also suggested that the exercise be extended in due course to water industry manual workers and to nurses.[74] The Chancellor further reported on low pay that the 5 per cent policy should be 'underpinned' by a minimum increase of £3.50, which would apply in both the private and public sectors.

On the eve of the National Day of Action, Peter Shore, Secretary of State for the Environment, took part in the London Weekend Television (LWT) programme *Weekend World*. His briefing notes reveal the key points of the government's case of special help for the low-paid, including a rise in child benefit. The government could also point to the introduction of the 'underpinning' of £3.50. He was also advised to argue that in any 'wage free-for-all' the lowest paid would lose out and that comparability studies were not necessarily the answer as there were no clear analogues.[75] Shore was briefed to argue the government's official position that the 5 per cent pay policy was the best way forward for defeating inflation and was also in the best interests of the low paid.

Eventually, on 14 February 1979, the government and the TUC published a patched up version of the social contract, which became known as the St Valentine's Day Concordat.[76] This document had been cobbled together somewhat hastily, mainly the work of Callaghan's principal private secretary, Kenneth Stowe, and David Lea, TUC Assistant General Secretary, and other union representatives. Callaghan secured immediate Cabinet approval for the new agreement before it became known in the Labour Party or leaked in the press. The Concordat, designed with the general election in mind (either in the summer or at the end of the full parliamentary term in October 1979), planned a reduction in the annual rate of inflation to 5 per cent within three years. The new arrangement set out long-term and mid-term objectives, including: guidance by the TUC on strikes, including strike ballots; maintenance of essential services; and peaceful picketing.[77] Other issues, such as pay comparability, a national economic assessment,

---

74 Cabinet conclusions, 11 January 1979, CAB 128/65(3).
75 Brian Abel-Smith to Pater Shore, 19 January 1979, Lord Peter Shore papers, British Library of Political Science, London, 11/90.
76 *The Economy, the Government and Trade Union Responsibilities: Joint Statement by the TUC and the Government* (London: HMSO, February 1979).
77 Cabinet conclusions, 8 February 1979, TNA CAB 128/65(5); Cabinet conclusions, 15 February 1979, TNA CAB 128/65(4).

pay relativities, TUC monitoring of strikes and the drafting of 'no strike' agreements in essential services, were left to a group of ministers, chaired by the Chancellor of the Exchequer, to be worked out in detail.[78] A somewhat unconvinced Donoughue was reassured on hearing Callaghan present the new Concordat with the TUC to the Commons: 'I must admit that it is better than I had expected. There is still nothing on *current* pay, but quite big concessions on union behaviour, and it is a fairly firm commitment to get inflation down to 5% over three years', he observed.[79]

While most of the public sector claims had been handled by the end of February 1979, the government's problems were not over. There were still claims from nurses, teachers and the civil servants. Donoughue noted that the civil service was the 'professional body that was supposed to be administering the Government's anti-inflation policy in general and the 5 per cent norm in particular'. The civil servants' claim on average was for 26 per cent and for the senior grades as much as 48 per cent. Donoughue's explanation was that the Civil Service Pay Research Unit made comparisons with the very highest pay grades in the private sector, but made no allowance for civil service privileges such as job security and inflation-proofed pensions.[80]

While the NHS claim was not finally settled until the eve of the Labour government's downfall on losing the vote of confidence on 28 March, the 1979 civil service strike can be considered the last major industrial action of the 'winter of discontent'. Between 23 February and 2 April, civil servants in Britain in the Civil and Public Services Association (CPSA) and Society of Civil and Public Servants (SCPS) unions, including many who had never taken industrial action before, staged a series of one-day strikes and finally accepted the formula of 9 per cent plus £1 a week with two later increases (up to 26 per cent by January 1980). The origins of the dispute can be found in the government's refusal to reintroduce annual pay research involving outside occupations, which had been suspended only one year after the 1974 strike settlement. By October 1978, the unions had assembled contingency plans for selective stoppages to start on 23 February 1979, which were approved by a large majority of union members, but heavily criticised by the Prime Minister in Parliament. John Mallinson, a member of the civil service First Division Association (FDA), recalled attitudes in the civil service, including severe disapproval from senior FDA staff about taking part in the National Day of Action, as well as an official letter of censure from the Law Society for his participation.[81]

---

78 Morgan, *Callaghan*, p. 671.
79 Donoughue, *Downing Street Diary, Volume Two*, p. 444 (diary entry: 14 February 1979).
80 Bernard Donoughue, *Prime Minister: The Conduct of Policy Under Harold Wilson and James Callaghan* (London: Jonathan Cape, 1987), pp. 181–2.
81 John Mallinson was a solicitor in the Department of Trade and Industry. 'I felt politicised by the event [the National Day of Action]. A solidarity gesture for me. I was not supposed to belong to a political party or take action as a civil servant. I came out …

The industrial action in the British civil service sheds interesting light on the public sector disputes towards the end of the 'winter of discontent'. The unions claimed 90 per cent support (management estimated support at 50 per cent) for the one-day strike held on 23 February. The selective action that followed included a ban on overtime and on the use of private cars for official business, as well as a refusal to undertake the work of other grades or to travel on official business in personal time. In addition, a series of selective strikes was arranged in government regional offices and different courts of law, many with computer installations, where the withdrawal of a few staff would have the maximum effect. Often, action was taken in geographical areas with no history of trade union militancy. Though the civil service unions were becoming more militant – even, remarkably, the FDA urged top management to support an all-out strike on 2 April – the industrial action was planned to limit any adverse impact on the general public. On 2 April there was a very high turn-out of 250,000–300,000 civil servants from virtually every department for the one-day strike that led to the settlement on 11 April of 9 per cent immediately (plus £1 for lower grades), 5 per cent in August 1979 and a further increase on 1 January 1980. By this stage, the election campaign was underway and union leaders argued that no better resolution would be possible. A historian of civil service unionism summed up the industrial action:

> the major impetus to the dispute was government insistence on maintaining a 5 per cent pay limit in the face of established procedure which had recommended more than 5 per cent … reluctance to break its own 5 per cent guideline precipitated the dispute, not nascent class militancy of Civil Servants working in clerical factory situations.[82]

Remarkably, shortly before the government fell in late March 1979, it was still endeavouring to maintain the fiction of a 5 per cent policy that had 'popped out' in a radio interview in the New Year.

In the face of the mounting difficulties caused by the public sector strikes, Callaghan's biographer noted that for several weeks the Prime Minister showed no leadership and seemed afflicted by despair:

> The Prime Minister had become the embodiment of Durkheim's *anomie*. He complained that colleagues and civil servants in department after department were giving way to union pressure in a spineless way (David Ennals at Health was a particular target). After a Cabinet meeting in late January,

---

[the] majority of my colleagues didn't want to strike and used "lawyer–client relationship" as a get-out … inflation had eroded our pay … the 5 per cent guideline – but did it have a legal base? We asked for more than 5 per cent.…We did not come out for a pay claim, but in a solidarity move.' Interview: John Mallinson, Highbury, London, 16 November 2011.

82 Michael P. Kelly, *White-Collar Proletariat: The Industrial Behaviour of British Civil Servants* (London: Routledge, 1980), pp. 113–19.

he asked his press officer Tom McCaffrey almost pathetically 'How do you announce that the Government's pay policy has almost collapsed?'[83]

In Downing Street, Bernard Donoughue had observed the crisis at the heart of a government endeavouring to handle the overwhelming tangle of wage negotiations. However, it was 'all very quiet', with a sombre mood of 'quiet despair' rather than 'people dashing around desperately trying to rescue the situation'. He noted:

> Incidentally, the flow of papers has completely stopped.... Ken Stowe says this is just like 1974: Whitehall has come to a total halt while they wait to see which way the cat will jump politically.... After [parliamentary] Questions [in the Commons] the PM made a statement about the [road hauliers'] strike situation. He announced the new voluntary code for picketing. It didn't go well. Most people don't want to know what Moss Evans will do. They want to know what the government will do.

On 22 January Donoughue had observed:

> Now today we have the 'day of Action', a national strike by 1.5 million public service workers. For many of them, this will be the first action they have ever seen, as they certainly never do a day's work for whichever local authority overpays them.

He added that the consequences of this militant union onslaught undermined the government, particularly the Prime Minister, who had lost his sense of direction – at one point announcing that if necessary he would cross a picket line. Donoughue, who wanted to take a tough stand with the unions, also recorded:

> It is very depressing to see how some ministers have given up ... several of them – Ennals, Foot, Silkin, Orme – seem to believe all we have to do is to 'give them the money'. They surrender at the first sign of union militancy.... Watching this happen, it strikes me how governments are beaten – from within and without.[84]

Then, on 1 March the results of the devolution referenda in Wales and particularly in Scotland dealt the government a deadly blow that led eventually to a lost vote of confidence and ultimate electoral defeat.[85] Bernard Donoughue described the demoralisation that eventually set in, with Cabinet ministers in a minority administration beset by a long period of industrial unrest and general political misfortune:

> It was a curious experience to be in a government that knows that it will inevitably be defeated before long. It was like being on the sinking

---

83 Morgan, *Callaghan*, p. 664.
84 Donoughue, *Downing Street Diary, Volume Two*, pp. 425–33 (diary entries: 18–23 January 1979)
85 These events are discussed in detail in chapter 8.

Titanic, although without the music. Neither ministers nor civil servants did anything. No policy papers were circulated and there was no serious attempt to follow up the recent new agreement with the TUC [the 'St. Valentine's Day Concordat']. The only thing that did take place, regrettably, was the setting up of the Standing Commission on public sector pay comparability under the distinguished Chairmanship of one of its authors, Hugh Clegg.[86]

On 26 March Professor Hugh Clegg of the University of Warwick, who had been a member of the Donovan Commission on Trade Unions and Employers' Associations in 1968, was appointed somewhat hurriedly as chair of the Standing Commission on Pay Comparability in the Public Sector. For the Callaghan government, the Commission had been seen as part of a new social contract in the St Valentine's Day Concordat. Clegg recalled that 'comparability' had emerged during pay discussions between the government and the public sector unions in early 1979 as a means of settling pay disputes by comparison with other groups of workers. He wrote:

> Eventually their disputes were settled by pay increases of about 9–10 per cent (not 5 per cent) and a reference of their claims to a comparability commission … to determine whether there was more to come by establishing acceptable bases of comparison, including comparisons with terms and conditions for other comparable work and … maintaining appropriate internal relativities.

Altogether in the two years it existed (largely under the Thatcher government) the Commission dealt with 25 different groups of public servants (mainly local government manual workers, hospital manual workers, nurses and teachers) totalling almost 2.5 million employees.[87]

Over 30 years on, the 'winter of discontent' continues to resonate in the popular memory, particularly in terms of iconic images associated with public sector unionism. It was this sector of trade unionism which had witnessed remarkable growth in terms of membership and militancy in industrial relations. By 1979, public service workers represented nearly 40 per cent of trade unionism in Britain, compared with less than 15 per cent in 1911. From 1911 to 1979, while trade union membership quadrupled, there was a ten-fold expansion in public services. Of the four unions (NUPE, COHSE, GMWU, TWGU) chiefly involved in the National Day of Action on 22 January 1979, the leading union, NUPE, had a membership of 140,054 in 1950 but sustained recruitment of manual workers (particularly women part-timers), especially in the NHS and local government resulted in a 374 per cent expansion.[88]

---

86 Donoughue, *Prime Minister*, p. 183.
87 Hugh Clegg, 'How public sector pay systems have gone wrong before', in John Gretton and Anthony Harrison (eds), *How Much Are Public Servants Worth?* (Oxford: Basil Blackwell, 1982), pp. 7–8. Interview: Fred Jarvis, Bloomsbury, London, 22 June 2010.
88 Fryer, 'Public service trade unionism in the twentieth century'.

Yet Peter Shore, who as a Cabinet departmental minister had been at the centre of the 'winter of discontent', later wrote in graphic terms about the impact of the public sector workers' industrial action:

> Not only were these pay claims massive and incontestably inflationary, industrial action was ruthlessly applied in total disregard of the interests of the public and of the effects on the community. So we had the outrage of serious threats to the nation's food supply; of grave-diggers refusing to bury the dead; of official and unofficial shop stewards and pickets deciding who was to be allowed into the nation's hospitals to receive treatment; of stinking heaps of uncollected refuse in the streets of our cities.... In his memoir, Callaghan tells us that: 'my instinct was in favour of doing so (declaring a State of Emergency) as a demonstration of our determination, but it was argued that it was very uncertain whether a declaration would do much practical good.' Callaghan's instinct was correct. The armed forces should have been deployed to clear the refuse, dig the graves, ensure the water and the essential supplies. They were not.[89]

For Clegg, it was ironic that, for most of the post-war years, governments of both political colours had used their position as the major paymaster to control pay in the public sector – in the civil service, in the NHS and in education – as well as being influential in the nationalised industries and with local authorities as an example to the private sector. Yet incomes policies in 1970–72 and 1972–74 had been undermined by strikes in the nationalised coalmines. Moreover, in his view, the wave of public sector strikes in the 'winter of discontent' smashed the Callaghan government's incomes policy and culminated in defeat at the May 1979 general election.[90]

---

89 Peter Shore, *Leading the Left* (London: Weidenfeld & Nicolson, 1993), pp. 118–19.
90 Clegg, 'How public sector pay systems have gone wrong before', pp. 3–4.

Chapter Six

Media coverage

On 22 January 1979, Tony Benn noted in his diary: 'Today was the Day of Action for local government employees and 1.25 million workers took the day off. The press is just full of crises, anarchy, chaos, disruption – bitterly hostile to the trade union movement. I have never seen anything like it in my life.'[1]

At the peak of the 'winter of discontent', the National Day of Action became the greatest industrial stoppage since the General Strike of May 1926. On 22 January 1979 around 1.5 million public sector workers took part in major demonstrations and rallies in London, Birmingham, Glasgow, Belfast and elsewhere. Benn, the Energy Secretary, saw at first hand the large gathering of public sector workers who had journeyed to London to demonstrate outside Parliament:

> Went over to the House of Commons, and outside St Stephen's Entrance there were 70,000 local government demonstrators who had come to protest against low pay. It was bitterly cold. There were gravediggers, caretakers, ambulance drivers – in short, our constituency – appealing for more money to keep public services going. They were very friendly to me. Tony, how are you? ... keep it up.

Earlier in the day, Benn had attended the Trades Union Congress (TUC)–Labour Party Liaison Committee, where he observed the trade union leadership's lack of power in the face of the revolt by their rank-and-file members. He noted:

> Len Murray [TUC General Secretary] looked poorly; he is powerless now, he's lost all his vitality by going along with policies that were not in the interests of the trade union movement. The union leaders simply have no

---

1 Tony Benn, *Conflicts of Interest: Diaries 1977–80*, edited by Ruth Winstone (London: Arrow Books, 1991), p. 433 (diary entry: 22 January 1979).

strength left. David Basnett [General Secretary of the General Municipal Boiler Makers' Union (GMBU) and one of the great architects of the pay policy] is now absolutely outflanked by his rank and file.[2]

However, from 10 Downing Street, at the centre of government, Bernard Donoughue had a different view of the National Day of Action, particularly after the weekend press had been 'full of the collapse of our pay policy and of the government with it'. Noting the demoralising effect on government, the head of the Downing Street Policy Unit – also in favour of the Prime Minister declaring a state of emergency – penned an acerbic observation in his diary about the 1.5 million public service workers who were taking strike action across Britain on 22 January. He added that the next day there would also be one of the national railway strikes. 'Apparently the British, never very keen on hard work, have decided on permanent inactivity', he concluded.[3]

Benn's instinctive sympathy for those demonstrating during the 'National Day of Action' in London and elsewhere was in sharp contrast to Donoughue's vitriolic attack, more comparable to the hostile media coverage in the popular press at the height of the 'winter of discontent'.[4]

Ever since the scare surrounding the Zinoviev letter during the 1924 general election campaign, which allegedly contributed to the downfall of the first Labour government, relations between the Labour Party and the capitalist press had often been tense.[5] Nearly 70 years later, the *Sun* newspaper's triumphant 1992 banner headline 'IT'S THE SUN WOT WON IT!' took the credit for returning John Major to 10 Downing Street for a fourth successive Conservative election victory. It summed up Labour's worst fears

---

2   *Ibid.*

3   Bernard Donoughue, *Downing Street Diary, Volume Two: With James Callaghan in No. 10* (London: Jonathan Cape, 2008), p. 428 (diary entry: 22 January 1979).

4   A leading left-wing critic of the media, Benn was no stranger to personal attacks made by the media as well as politicians. A year and a half earlier, for example, he had written: 'One interesting thing at the moment is the way the flamethrower of the press is being turned on me again as it was during the Common Market Referendum campaign. They have five lines of attack: that I am mad, ambitious, incompetent, a hypocrite and a red. This week I appear to be all of these at once. Alan Watkins describes me as a boy inventor – the next thing to a mad professor.' Benn, *Conflicts of Interest*, p. 165 (diary entry: 12 June 1977).

5   The ghost of the forged Zinoviev letter – purported to have sealed the fate of Ramsay MacDonald's fledgling government in 1924 – haunted Labour's memory during the twentieth century. In 1998 Robert Cook, the new Labour Foreign Secretary, commissioned a fresh inquiry into the controversy. Despite access to closed British and Russian archives, historian Gill Bennett found no evidence of a Foreign Office conspiracy to discredit the Russians and the 1924 Labour administration. Gill Bennett, *A Most Extraordinary and Mysterious Business: The Zinoviev Letter of 1924* (London: Foreign and Commonwealth Office, 1999). See also John Shepherd and Keith Laybourn, *Britain's First Labour government* (Basingstoke: Palgrave Macmillan, 2006), pp. 161–84; John Shepherd and Keith Laybourn, 'Labour's red letter day', *BBC History Magazine*, vol. 5, no. 12, December 2004, pp. 22–5.

and suspicions about the hostility of the Tory-supporting popular press. A defeated Neil Kinnock complained bitterly that the press had 'enabled the Tory Party to win yet again when it could not have secured victory on the basis of its own record, its programme or its character'.[6]

The role of the media coverage of the British 'winter of discontent' raises a number of interesting historical and methodological questions.[7] Particular attention in this chapter is given primarily to how the media – the national and local press, television and radio – reported the causes, character and impact of 'winter of discontent' in Britain. Press hostility towards the unions was particularly unrestrained during the industrial unrest of September 1978 to March 1979, at a time when trade union membership peaked at 13 million.

A hostile attitude of Labour governments towards the media (particularly a Tory-supporting national press) has a long history. Jean Seaton has written: 'union bashing is one of the conventions of the British media'.[8] How far in the 1970s did the unions remain scapegoats for the crisis in the British state and the 'winter of discontent'? As a result of the unsympathetic coverage of trade unionism, especially in the press, in 1977 the TUC established its Media Working Group under the chairmanship of Moss Evans. A number of reports and pamphlets on the media, mainly of high quality, were

6   Cited in David McKie, '"Fact is free but comment is sacred"; or was it *The Sun* wot won it?', in Ivor Crewe and Brian Gosschalk (eds), *Political Communications: The General Election Campaign of 1992* (Cambridge: Cambridge University Press, 1992), p. 121.
7   There is an extensive literature on the British media, including: James Curran and Jean Seaton, *Power Without Responsibility: The Press and Broadcasting in Britain* (London: Routledge, 1997); Jeremy Tunstall, *The Media in Britain* (London: Constable, 1983); Jean Seaton and Ben Pimlott (eds), *The Media in British Politics* (Aldershot: Avebury, 1987). The main published sources on the media concerning the 'winter of discontent' include: James Thomas, *Popular Newspapers, the Labour Party and British Politics* (Abingdon: Routledge, 2005); James Thomas, 'Bound by history: the winter of discontent in British politics, 1979–2004', *Media, Culture and Society*, vol. 29, no. 2, March 2007, pp. 263–83; Colin Hay, 'Chronicles of a death foretold: the winter of discontent and construction of the crisis of British Keynesianism', *Parliamentary Affairs*, vol. 63, no. 3, July 2012, pp. 446–70; Colin Hay, 'Narrating crisis: the discursive construction of the winter of discontent', *Sociology*, vol. 30, no.2, 1996, pp. 253–77; Jean Seaton, 'Trade unions and the media', in Ben Pimlott and Chris Cook (eds), *Trade Unions in British Politics* (London: Longman, 1982), pp. 272–90; Roy Greenslade, *Press Gang: How Newspapers Make Profits From Propaganda* (Basingstoke: Macmillan, 2003); Michael Cockerell, *Live From Number 10: The Inside Story of Prime Ministers and Television* (London: Faber & Faber, 1988); Lance Price, *Where the Power Lies: Prime Ministers v. the Media* (London: Simon & Schuster, 2010); John Cole, *How It Seemed to Me: Political Memoirs* (London: Weidenfeld & Nicolson, 1995); Geoffrey Goodman, *From Bevan to Blair: Fifty Years Reporting From the Political Front Line* (London: Pluto Press, 2003); Dominic Wring, *The Politics of Marketing the Labour Party* (Basingstoke: Palgrave Macmillan, 2005); Laura Beers, *Your Britain: Media and the Making of the Labour Party* (Cambridge, MA: Harvard University Press, 2009).
8   Seaton, 'Trade unions and the media', p. 272.

published by the TUC, including a valuable study of coverage by the press, television and radio of the January and February 1979 industrial disputes.[9]

In 1984 William Rodgers, Minister of Transport in the Callaghan Cabinet, put forward the remarkable assertion that 'the reporting of the strike [the road hauliers' dispute] by newspapers, television and to some extent radio was dramatic and had much more impact on opinion than the public's own direct experience of the strike'.[10]

The present chapter attempts to assess in what ways media coverage shaped people's perceptions of the industrial disorder that dominated those months. To what extent, for instance, was the enduring memory of 'crisis Britain' essentially media-created, as has been suggested by Colin Hay?[11]

The 1970s was a key decade in the politics and ownership of the national press in Britain. At the 1974 general election, in terms of the numbers of copies of national daily newspapers purchased, slightly more than 40 per cent supported the Conservative Party. By the time of the 'winter of discontent', the TUC pointed out that nearly 70 per cent of the British national daily newspapers had a definite pro-Conservative and anti-trade union editorial policy.[12] At the same time, there were significant connections between the media and the modern international world of business. A prime example for the TUC was 'News International, which owns *News of the World* and the *Sun*, [and] is part of an international Australian company with extensive commercial interests in paper manufacture, engineering, transport and publishing'.[13]

Of the various changes in the press in the late 1970s, the most significant was the alteration in the ownership, and eventual political affiliation, of the *Sun,* which became the Britain's best-selling tabloid newspaper. In November 1969, the International Press Corporation (IPC), which owned around 200 titles, including the *Sun* and the *Daily Mirror* – both Labour-supporting newspapers – had sold the *Sun* at a giveaway price to a young Australian-born American tycoon, Rupert Murdoch. At the time, the *Sun's* circulation was around a million copies; by late 1973 this had increased to 3 million and the paper eventually overtook the *Daily Mirror* in 1978. Murdoch transformed the *Sun* into a daily version of his *News of the World* Sunday paper (also acquired in 1969), aided by aggressive promotion and the exploitation of pin-ups on page 3. As part of the endless tabloid circulation battle, Associated Newspapers closed the *Daily Sketch* in 1971

9 Trades Union Congress, *A Cause for Concern: Media Coverage of Industrial Disputes, January and February 1979* (London: TUC Publications, 1979).
10 William Rodgers, 'Government under stress: Britain's winter of discontent 1979', *Political Quarterly*, vol. 55, no. 2, 1984, p. 178.
11 Hay, 'Chronicles of a death foretold', pp. 446–70; Hay, 'Narrating crisis'.
12 Trades Union Congress, *A Cause for Concern.*
13 *Ibid.*

and relaunched the *Daily Mail* in tabloid format. By 1977, the *Daily Express* was also being published as a tabloid.[14]

The transformation of the *Sun* under Murdoch's ownership to an out-and-out Conservative-supporting newspaper was a gradual rather than an overnight change. A nominal supporter of the Labour Party, the *Sun* had been launched following the demise of the *Daily Herald* – Labour's main national daily newspaper from 1912 to 1964.[15] With falling sales and, in particular, collapsing advertising revenue, the IPC (previously the Mirror Group) decided finally to close the paper and re-open with a new title, the *Sun* – 'the only newspaper born of the age we live in'. However, as Tony Benn observed at the time, the debut issue was 'appalling ... basically the same minus the *Herald* political content'.[16]

During the Heath premiership, 1970–74, Murdoch's *Sun* supported the miners against the government and attacked Margaret Thatcher, Minister of Education, as 'Maggie Thatcher, Milk Snatcher!' when she ended free school milk. Nor did the paper support Thatcher in her successful Conservative leadership contest. In 1975 the *Sun* featured a 'Meet the Unions' series. However, in 1976 the paper began to attack the left wing of the Labour Party and the Callaghan government for economic incompetence that led to the crisis involving the International Monetary Fund (IMF). Yet it was not until 9 May 1978 that the *Sun* notched up the highest circulation of all the daily papers and explicitly announced a change of political affiliation by backing the Conservative candidate at the Ilford North by-election. The subsequent Conservative gain of this important Labour seat was seen by the party managers as evidence of growing electoral support among the C2 (skilled working-class) voters. The *Sun* pronounced that: 'it is Margaret Thatcher, not Jim Callaghan, who speaks for Britain these days'.[17]

In 1975 Gordon Reece had been recruited by Thatcher from EMI for a key appointment – as her personal public relations adviser and head of publicity. In 1978 he signed up a little-known advertising agency, Saatchi and Saatchi, to radically reshape Tory advertising, publicity and communications policy, and also encouraged the leader of the opposition to court the

---

14 Tunstall, *The Media in Britain*, pp. 83–6; Bill Grundy, *The Press Inside Out* (London: W. H. Allen, 1976), pp. 24–5, 45–6.

15 The *Daily Herald* had three main configurations: from 1912 to 1922, under the Christian socialist George Lansbury as editor/proprietor (during the First World War, the paper became a weekly pacifist left-wing publication); from 1922 to 1930 as a national daily under joint Labour Party and TUC control; and from 1930 until 1964 as a mass-circulation commercial Labour daily published by Odhams Press. For the *Daily Herald*, see Huw Richards, *The Bloody Circus: The Daily Herald and the Left* (London: Pluto Press, 1999); John Shepherd, *George Lansbury: At the Heart of Old Labour* (Oxford: Oxford University Press, 2004), pp. 138–57.

16 Tony Benn, *Out of the Wilderness: Diaries 1963–67* (London: Hutchinson, 1987), cited in Richards, *The Bloody Circus*, pp. 178–9.

17 See Thomas, *Popular Newspapers*, pp. 74–6.

tabloid press. Murdoch's *Sun* and *News of the World* were now strategically in the Conservative camp. The collapse of the Labour government's pay policy and the industrial unrest of the 'winter of discontent' provided the Tory opposition with an unforeseen and fortuitous opportunity to reshape party electoral fortunes.[18]

By the 1979 'winter of discontent', there were five main national daily tabloid publications:

1. *Sun* (circulation nearly 4,000,000; readership nearly 12,000,000);
2. *Daily Mirror* (circulation 3,783,000; readership 11,603,000);
3. *Daily Express* (circulation 2,458,000; readership 6,807,000);
4. *Daily Mail* (circulation 1,973,000; readership 5,423,000);
5. *Daily Star* (no statistics available).[19]

In 1977 the Beaverbrook family had sold Express Newspapers to Victor Matthew's Trafalgar House Investments. In turn, Express Newspapers launched the Manchester-based *Daily Star* in direct competition with the *Daily Mirror* and the *Sun*. In the 1970s there was also a significant change to the range of broadsheets published in Britain. An American oil company, Atlantic Richfield, acquired the 175-year-old *Observer* in 1977 and in 1981 sold the paper to 'Tiny' Rowland's Lonhro company. On 30 November 1978, in response to an industrial dispute, ostensibly over the introduction of new technology, Times Newspapers stopped publishing the five titles in its stable: *The Times* and *Sunday Times*, as well as *Times Higher Education Supplement*, *Times Educational Supplement* and *Times Literary Supplement*.[20] While the tabloid press was engaged in a fiercely contested circulation war in the 1970s, the closure of *The Times* benefited both the sales and the advertising revenue of its rivals: the *Financial Times*, the *Guardian* and the *Daily Telegraph*. Likewise, the suspension of the *Sunday Times* resulted in increased sales and advertising income for its competitors: the *Observer* and the *Sunday Telegraph*. At the same time there were other developments, principally with the *Daily Mail*, which had been the only newspaper to back Thatcher in the 1975 Conservative Party leadership contest. Under the new editorship of

---

18 Tim Bell, 'The Conservatives' advertising campaign', in Robert M. Worcester and Martin Harrop (eds), *Political Communications: The General Election Campaign of 1979* (London: George Allen & Unwin, 1982), pp. 11–26; Michael Cockerell, 'Reece, Sir (James) Gordon (1929–2001)' in Lawrence Goldman (ed.), *Oxford Dictionary of National Biography* (Oxford: Oxford University Press, 2009), pp. 894–6. Thatcher and the Tory opposition 1975–79 are discussed in more detail in chapter 7.

19 Michael Bilton and Sheldon Himmelfarb, 'Fleet Street', in David Butler and Dennis Kavanagh (eds), *The British General Election of 1979* (London: Macmillan, 1980), pp. 231–3.

20 For the complex causes of this extended industrial dispute between the Thomson management and the print unions (over the 'management's right to manage'), see Simon Jenkins, 'Why *The Times* and *Sunday Times* vanished', *Encounter*, August 1979, pp. 59–69.

David English, appointed by proprietor Vere Rothmere, after he had closed the *Daily Sketch*, the *Daily Mail* was published as a tabloid newspaper.

The 'winter of discontent' still resonates within the popular memory today, particularly the public sector disputes in January and February 1979. These strikes became more prominent because of the media coverage, particularly in the tabloid press. The extent of coverage of the industrial disputes, particularly in January and February 1979, at the peak of the 'winter of discontent', produced strong criticisms of the way the media frequently portrayed trade unionists. As a result, later that year the TUC's Media Working Group published *A Cause for Concern: Media Coverage of Industrial Disputes, January and February 1979*, to increase public awareness of how the trade union movement was depicted in the press and broadcasting. Anti-union propaganda was fuelled by dramatic headlines which portrayed Britain almost 'at war', compared to the praise of the 'Dunkirk spirit' for those not on strike. A two-page spread of the TUC publication, featuring 18 national and provincial newspaper headlines, displayed the attitude of the press on industrial stoppages. These included: *Sun*, 1 February 1979, 'Angry mums rolled up their sleeves and went into action yesterday against hospital strikers threatening the safety of their sick children'; *Yorkshire Post*, 23 January 1979, 'Lives at risk as strikers show no mercy'; *Daily Mirror*, 18 January 1979, 'Britain is being held to ransom as industrial chaos grips the country'; *Northern Echo*, 29 January 1979, 'More hardship is on the card from today as hospital and council workers threaten the big squeeze if they don't get their way over pay'; *Morning Star*, 17 January 1979, 'Premier Callaghan last night launched an outrageous attack on the lorry drivers and the whole trade union movement'.[21]

By mid-February, opinion polls featured in the press revealed the growing demand for the limitation of trade union power. Yet most people's knowledge of unions, industrial relations and disputes was largely derived from the media, a likely indication of media influence on public opinion.

While the TUC publication readily acknowledged that many trade unionists in the past believed the mass media were biased against them, coverage of events of the 'winter of discontent' reached unparalleled dimensions in January and February 1979. As the TUC put it, 'For two months, trade unions and trade unionists were subjected to an unending series of attacks and abuses, which exceeded the experiences and expectations of even the most seasoned media watchers'. This onslaught had seriously affected public opinion, culminating in an 'almost universal cry for "reform" of trade unions'.[22]

This TUC publication also provided a rich source of detailed evidence, much of it drawn from official statistics, such as the official figures for days

---

21 Trades Union Congress, *Cause for Concern*, pp. 20–1.
22 *Ibid.*, p. 5.

lost through strikes and other stoppages, which gave a more balanced view of industrial action and its impact than in the media. The Department of Employment *Gazette* recorded, for example, that 1,449,400 workers were involved in industrial disputes in January 1979, with a total of 2,585,000 working days lost. There were similar high figures, 1,690,000 and 4,331,000, for February 1979. Yet the respective numbers of individual stoppages, 277 and 244 (not reported in the media), were well below the average monthly total during the late 1970s. Similarly, in January 1979 the Department of Employment estimated that 235,000 workers were laid off as a result of the road hauliers' dispute, which contrasted sharply with scaremongering predictions by the Confederation of British Industry (CBI) and individual employers that 'millions of workers' would soon be laid off.[23]

The press often mixed up comment and fact in reporting strikes. Specific attention tended to be concentrated on major industries, such as the motor industry, the public sector and transport, deemed as more newsworthy, though other industries were relatively strike free. At the same time, the media not only reported industrial unrest but also largely ignored attempts to control and contain the impact of the industrial action, such as the introduction of voluntary codes of conduct. The TUC also claimed that even in 'the winter of discontent' more days were lost through injuries, accidents or sickness than the number lost through industrial stoppages. Usually, about 14 working days were lost through illness or injury per worker per year, compared with only 7 or 8 hours a year through strikes.[24] Moreover, comparisons with other industrial countries such as the United States, France and Germany revealed that Britain was roughly in the middle of the international league table of days lost through industrial action.

Despite the amount of research conducted on the media, relatively little attention has been given to the opinions of its readers, viewers and listeners. However, the *Sunday Times* did commission Market and Opinion Research International (MORI) to conduct a 'four-wave panel study' of the views of those groups during the 1979 general election.[25] This investigation revealed some interesting conclusions about British public perceptions of press bias and its influence on voting behaviour. While the great majority in 1979 considered that the broadcasting media were unbiased, twice as many thought BBC television to be biased towards the Tories (9 per cent) as to Labour (4 per cent).[26]

When questioned about the press, more people believed there was a bias towards the Conservatives than towards Labour. However, two-thirds of

23 Trades Union Congress, *A Cause for Concern*, pp. 8–9.
24 *Ibid.*, pp. 8, 10.
25 Peter Kellner and Robert M. Worcester, 'Electoral perceptions of media stance', in Robert M. Worcester and Martin Harrop (eds), *Political Communications: The General Election Campaign of 1979* (London: George Allen & Unwin, 1982), p. 57.
26 *Ibid.*, pp. 57–9.

Table 6.1 *Comparison of the newspapers readerships, 1979 (percentage of each group regularly reading each title)*

	General public	MPs	Trade union general secretaries	TUC delegates	Industrial/ labour press correspondents
Daily newspapers					
Daily Express	15	19	19	16	67
Daily Mail	11	37	11	19	67
Daily Mirror	24	23	19	41	77
Sun	25	15	11	12	48
Daily Star	5	n.a.	5	4	29
Daily Telegraph	8	54	35	23	72
The Times	n.a.	76	n.a.	n.a.	95
Guardian	1	48	72	64	81
Financial Times	1	45	41	16	100
Morning Star	n.a.	n.a.	26	27	43
Evening Standard	n.a.	50	26	12	67
Evening News	n.a.	29	12	8	57
Sunday newspapers					
News of the World	24	8	11	15	14
Sunday Mirror	22	7	16	30	24
Sunday People	21	5	19	20	14
Sunday Express	17	53	16	19	33
Sunday Telegraph	7	47	23	21	77
Observer	7	58	73	54	86
Sunday Times	n.a.	80	n.a.	n.a.	95

n.a., data not available.
Source: Peter Kellner and Robert M. Worcester, 'Electoral perceptions of media stance', in Robert M. Worcester and Martin Harrop (eds), *Political Communications: The General Election Campaign of 1979* (London: George Allen & Unwin, 1982), p. 66.

those surveyed answered that there was no newspaper bias at all (or replied 'didn't know'). The category of 'Election readership by party support' revealed that most Conservative voters read Conservative newspapers, but Labour electors read either the *Daily Mirror* or the *Sun* (formerly Labour). The *Sun*'s readership was 38 per cent Conservative and 52 per cent Labour, with 9 per cent voting Liberal. However, during the 'winter of discontent', the *Daily Mirror* was at times very hostile to the Labour government and the unions.

A comparison of the newspapers read by the general public and different 'elite groups' (MPs, trade union leaders, TUC conference delegates and industrial/labour press correspondents) revealed significant variations in their reading habits (table 6.1). It is not surprising that all the industrial/

labour correspondents (100 per cent) read the *Financial Times* or that the *Sun* and the *Daily Mirror* were the two most popular of the five leading dailies. In terms of the industrial disputes during the 'winter of discontent', the difference in newspaper readership between the trade union leadership and the general public (including trade union members) is particularly noteworthy. Only 11 per cent of the trade union general secretaries perused the *Sun* (*Daily Mirror* and *Daily Express* scored 19 per cent each). Yet 35 per cent were readers of the Tory-supporting *Daily Telegraph* and twice that number (72 per cent) studied the *Guardian* and 41 per cent the *Financial Times*. However, among the general public, just 1 per cent were readers of the *Guardian* or *Financial Times*, whereas their favourite papers were the *Sun* and the *Daily Mirror*, as well as on Sundays the *News of the World* and the *Sunday Mirror*.

One of the most interesting conclusions revealed by this 1979 study were the small numbers of readers of the *Mail*, *Express* and *Mirror* who thought their paper had a different political orientation (in editorials and elsewhere in the paper) from the one it actually held. Virtually all *Daily Telegraph* readers knew their paper was a Conservative paper. However, nearly 500,000 *Daily Mirror* readers did not think their newspaper supported Labour.[27] Yet *Sun* readers revealed a fascinating division, attributing party support to both major parties in equal measure: a third believed the paper supported Labour, a third Conservative, a quarter indicated 'don't know' and the remainder no particular party support.[28] Kellner and Worcester attributed this finding to the *Sun*'s change of political affiliation in the 1970s.[29]

After 1979 the events of the 'winter of discontent' became deeply etched in the national psyche as part of 'crisis Britain' of the 1970s and are known today even by those too young to have lived through it. While the winter of strikes featured in the 1979 general election campaign, the myths and realities of this turbulent period continued to be disinterred in the Conservative election campaigns of 1983, 1987 and 1992. According to John Whittingdale, Margaret Thatcher's political secretary, the Conservative Prime Minister always went into her campaigns in the 1980s armed with newspaper headlines from the 'winter of discontent', which she claimed would be repeated if a Labour government was returned. In 1985 Thatcher famously told the Conservative Party conference and the nation: 'Do you remember Labour Britain of 1979? It was a Britain in which union leaders held their members and our country to ransom ... a Britain that was known as the sick man of Europe'.[30]

---

27 *Ibid.*, pp. 61–2.
28 *Ibid.*, p. 62.
29 *Ibid.*
30 Margaret Thatcher, *Speeches to the Conservative Party Conference 1975–1988* (London: Conservative Political Centre, 1989), p. 109.

The most dominant 'winter of discontent' images in the media were of the strikes and stoppages by public service workers during January and February 1979. As already noted, on 22 January some 1.5 million workers in the public sector participated in a National Day of Action in London, Manchester, Belfast, Birmingham and other British cities and towns. This was the largest display of action since the General Strike of 1926; it was organised by the National Association of Local Government Officers (NALGO), the Confederation of Health Service Employees (COHSE), the National Union of Public Employees (NUPE) and the General Municipal Workers' Union (GMWU). Its origins were in the low-pay campaign by the unions for a minimum wage of £60 per week and a 35-hour working week. Hostile media reporting included a declaration that 'emergency operations, burials, school closures and rubbish disposal are among services threatened by industrial disruption which will be far more disruptive than the lorry drivers' strike'.[31] This was at a time when the number of those out of work rose; during January 1979 it did so by 90,968, to a total of 1,455,275.[32]

Most of the hostile reaction to the strikes by those 'who care for us from the cradle to the grave', as David Basnett, General Secretary of the GMWU put it, focused on the effects on the vulnerable and the poor, who were dependent on public services such as the National Health Service and workers in local authorities. The Archbishop of Canterbury, Dr Coggan, publicly condemned the 'pitiless' industrial action which damaged helpless parties not involved in the disputes.[33]

No industrial action produced more infamous headlines in the national press than the Merseyside gravediggers' and crematorium workers' strike by members of the GMWU in Liverpool. It resulted in funerals being postponed, families digging graves and even the possibility of burial at sea for corpses being stored in a local disused factory. On 1 February 1979, the *Daily Mail* carried a most powerful and effective banner headline on its front page, 'They won't let us bury our dead', which told the reader what to think. And the main story, by reporters Alan Young and Andrew London, opened with 'If you must bury your dead, you have to ask the strike committee first'. The account of the strike focused on 'bodies piling up in the city's mortuaries; some may have to be buried at sea ... according to Dr Duncan Dolton, Liverpool's Medical Officer'. Altogether, a powerful image of malevolent trade unionists was constructed based on few facts about the dispute. Yet only very brief details of the gravediggers' pay claim were reported: 'That is the incredible situation in Liverpool, where gravediggers are refusing to work until they get a 46 per cent pay rise'.[34]

---

31 *Daily Telegraph*, 20 January 1979, p. 1.
32 *Daily Telegraph*, 24 January 1979, p. 1.
33 *Daily Telegraph*, 26 January 1979, p. 8.
34 *Daily Mail*, 1 February 1979.

The provincial press provided readers with more balanced reporting. This gave attention to the underlying deep-seated grievances over low pay, abysmal (even dangerous) working conditions and life at home that culminated in industrial action by 60 Merseyside gravediggers and crematorium workers.[35] Even so, the 'bodies not being buried' stories continued to appear in the Conservative press to haunt a Labour government almost 30 years later.[36]

In the national press and on the nation's television screens, Leicester Square in London famously became 'Fester Square', as a result of the mountains of uncollected refuse (it was also reported that a rat appeared). In Cambridge, more than 50 emergency rubbish dumps were established to cope with nearly 300 dustmen and council outdoor workers on strike in early 1979. The local branch of the GMWU, at a special meeting outside the city council store yard in Mill Road, decided to continue the industrial action, which in the end lasted eight weeks. The local paper – not renowned for covering industrial disputes – reported the views of those on strike. The secretary of the Cambridge branch of the GMWU, Andrew Murden, commented on tensions within the local community caused by the industrial stoppage, which included the roads not being gritted:

> Many people have said to us 'Don't you care about the children not being able to get around?' We tell these people that our members have children too – but that our strike is the only weapon to help us fight our battle for a decent living wage.[37]

'How many old age pensioners have been starved to death by the lorry drivers?' the journalist Anna Coote asked in the *New Statesman*.[38] Her trenchant article critically examined on a virtual day-by-day basis the *Sun's* one-sided coverage of the road hauliers' dispute in January 1979 in order to assess how far the strike had affected the British economy. On 30 December 1978, the *Sun* had predicted a 'crippling' strike if the 20 per cent pay claim by 50,000 lorry drivers was not settled. The Road Haulage Association (RHA) declared that the strike would 'severely damage the nation'. On 3 January 1979, the industrial stoppage was given more prominence by the *Sun* with a banner headline: 'IRON RATIONS ... Housewives face strike threat ... millions face layoffs'. The next day, a 'wildcat' strike, according to the RHA and the Fruit and Vegetable Bureau, was endangering supplies of newsprint, meat and parcels, as well as fruit and vegetables.[39]

---

35 See, for example, *Liverpool Echo*, 25, 26, 29 January, 2, 3, 4, 5 February 1979. The gravediggers' and crematorium workers' strikes in Liverpool and elsewhere are discussed in more detail in chapter 5.

36 'Echoes of winter of discontent ... BODIES OF THE DEAD NOT BEING BURIED', *Mail on Sunday*, 12 October 2008, p. 1.

37 *Cambridge Evening News*, 26 January 1979, p. 1.

38 Anna Coote, 'Strike havoc probed', *New Statesman*, 26 January 1979, pp. 106–7.

39 *Ibid.*, p. 106.

Yet little attempt had been made to provide *Sun* readers with any idea of the various grievances that caused the road hauliers' strike or the attitude of the employers and the government pay policy. Not until 6 January did the *Sun* print any specific details of the lorry drivers' pay claim: 'The bosses' offer would push up basic rates from £53 to £60. The unions want £64.' Nor were there any interviews with those on strike or manning the picket lines, as could be found in some of the broadsheet national dailies. The only exception was on 17 January, when the *Sun* carried a banner headline: 'BREAKFAST BLUES: Supplies NOT getting through, says food boss'. Alongside this news item, the paper quoted Bill Astbury, chairman of the Greater Manchester strike committee: 'If we can't afford the food why should anyone else have it?' On the same page, the paper printed a sidebar story on a familiar theme from the previous week: 'What crisis? It's just a spasm, says Jim', which alluded to the Prime Minister's response to a bombardment of parliamentary questions on the road and rail strikes: 'I think there is a spasm that the trade union movement – and indeed many workers in this country – are going through'.[40]

Yet earlier, on 8 January, another dimension had been added to the *Sun's* narrative when the paper welcomed Thatcher's promise to 'crack down on state benefits' for strikers, praising it as 'a ray of sunshine to strike-torn battered Britain'. On 9 January, according to the *Sun*, the road hauliers' strike had taken Britain to the 'brink of a disaster that will make Ted's [Ted Heath's] three day week seem like a golden age'. For good measure, the newspaper warned in racist language of a 'massive' dirty jobs strike by 'the shock troops of NUPE under Fuhrer Alan Fisher'. In reporting the road hauliers' strike, the *Sun* left no stones unturned. Three days later, a series of prominent stories on the impact of the dispute became increasingly apocalyptic: 'FAMINE THREAT … 1,000 old people may die each day'; followed by 'HELPLESS! 3 million face dole queue'; then, on 15 January, the Director of the CBI, Sir John Methven, gave an unbelievable warning that 'the pickets are holding the country to ransom' and there was a story from near Abergavenny, south Wales, of 'SHOTS FIRED AT PICKETS'.[41]

In January 1979, Christopher Hitchens' article in the *New Statesman* on the depiction of violence during the road hauliers' strike challenged the coverage by the *Daily Mail* of an incident involving a lorry driver hauled from his cab and beaten up by four mobile motorway pickets who had followed him for 100 miles. Hitchens claimed that the *Daily Mail*'s version had inaccuracies, including 'eight direct misstatements of fact', which he outlined in detail his piece.[42] Hitchens' investigative journalism concluded

---

40 *Sun*, 17 January 1979, pp. 1–2.
41 Coote, 'Strike havoc probed', p. 106.
42 Christopher Hitchens, 'The *Daily Mail* does it again', *New Statesman*, 2 February 1979, p. 136.

with a reference to the Labour Party's longstanding suspicions of the British press:

> The *Daily Mail* has long been famous for two things: its bitter and hysterical hatred of the Labour movement and its abysmal failure as a newspaper to get at the truth. Sometimes, as in the celebrated case of the Zinoviev letter, the political bias and rank dishonesty merge in the same story.[43]

The *Daily Mail* in turn then commented on the piece in the *New Statesman*. The following week Hitchens concluded: 'Briefly the *Daily Mail* has published an article many times the length of the original, and still cannot produce any worthwhile evidence to justify their inflammatory treatment of the incident'.[44]

More detailed articles that contextualised the strikes during the 'winter of discontent' were virtually confined to the quality broadsheets, such as the *Financial Times* and the *Guardian*,[45] and journals like the *New Statesman*, the *Economist*, *New Society* and the *Spectator*. However, two rare exceptions in the general media coverage of the 'winter of discontent' were a two-page article 'Portrait of the poor' by the investigative journalist John Pilger, in the *Daily Mirror*, about the desperate lives of public sector workers and their families – caretakers, hospital workers and local government employees in the prosperous university city of Oxford, who formed part of the 4.5 million living on a basic 'poverty wage' – well below the average industrial earnings – of no more than £55 per week with little opportunity.[46] Surprisingly, on the National Day of Action the London Conservative-supporting paper, the *Evening Standard*, published a two-page feature with six brief case studies (and photographs) of low-paid workers in the capital city – the gardener, the domestic, the gravedigger, the nurse, the porter and the caretaker.[47] However, on 14 February the paper censured the London Borough of Camden for agreeing the NUPE pay claim of a minimum wage of £66.67 for a 35-hour week for manual workers and described Camden as 'the most incorrigibly spendthrift local authority in this city, if not all Britain'.[48]

The trade union movement's attitude towards the mass media was demonstrated in different ways during the 'winter of discontent'. As Jean Seaton observed: 'a growing concern was given urgency by the way in

---

43 *Ibid*. For further discussion of the Zinoviev letter, see p. 109.
44 Christopher Hitchens, '"Ghost" writing at the *Daily Mail*', *New Statesman*, 9 February 1979.
45 See, for example, 'The factors fuelling the lorry drivers' strike', *Financial Times*, 11 January 1979, p. 20; 'The justified grievances of Britain's low paid workers', *Guardian*, 2 January 1979, p. 13.
46 See John Shepherd, 'Labour wasn't working', *History Today*, vol. 59, no. 1, January 2009, p. 48.
47 'After thirty years … the gardener who gets £58 a week', *Evening Standard*, 22 January 1979, pp. 14–15.
48 *Evening Standard*, 14 February 1979.

which the disputes of 1978–79 were represented. Many of the lowest-paid workers in the public sector, who had never been previously on strike, were appalled to find themselves pilloried as inhumane blackmailers'.[49]

On 1 February 1979 the *Express* carried a banner headline on its front page – 'MAGGIE'S WAR CRY' – supported by a direct quote from Margaret Thatcher: 'If someone is confronting our essential liberties, if someone is inflicting on-going harm – by God, I'll confront them'. In a radio interview, Thatcher confirmed she would be prepared to: 'take on militants hitting at the elderly, the sick and children, or threatening law and liberty'.[50] The centre spread of the same issue, under the caption 'WHAT DO YOU THINK OF IT SO FAR?', featured photographs of mounting uncollected rubbish – a potential health hazard – in Soho, plus two volunteers cleaning a ward in the Westminster Children's Hospital.[51]

Over several weeks, the *Express* mainly targeted public sector workers. On 2 February a one-word banner headline declared 'ENOUGH!', before outlining Thatcher's 'battle plans' to TAX social security benefits to strikers and their families; to REFUSE benefits for wildcat strikers; to DELAY tax refunds to strikers; to MAKE strikes illegal in essential public services, including the gas and electricity industries; and to OUTLAW sympathy strikes.[52] Public sector workers on strike in the National Health Service were left in no doubt about the newspaper's condemnation of their behaviour. On 2 February, the paper published a massive banner headline – 'SICK, SICK, SICK: After the ill, the bereaved, the elderly – it's the children's turn to suffer hospital chaos'. The front-page report described a four-hour strike by porters and kitchen staff at the Great Ormond Street Hospital for Children, where Audrey Callaghan, the Prime Minister's wife, was chair of the board of governors, and a 24-hour strike at the Queen Elizabeth Hospital for Sick Children in the East End. The paper carried a statement by the Great Ormond Street shop steward: 'We have chosen this form of industrial action to cause minimum disruption, while making our case for our pay claim. I must stress we do not want the children to suffer.'[53]

Outside the five popular 'dailies' (*Mail, Express, Mirror, Sun, Star*), the most widely read paper among the broadsheets was the *Financial Times* (*FT*). It was widely read by the 'elites', including MPs, trade union leaders and especially industrial and labour correspondents (see table 6.1). On 9 January 1979, the *FT* devoted page 7 to 'UK news', which gave factual summaries of the extent of the industrial disputes, including reports on the effects of the lorry drivers' strike, the forthcoming train drivers' stoppage and accounts of industrial democracy by the TGWU General Secretary,

---

49 Seaton, 'Trade unions and the media', p. 273.
50 *Daily Express*, 1 February 1979, p. 1.
51 *Ibid.*, pp. 20–1.
52 *Daily Express*, 2 February 1979, p. 1.
53 *Ibid.*

Moss Evans, and a short piece entitled 'Tories wary of Thatcher's union plans'.[54] On 11 January, besides similar reports on the industrial disputes, the *FT* carried an informative article – 'Ulster close to state of emergency' and also 'The factors fuelling the lorry drivers', an examination of the causes of the nationwide dispute.[55] On 13 January, at the height of the 'winter of discontent', the paper's political editor, Malcolm Rutherford, provided a similar analysis of the Callaghan government's handling of that dispute under the heading 'The biggest union challenge since 1974'.[56]

After the 'winter of discontent', Geoffrey Goodman, industrial editor of the *Daily Mirror*, questioned whether biased or inaccurate reporting had any significant effect on industrial relations in Britain.[57] He observed that 'one of the most widely held beliefs in our society is that the press, and indeed, the whole of the media do a rather poor job of reflecting the true nature of Britain's industrial relations'. He declared that this was a belief – 'that the media are incapable of getting things right' – shared by both sides of industry, whether it was senior of middle managers, trade union leaders, local officials or shop stewards. A major criticism levelled against the media coverage of industrial conflicts was its sensationalism. In particular, the media were often accused of concentrating on the impact of a strike, with little or no effort to investigate the underlying issues or grievances. According to Goodman, in some cases the presence of television cameras might escalate or draw out an industrial stoppage.[58]

Two important factors about the five daily popular titles were their rivalry over circulation and their developing technology in terms of news production. As Michael Bilton and Sheldon Himmelfarb noted at the time, news presentation was very much governed by technology, design and layout. On the front pages, tabloid writers deployed banner headlines, designed to remain in the readers' minds in a subliminal fashion favoured by advertising agencies, plus 'straplines' in smaller type to direct the reader to the main text. The written text was used in a subordinate function in the space between the main headline and the bottom of the page. This development

---

54 *Financial Times*, 9 January 1979, p. 7.
55 *Financial Times*, 11 January 1979, p. 20.
56 *Financial Times*, 13 January 1979, p. 16.
57 Geoffrey Goodman CBE, journalist, historian and broadcaster, has written for a number of national newspapers, including the *Manchester Guardian*, *News Chronicle*, *Daily Herald*, *Sun* and *Daily Mirror*. He was a member of the Royal Commission on the Press (1977) and joint author (with David Basnett, General Secretary of the GMBU) of the resulting minority report (Cmnd 6810), July 1977. David Basnett and Geoffrey Goodman, *Royal Commission on the Press: Minority Report* (London: Labour Party, 1977). See also Sean Tunney, *Labour and the Press: From New Left to New Labour* (Brighton: Sussex Academic Press, 2007), pp. 39–42, 51–2, 53, 154 n. 37. Interview: Geoffrey Goodman, Congress House, London, 22 July 2008.
58 Geoffrey Goodman, 'The impact of the media on industrial relations', *Personnel Management*, vol. 11, no. 3, October 1979, pp. 44–7.

in technology, design and layout provided a distinctive style to the portrayal of the 'winter of discontent' by the popular press.[59]

As James Thomas has written, the industrial disruption during the 1978–79 winter provided 'the first major illustration in the popular press' of reporting strikes by 'low-paid oil tanker drivers, road haulage workers, lorry drivers and public service unions'.[60]

Various negative images were repeatedly presented of Labour Britain, principally the tyranny of union power – with headlines such as – 'UNDER SIEGE' from the 'tyranny of pickets';[61] 'RULE AND FEAR' and reeking of 'sheer gangsterism';[62] 'MILES OF MISERY' and 'CHAOS ON ALL SIDES'.[63] Such tyranny was said to be the result of government failure, and especially of the Prime Minister, who failed to confront 'the over-weening power of the trade union barons',[64] in particular after his return from the international summit in Guadeloupe. The disastrous press conference at Heathrow was captured with the memorable headline 'Crisis? What crisis?'[65]

By 9 January, even before Callaghan's return home, the *Sun*'s coverage of the Guadeloupe summit focused on providing images of Britain's missing Prime Minister, using familiar naval terms: 'Cap'n Jim and the sinking ship'. The newspaper told its readers that 'key members of the Cabinet' were bravely tackling Britain's worst 'industrial shambles for years. And where is the Prime Minister?'[66] According to the *Sun*, unfortunately 'Sunny Jim' was still 4,000 miles away – not in Guadeloupe but on 'a little winter break' in Barbados. As Bernard Donoughue readily acknowledged, Callaghan's cardinal error was to extend his stay abroad by agreeing to visit Tom Adams, Prime Minister of Barbados. Donoughue later observed:

> Tom McNally and Roger Stott have both returned from their constituencies in the North-West very chastened. They now realise that staying on in Barbados was a mistake, that the PM's conference at Heathrow was a mistake and that they completely misread the situation at home. They met a lot of hostility in the Manchester area, which has had a very tough time, and pictures of them bathing in the Caribbean sun were not much appreciated.[67]

Sun readers, though, may not have noticed the appalling racist language used in the remainder of the paper's editorial about the pending expansion

59 Bilton and Himmelfarb, 'Fleet Street', pp. 237–8; see also Vance Packard, *Hidden Persuaders* (Harmondsworth: Penguin, 1981).
60 Thomas, *Popular Newspapers*, p. 78.
61 *Daily Mail*, 8, 18 January 1979.
62 *Daily Express*, 15 January 1979, pp. 1–2.
63 *Sun*, 23 January 1979, p. 1.
64 *Sun*, 23 January 1979.
65 *Sun*, 11 January 1979.
66 *Sun,* 9 January 1979, pp. 2, 4.
67 Bernard Donoughue, *Downing Street Diary, Volume Two*, p. 423 (diary entry: 15 January 1979).

of industrial unrest: 'And the shock troops of NUPE under the *Fuhrer* Alan Fisher [emphasis added] are preparing a massive dirty job strike on January 22'. For good measure, the paper carried a political cartoon by Franklin depicting the Prime Minister on a deck chair on a Caribbean beach watching his ship, the *Crisis Britain*, sinking out at sea. The caption read: 'Jim handled the helm with a masterly grip, pity it wasn't attached to the ship'.[68]

In terms of handling the media, James Callaghan, on becoming Prime Minister in April 1976, was probably the most accomplished politician since the Second World War. His biographer, Ken Morgan, considers Callaghan, who made his first radio broadcast in London just before VJ Day 1945, was a natural for the new post-war television age. His unfussy style displayed at Westminster, as one of the 200 new Labour MPs, transferred comfortably for television and radio broadcasts. He was always in demand for Labour Party election broadcasts and had a good presence before the television cameras. In the 1950s Callaghan made regular media appearances, most successfully as a panellist on the weekly BBC current affairs programme *In The News*, and later when it transferred to the new ITV channel as *Free Speech*. Callaghan was also a practised journalist, contributing to a number of publications, including a weekly column, 'The intelligent woman's guide to world affairs', for the Labour-supporting *Women's Sunday Mirror*.[69]

According to Michael Cockerell, by the 1970s, Callaghan's acknowledged ability with the media had been built on 20 years of television appearances. Tom McNally, his chief political adviser 1974–79, stated: 'Jim was the supreme TV professional'. In 1962, the *Daily Telegraph* declared that 'he packed a better television punch than practically anyone on the Labour front bench'.[70] Callaghan's masterful appearance on the BBC programme *Nationwide* – when Thatcher's popularity was increasing among Labour voters – had helped the Prime Minister reach a new target audience. McNally told Cockerell: 'We were absolutely amazed by the post bag afterwards. We had tapped into the working-class female audience which was almost totally absent from Panorama.'[71] When Callaghan was Foreign Secretary, he shrewdly declined to be interviewed during the 1976 Labour Party leadership contest, unlike the other contestants. Instead, Callaghan skilfully managed the media to project his image as the august Foreign Secretary and international authority on the global stage above the electoral fray.

It was remarkable, therefore, that, during his final months as Prime Minister, he probably made his greatest error in deciding not to call the

68 *Sun*, 9 January 1979, p. 4.
69 Kenneth O. Morgan, *Callaghan: A Life* (Oxford: Oxford University Press, 1997), pp. 108–9.
70 Michael Cockerell, *Live From Number 10: The Inside Story of Prime Ministers and Television* (London: Faber & Faber, 1988), pp. 228–32.
71 *Ibid.*, p. 236.

general election that autumn. First, he allowed speculation to mount for several weeks that he would call a general election. Secondly, Callaghan famously mismanaged relations with the media before deciding to defer the general election without telling his colleagues and political advisers.[72] Finally, in his short television broadcast on 7 September 1978 to the nation, he left almost to the end his surprise announcement 'So I shall not be calling for a general election at this time'.[73] This allowed Margaret Thatcher to underline the nonsense of going on television to announce no election. According to Bernard Donoghue, Callaghan's decision to put off the election could be explained by his enjoyment of the 'mystery and the drama and especially misleading the press, whom he held in even greater contempt than did Harold Wilson'. Donoughue noted: 'I think he kept *both* options open [of holding or deferring the general election] until nearly the last moment ... and he did not tell anybody because he wanted to make fools of the hated press, which he did'.[74] Joe Haines, Harold Wilson's press secretary, proposed that a professional information officer, rather than a professional diplomat, should head the news department at the Foreign and Commonwealth Office. Haines nominated a Scot, Tom McCaffrey, Director of Information at the Home Office, who had previously worked with Jim Callaghan from 1967 to 1970, and had also been a former deputy press secretary at Number 10 Downing Street. McCaffrey was regarded as a 'safe pair of hands', unlikely to make mistakes. Callaghan appointed him on becoming Foreign Secretary and also secured Tom McNally, head of the Labour Party's international department, as his special adviser at the Foreign Office. Callaghan's team were therefore in place when he became Prime Minister on 5 April 1976 and served with him until Labour's defeat in the general election of May 1979.

During the 'winter of discontent' Callaghan participated in an international summit on the Caribbean island of Guadeloupe in the French West Indies in early January 1979 with President Jimmy Carter, President Giscard d'Estang and Chancellor Helmut Schmidt on the Strategic Arms Limitation Talks (SALT). As we have seen already, on 11 January 1979 the

---

72 His principal private secretary, Sir Ken Stowe, appears to have been the only person informed by the Prime Minister during the summer, though Michael Foot and Denis Healey had an indication ahead of the announcement to the Cabinet. His closest political advisers, Tom McNally and Sir Tom McCaffrey, had been kept in the dark, as well as Callaghan's parliamentary private secretary, Roger Stott. Callaghan's biographer later observed: 'Almost all Callaghan's likely allies reacted in a negative or hostile way'. Morgan, *Callaghan*, p. 644.

73 For the full text of the broadcast, see James Callaghan, *Time and Chance* (London: Politico's, 2006), pp. 516–17.

74 Bernard Donoughue, *Prime Minister: The Conduct of Policy Under Harold Wilson and James Callaghan* (London: Jonathan Cape: 1987), pp. 163–6; Bernard Donoughue, *The Heat of the Kitchen: An Autobiography* (London: Politicos, 2003). Interview: Lord Bernard Donoughue, House of Lords, 6 July 2010. For more discussion of Jim Callaghan's decision to defer the general election in the autumn 1978, see chapter 2.

Sun carried one of its most famous headlines, 'Crisis? What crisis?', after Callaghan mishandled an impromptu press conference at Heathrow airport on his return and tried to convey that he had been completely in touch with domestic events while abroad.[75]

On the return flight, about two hours from Heathrow, Callaghan had decided to meet the reporters and television crews at the airport for a press conference, rather than return direct to Downing Street, as it would give him the opportunity to display his leadership qualities on returning to Britain. Michael Cockerell noted that 'the Prime Minister planned to put Britain's problems in a world context and take a swipe at the *Daily Mail* whose photographer with a telescopic-lens had caught him swimming'.[76]

In this famous encounter he appeared complacent about the growing industrial anarchy at home while he had been abroad. At the badly organised conference, Callaghan was asked by an *Evening Standard* journalist: 'What is your approach, in view of the mounting chaos in the country at the moment?' The Prime Minister retorted:

> Well, that's a judgement that you are making, and I promise you that if you look at it from the outside, and perhaps you are taking rather a parochial view at the moment, I don't think that other people in the world would share the view that there is mounting chaos.[77]

This was transformed overnight to become one of the *Sun*'s most famous banner headlines emblazoned on its front page, 'Crisis? What crisis?' Walter Terry, the *Sun*'s political editor, observed that 'Sunny Jim' had 'ticked off reporters', commenting 'please don't run down your country by talking about chaos'.[78]

The media – kept at arm's length – helped to destabilise the Prime Minister, particularly the *Daily Mail*'s with its 'swimming' photograph.[79] From Downing Street, Donoughue, who had wanted the Prime Minister to return to Britain early, noted: 'I think they are mistaken to sit out there in the sun, with photographs of them lazing on beaches surrounded by topless women, while this country is increasingly paralysed. There will be a backlash and it won't help the PM's authority [with the unions].'[80]

Lord McNally later recalled:

75 Sunday 11 January 1979, TNA PREM 16/2050.
76 Cockerell, *Live From Number 10*, p. 243. The Heathrow press conference on 10 January 1979 can be seen at http://news.bbc.co.uk/onthisday/hi/dates/stories/january/10/newsid_2518000/2518957.stm.
77 'Interview with the Prime Minister, the Rt. Hon. James Callaghan, M.P., at Heathrow Airport after talks in Guadeloupe and Barbados', 10 January 1979, TNA PREM 16/2050.
78 *Ibid.*
79 Interview: Lord Tom McNally, House of Lords, 23 June 2007.
80 Donoughue, *Downing Street Diary, Volume Two*, p. 418 (diary entry: 9 January 1979).

a press conference at the airport would have a big impact (like Callaghan's highly successful 1974 airport press conference during the Heath government's three-day week) ... but he had been niggled. During the trip the British media were keen to get a photograph of him in his swimming trunks and indeed the *Daily Mail* had managed to get a photograph, not too glamorous of either of us, in the surf in Barbados. I remember him saying 'How did they get this?' The security guy said we estimate that the boat was at least 4,000 yards out when they took that photograph. But this niggled him. I remember him saying Helmut Schmidt went off for a holiday in Mexico after the Guadeloupe [summit] and the German press don't go berserk about it. Carter goes off to Camp David and it's only our Press that get us.... In the end the niggle worked. When he got back the plan was he would give this short sharp message about the state of the nation. But with a confident message that he had been doing serious work abroad, and he had been kept abreast of the issues and he was going back to Downing Street, he was in charge, pull yourselves together and let's get on with the job. Instead of which, this quote got him ... he made this comment ... sometimes things don't look so bad abroad as they do here ... all that I can tell you ... ITN have an archive footage of that press conference and I am standing at Jim's shoulder and if you carefully look at my face as he is speaking you can tell that I think he's losing it ... I felt this is going to sound very complacent. The *Sun* caught the mood, if not the words, with 'Crisis? What crisis?' and that added to the tail spin at the time.[81]

'Crisis? What crisis?' has now become enshrined in political folklore and has been revamped in many contexts. It will always be associated with Jim Callaghan, in the same way the famous 'pound in your pocket' phrase in the 1967 post-devaluation Labour television broadcast is indelibly associated with his predecessor, Harold Wilson.

During the 'winter of discontent', 'Crisis? What crisis?' was duplicated in different formats by the tabloid press. 'COME OFF IT, JIM' proclaimed the *Daily Express* on its front page, with various straplines, including, 'The man in the crumpled suit who turned his back on crisis-ridden Britain', illustrated by a rear photograph of the Prime Minister entering Number 10 Downing Street captioned 'Inaction man: Premier, suit crumpled, comes home to No. 10 yesterday'.[82] The *Daily Mail* on its front page named Callaghan as 'THE OSTRICH PRIME MINISTER: He's back from the beaches but his head is still in the sand.' Above a photograph of Callaghan was the caption: 'The only man in Britain who does not see a crisis'. The paper's front page carried a two-pronged message for its readers – that the Prime Minister had been away on the hot Caribbean beaches, alongside his myopic view of the industrial problems awaiting him at home, while the British nation suffered in the arctic winter. These were spelled out as bullet

---

81 Interview: McNally.
82 *Daily Express*, 11 January 1979, p. 1.

points: the lorry drivers' strike; ICI losing millions of pounds; a national food shortage in the country; farmyard animals starving; a national rail strike next week; the stock market going down.[83]

After Callaghan's return, the tabloid press highlighted his 'lack of leadership or action' in the banner headlines: 'IS ANYONE RUNNING BRITAIN?[84] and 'WHAT THE BLOODY HELL IS GOING ON, JIM?'[85]

After Labour's defeat in the 1979 general election, the resentment against what was seen as a press campaign against the unions broke out in a bitter dispute in the press and broadcasting debate at the annual TUC conference in Blackpool, September 1979. The NUPE General Secretary, Alan Fisher, opened the debate on the 'media coverage of industrial disputes, January and February 1979':

> this is not an attack on journalists. Some of my best friends are journalists … I wonder who these people are who write things about us. Where are they? Who was it called me Hitler in January? Who was it called me Mussolini? Genghis Khan? I am a murderer although nobody died through what happened … what worries me about what happened last winter is partly what happened to my members, people who had never been on strike before in their lives and went on strike because they believed their bloody pay was too low, disgracefully low. Who were the people who crept and crawled around them for comment outside the hospital gates, on refuse tips and in the streets? They were journalists, some of them.[86]

Reflecting on his career in journalism, Geoffrey Goodman noted the tensions captured in the press during the winter of 1978–79:

> those of us covering those final days of the Callaghan government, through the appalling confusion in that 'winter of discontent', could visibly see the writing on the wall for the Labour government, may be even for the trade unions. So it was to be.[87]

---

83 *Daily Mail*, 11 January 1979, p. 1.
84 *Sun*, 7,8, February 1979, p. 1.
85 *Daily Mail*, 1 February 1979, p. 1.
86 *Report of the 111th Annual Trades Union Congress*, Blackpool, September 1979, pp. 585–6.
87 Geoffrey Goodman, 'The role of the industrial correspondents', in John McIlroy, Nina Fishman and Alan Campbell (eds), *British Trade Unions and Industrial Politics. Volume One: The Postwar Compromise, 1945–64* (Aldershot: Ashgate, 1999), pp. 23–36.

Chapter Seven

The Conservative Party and the 'winter of discontent'

At the height of the industrial unrest of the 'winter of discontent', Margaret Thatcher's party political broadcast (PPB) on 17 January, which had been filmed the previous day in the party leader's room at the House of Commons, was a turning point in Conservative political fortunes.[1] As she observed in her memoirs, it was no conventional television broadcast. The Conservatives had suddenly soared to a 20-point lead over Labour in the opinion polls and this had dramatically altered the political weather in Britain. In the broadcast Thatcher offered in the national interest to support the Callaghan government in dealing with the escalating industrial troubles.[2]

The leader of the opposition addressed the nation by opening with a disclaimer:

> Yes, technically this is a Party Political Broadcast on behalf of the Conservative Party. But tonight I don't propose to use the time to make party political points. I don't think you would want me to so. The crisis that our country faces is too serious for that. And it is our country, the whole nation that faces this crisis, not just one party or even one government. This is no time to put party before country. I start from there.[3]

---

1 In 1978 the influential public relations consultant Gordon Reece, Margaret Thatcher's Director of Publicity, had hired the then little-known advertising agency Saatchi and Saatchi to work for the Conservative Party. The original PPB had been filmed on the unsheltered roof of a Tottenham Court Road building in London. Tim Bell, Saatchi and Saatchi's managing director, scrapped the first version for the totally reworked PPB televised on 17 January. Mark Hollingsworth, *Tim Bell: The Ultimate Spin Doctor* (London: Hodder & Stoughton, 1997), p. 68; Michael Cockerell, 'Reece, Sir (James) Gordon (1929–2001)', in Lawrence Goldman (ed.), *Oxford Dictionary of National Biography 2001–2004* (Oxford: Oxford University Press, 2009), pp. 894–96. Interview: Michael Cockerell, Notting Hill, London, 4 April 2011.

2 Margaret Thatcher, *The Path to Power* (New York: HarperCollins, 1995), pp. 429–30; John Campbell, *Margaret Thatcher, Volume One: The Grocer's Daughter* (London: Vintage, 2007), pp. 422–3.

3 For a full transcript and video of Margaret Thatcher's PPB, 17 January 1979, see 'Conservative Party political broadcast (winter of discontent)', Margaret Thatcher papers, Churchill Archives Centre, CCOPR 71/79.

Speaking straight to camera in her nine-minute television broadcast, Thatcher brought to her audience's mind the day-to-day scenes of industrial unrest in Britain. Particular mention was made of the robust picketing that threatened to paralyse the country and its impact on the old, young children, the vulnerable and sick. To restrict the power of the unions, she said: 'we should attempt inside Parliament to reach agreement on three areas where ... there is agreement outside Parliament: amending the law on picketing, secret ballots to make unions more democratic and no-strike agreements in essential public services in return for guarantees on pay'. Thatcher concluded:

> these are three concrete proposals for a common effort to meet a common danger. I hope that Mr. Callaghan and his colleagues will give them a fair wind. I don't claim they would provide an immediate answer to all our problems. But they would help to restore a measure of peace and sanity to a worsening situation.... We have to learn again to be one nation, or one day we shall be no nation.[4]

Surprisingly, despite the relatively few lines Thatcher gave the matter in her PPB, she had debated whether to use the opportunity for an assault on the failings of the government or whether to extend her offer of support made in Parliament the day before.[5] Her first inclination had been to lay into Callaghan and his ministers over their collective failure to handle the industrial difficulties, until persuaded by her chief media advisers to take a new line, in the interests of national unity in troubled times. 'Spin doctor' Tim Bell noted Thatcher's reaction: 'You're asking me to let Callaghan off the hook'. She was persuaded by the chairman of the Conservative Party, Lord Thorneycroft, and her adviser, Chris Patten, to adopt a change of strategy that would 'put country before party'.[6]

By common consent, Thatcher's PPB, with its seemingly non-partisan style, was a media triumph. The next day the *Daily Mail* published the whole broadcast under the headline: 'WHY WE MUST BE ONE NATION, OR NO NATION!' Similar coverage in the *Daily Telegraph* also quoted Thatcher direct: 'There will be no solution to our difficulties which does not include some restriction on the power of unions.... And if that case is overwhelming, then in the national interest surely Government and Opposition should make common cause on this one issue.'[7]

From the leader's office, Matthew Parris (her political secretary) told Thatcher: 'this morning alone you received some 700 letters [about the industrial unrest]. About a third actually mentioning your television talk ...

---

4 *Ibid.*
5 For Thatcher's offer of support for trade union reform in the parliamentary debate the day before, see below.
6 Hollingsworth, *Tim Bell*, pp. 68–9.
7 *Daily Mail*, 18 January 1979, p. 1; *Daily Telegraph*, 18 January 1979, p. 1.

the "non-party" tone of what you said has impressed many who mention it'.[8] Tim Bell observed: 'my feeling is that this broadcast won her the election'.[9] One of Thatcher's main speechwriters, Ronald Millar, the playwright and actor, also summed up her performance: 'For the first time she sounded like a national leader ... it did more to swing the country behind her than any subsequent speech'.[10]

The PPB had put the Labour government on the back foot as Thatcher took the initiative. Callaghan's predictable refusal to accept Thatcher's proposals left her free to attack the abuses of trade union power and demand legislation to curb its excesses. At the same time, the picture of 'crisis Britain' was richly exploited by Conservative politicians and their press supporters in the 1979 election and at subsequent general elections up to 1992.[11]

During the last months of the Callaghan administration the collapse of the government's pay policy during the industrial unrest of 1978–79 revived the fortunes of the Conservative Party. Margaret Thatcher was galvanised from a cautious and hesitant leader of HM opposition – lagging behind Prime Minister Callaghan in the personal approval ratings – into a likely Prime Minister in waiting. This chapter examines the development and character of Conservative trade union policy during Thatcher's leadership of the opposition from 1975 to 1979 and gives particular attention to the impact of the 'winter of discontent' as the major turning point in Conservative electoral fortunes that eventually culminated in the May 1979 election victory.[12]

---

8 Matthew Parris to Thatcher, 22 January 1979, Thatcher papers, Churchill Archives, THCR 261/150.

9 Tim Bell, 'The Conservatives' advertising campaign', in Robert M. Worcester and Martin Harrop (eds), *Political Communications: The General Election Campaign of 1979* (London: George Allen & Unwin, 1982), p. 22.

10 Ronald Millar, *A View From The Wings: West End, West Coast, Westminster* (London: Weidenfeld & Nicolson, 1993), p. 247.

11 For discussion of the role of the media, see chapter 6.

12 There is an already extensive literature on Margaret Thatcher and the history of the Conservative Party, although this note does not include works forthcoming at the time of her death in April 1913. The major secondary sources for the party's period in opposition 1974–79 include: Dennis Kavanagh, 'The making of Thatcherism 1974–1979', in Stuart Ball and Anthony Seldon (eds), *Recovering Power: The Conservatives in Opposition Since 1867* (Basingstoke: Palgrave Macmillan, 2005), pp. 219–41; Robert Saunders, 'Crisis? What crisis? Thatcherism and the seventies', in Ben Jackson and Robert Saunders (eds), *Making Thatcher's Britain* (Cambridge: Cambridge University Press, 2012), pp. 25–42; Peter Dorey, *The Conservative Party and the Trade Unions* (London: Routledge, 1995), pp. 122–55; Andrew Taylor, 'The Conservative Party and the trade unions', in John McIlroy, Nina Fishman and Alan Campbell (eds), *The High Tide of British Trade Unionism: Trade Unions and Industrial Politics, 1964–79* (Monmouth: Merlin Press, second edition 2007), pp. 151–86; Andrew Taylor, 'The party and the trade unions', in Anthony Seldon and Stuart Ball (eds), *Conservative Century: The Conservative Party Since 1900* (Oxford: Oxford University Press, 1994), pp. 499–546; Andrew Taylor, 'The "Stepping Stones" programme: Conservative Party thinking on trade unions, 1975–9', *Historical Studies in Industrial Relations*, vol. 2, spring 2001, pp. 109–33; Brendan Evans, *Thatcherism and*

The 'winter of discontent' represented a watershed in late twentieth-century British politics. Margaret Thatcher in her memoirs devoted more than 10 pages to reviewing the events of the winter of 1978–79, focusing on the Conservative Party's attitude to the trade unions, including the development of the radical 'Stepping Stones' programme by John Hoskyns and Norman Strauss, about which members of her shadow Cabinet expressed differing degrees of doubt.[13]

Most particularly, Thatcher recalled that the industrial troubles which beset Callaghan's government contributed to the electoral gains of the Conservatives in 1979. Yet it can be questioned whether the Conservative Party leader was as fully aware at the time of the benefits of exploiting the political advantage afforded by the 'winter of discontent' as she retrospectively suggested in her memoirs: 'I have also described how I decided to seize the initiative in January 1979. Between the summer of 1978 and the dissolution of Parliament in March 1979 outside events, above all that winter's strikes, allowed me to shift our policies in the direction I wanted.'[14]

After the policy failures and u-turns of the Heath government, and two general election defeats, in February 1974 and October 1974, the Parliamentary Conservative Party had sought a new start in electing Margaret Thatcher as leader.[15] As Hugo Young observed, not only was she different to her predecessors as the first woman to hold the post, but also she was an outsider – a combination that largely shaped how she led her party. Moreover, Thatcher did not win the leadership as a right-winger, but rather as the candidate who challenged the former Prime Minister, when insiders within the party hesitated. Heath's defeat was attributable to personal as well as ideological factors.[16] He had lost three general elections, in 1966 and 1974, and was personally unpopular with many Conservative MPs. Heath had refused at first to resign, as he did not wish to be succeeded by a right-wing Conservative.

Thatcher became Tory leader when Britain seemed in apparent irreversible economic decline at the time of the ending of the post-war Bretton Woods agreement on stabilising world currencies and the global shock of a

---

British Politics 1975–1999 (Stroud: Sutton Publishing, 1999); Peter Dorey, 'Between principle, pragmatism and practicability: the development of Conservative Party policy towards the trade unions in opposition, 1974–1979', in David Broughton, David M. Farrell, David Denver and Colin Rallings (eds), *British Elections and Parties Yearbook 1994* (London: Frank Cass, 1995), p. 29. For Margaret Thatcher, see: Hugo Young, *One of Us: A Biography of Margaret Thatcher* (London: Pan Books, 1990); Campbell, *Margaret Thatcher, Volume One*; Thatcher, *The Path to Power*.

13 For the 'Stepping Stones' programme, see this chapter, pp. 138–40.
14 Thatcher, *The Path to Power*, p. 435. See also Evans, *Thatcherism and British Politics*, pp. 47–8.
15 Conservative Party leadership election results, 1975: first ballot, Margaret Thatcher (130 votes), Edward Heath (119), Hugh Fraser (16); second ballot, Margaret Thatcher (146), William Whitelaw (79), Geoffrey Howe (19), James Prior (19), John Peyton (11).
16 Young, *One of Us*, pp. 95–102.

quadrupling of oil prices by the Organization of the Petroleum Exporting Countries (OPEC). The Conservative Party seemed ready to return to a form of traditional Conservatism. This could be witnessed particularly in its attitudes and thinking on industrial relations and trade union reform, economic management and the role of the state.

The bitter experience of the Heath government's 1971 Industrial Relations Act, the miners' strikes 1972 and 1974, five states of emergency in four years and the 'three-day week' left enduring memories of trade union power in Conservative minds and a difficult legacy, particularly with regard to the unions, for the new party leader. While in opposition from 1974 to 1979, the development of party policy on union reform became an important issue, mainly characterised by considerable caution and circumspection.[17] However, the belief that Thatcherism – as a political strategy to roll back the post-war British state, end socialism and tame trade union power – was established during Thatcher's early years of leadership in opposition, or that a blueprint for government was produced between 1975 and 1979, has been successfully challenged.[18] In particular, the question of industrial relations and pay policy revealed clear divisions within the Tory leadership and the Parliamentary Conservative Party during the years of opposition.

By contrast, Labour's claim to be able to work with the unions – unlike the Tories – was enshrined in the social contract with the Trades Union Congress (TUC), which was successful at first, extending union rights and social benefits. On returning to office in 1974 Labour swiftly settled the miners' strike that had contributed to the downfall of the Heath government. As part of the social contract, at the Department of Employment, Michael Foot and Albert Booth, drawing on expert advice from Lord Wedderburn and others, piloted six major pieces of legislation through Parliament in two sessions at Westminster: the Health and Safety at Work Act and the Trade Union and Labour Relations Act (TULRA) in 1974, the establishment of the Advisory, Conciliation and Arbitration Service (ACAS), the Employment Protection Act (EPA) and the Sex Discrimination Act in 1975, and the TULRA Amendment Act in 1976. Foot's biographer, Kenneth O. Morgan, observed: 'Foot's holy grail was always to succeed in recasting the framework of industrial law'.[19] However, to the abhorrence of the Conservative Party, union immunities had been considerably increased, making legal reform seem essential. Yet to accomplish this with trade union cooperation rather than confrontation and without loss of electoral support would require caution and moderation.[20]

---

17 Dorey, 'Between principle, pragmatism and practicability'.
18 Kavanagh, 'The making of Thatcherism'. For 'little evidence of a "grand strategy" concerning union reform', see Taylor, 'The party and the trade unions', p. 532.
19 Kenneth O. Morgan, *Michael Foot: A Life* (London: HarperCollins, 2007), pp. 292–8.
20 Taylor, 'The party and the trade unions', pp. 528–9.

Peter Dorey has argued that the Parliamentary Conservative Party during those years of opposition could be divided into three groups with different perspectives on trade union policy. First, one section of the party believed that industrial harmony could be secured by a primarily neo-corporatist approach to industrial relations – in the tradition of what was generally known as 'one-nation Toryism' – by involving trade union leaders in tripartite discussions and decision-making. Any attempt to legislate in industrial relations risked provoking the kind of reaction associated with the Wilson government's *In Place of Strife* in 1969 and the Heath government's 1971 Industrial Relations Act. However, in opposition, the neo-corporatist strategy was fading within Conservative circles after the travails of the Heath government's industrial relations policy.

A second group could be identified among the Conservative ranks, those who wished to secure trade union reform by legislation but, at the same time, taking on board the lessons learned from the introduction of the 1971 Industrial Relations Act.

The third point of view was an uncompromising approach, held by a minority within the Parliamentary Conservative Party, based on the hard-nosed belief that the unions should be brought within the rule of law. In other words, the reinstatement of the 1971 Tory Industrial Relations Act should not have been abandoned after the Act's repeal by the Labour government. Indeed, its abandonment had, for many Conservatives, indicated that the party leadership was badly out of touch with attitudes towards trade union reform among ordinary constituency members.[21]

In her 1975 shadow Cabinet, where Thatcher was outnumbered by Heathite ministers, Thatcher retained Jim Prior as shadow Secretary of State for Employment and he then served as Secretary of State for Employment from May 1979 to 14 September 1981 in her first Cabinet. He thus remained the main Conservative spokesman on the trade unions, industrial relations and employment policies for eight years.[22]

Nicholas Ridley later stated 'why she kept him on has always eluded me: he was a landowner and farmer, a patrician Tory, very much on the left side of the Party and not at all in sympathy with her views'.[23] In her memoirs, Thatcher recognised that Jim Prior was a figure of moderation in handling the unions and described him as 'the right man in the right position'.[24]

---

21 Dorey, *The Conservative Party and the Trade Unions*, pp. 124–5.
22 Jim Prior had entered Parliament in 1959, the same year as Margaret Thatcher, and had served in Edward Heath's government, 1970–74. After Thatcher had roundly defeated Heath for the party leadership on the first ballot, Prior was one of five candidates who stood against her on the second ballot. Jim Prior, *A Balance of Power* (London: Hamish Hamilton, 1986). Interview: Lord Jim Prior, Beccles, 11 November 2011.
23 Nicholas Ridley, *'My Style of Government': The Thatcher Years* (London: Hutchinson, 1991).
24 Thatcher, *The Path to Power*, pp. 288–9.

Sir Geoffrey Howe, the architect of Heath's 1971 Industrial Relations Act, also recalled the role of Jim Prior, who was a member of the Conservative Party's Economic Reconstruction Group (with Keith Joseph, David Howell and Ian Gilmour), in assembling the most significant policy document during this period of opposition, *The Right Approach to the Economy*.[25]

Prior believed firmly that the Conservatives should broadly accept the existing trade union law and should adopt a conciliatory rather than confrontational approach to the trade union leaders, bearing in mind Labour's main claim to be the natural party to work harmoniously with the trade union movement.[26]

Sir Keith Joseph was a central figure in the Conservative Party in what was termed 'the New Right' and most influential as the 'father of Thatcherism'. Inspired by the ideas of F. A. Hayek and Milton Friedman, Joseph's mission was to change the economic and social direction of the country, from the post-war settlement based on Keynesianism and political consensus to a free-market economy. Stephen Wade, later a Conservative councillor, remembered his impression as a young man of Margaret Thatcher's impact on the Tory leadership during the opposition years of 1975–79 and beyond: 'A distinctive Thatcherite ideology that started to come through.… As a student, it came across to me as a combative sort of ideology that said *we aren't defeated, we don't have to surrender, it doesn't have to be like this, it can be different*'. He added that, at university, the broad left and associated Trotskyist movements gave him:

> the misleading feeling that some form of Communism, ultra Socialism, was inevitable … that industrial strife, the decline of Britain as a world power, the decline of standards of living and the inexorable slide towards a Soviet style economy, was inevitable and *would happen*. That feeling pervaded a large sector of the Tory party … you could never denationalise anything because it would be re-nationalised by the Labour Government … you had to somehow get some sort of social democratic accommodation with them … Margaret Thatcher called them *the wets*. They had accepted the post-war consensus that Britain was in inexorable decline post-Empire, and that decline didn't only mean giving up the colonies, it meant surrendering to the historic inevitability of Marxism.… Thatcher gave us an alternative. She gave us Friedman, Hayek and Burke, an alternative philosophy, an alternative, more pugnacious style of Conservatism.[27]

With Margaret Thatcher, Keith Joseph had founded in 1975 the Centre for Policy Studies (CPS), the free-enterprise think-tank that challenged

---

25 *Ibid.*, pp. 100–1.
26 Interview: Prior.
27 Interview: Stephen Wade, Dry Drayton, 15 January 2012. Barrister Stephen Wade was a Conservative councillor on Brighton and Hove City Council, 1996–2003, and chairman of Hove and Portslade Conservative Association, 1998–2001.

the Conservative Research Department and Conservative Central Office.[28] Alongside other right-wing think-tanks, including the established Institute of Economic Affairs and the Adam Smith Institute, the CPS provided key ideas on monetarism, free markets and trade union reform, as an alternative economic strategy to the post-war political consensus.[29]

Thatcher had earlier been a supporter of Joseph, whose major speeches marked him out as the main candidate on the right of the Conservative Party. In April 1974, in becoming a convert to monetarism, he famously declared that he had only just become a Conservative. Between 1974 and 1977, in speeches and pamphlets that took up the ideas of Alfred Sherman, the Director of the CPS, Joseph challenged both the political consensus of the mid-1970s and Keynesian economic policy. He was convinced that Keynes had been misrepresented. Instead, Joseph advocated the social market, monetarism, sound finance and the merits of entrepreneurial capitalism.[30]

Thatcher's path to the leadership became clear when Joseph ruled himself out of the contest. He had previously told Patrick Cosgrave, writer, journalist and one-time adviser to Margaret Thatcher, who had been contacted about a plot to make William Whitelaw Conservative leader, that he was definitely a candidate.[31] But in a controversial speech in Birmingham in November 1974, his references to social deprivation and poor large families – 'the balance of the human stock is threatened' – raised associations with eugenics that caused a press furore in the same city in which Enoch Powell had spoken about immigration and 'rivers of blood' only a few years earlier. Instead, Joseph became Thatcher's intellectual guru, and filled a gap on the right of the party following the departure of Powell. Thatcher summarised Joseph's contribution to this early period of her party leadership: 'It was Keith who really began to turn the intellectual tide back against socialism. He got our fundamental intellectual message across, to students, professors, journalists, the "intelligentsia" generally'.[32]

Between 1974 and 1977, Joseph spoke at over 150 universities and polytechnics – though sometimes denied a platform, as at the London School of Economics (LSE) or given a hostile and noisy reception. Many of these speeches were subsequently published: *Monetarism Is Not Enough*; *Conditions for Full Employment*; *Why Britain Needs a Social Market Economy*; and a collection of seven speeches in *Reversing the Trend: A Critical Re-appraisal of*

28 Simon Burgess and Geoffrey Alderman, 'Centre for Political Studies: the influence of Sir Alfred Sherman', *Contemporary Record*, vol. 4, no. 2, November 1990, pp. 14–15.

29 Andrew Denham and Mark Garnett, *British Think-Tanks and the Climate of Opinion* (London: University College London Press, 1998).

30 Brian Harrison, 'Joseph, Keith Sinjohn. Baron Joseph (1918–1994)', in H. C. G. Matthew and Brian Harrison (eds), *Oxford Dictionary of National Biography* (Oxford: Oxford University Press, 2004), pp. 781–728.

31 Obituaries for Patrick Cosgrove, *Daily Telegraph*, 17 September 2001; *Guardian*, 17 September 2001.

32 Morrison Halcrow, *Keith Joseph, A Single Mind* (London: Macmillan, 1989), p. 97.

Conservative Economic and Social Policies (1975). In 1979, he co-authored with Jonathan Sumption Equality, arguing for 'more millionaires and more bankrupts'.

At the peak of the 'winter of discontent', on 5 February 1979, Joseph gave a talk on trade unions to the Conservative Bow Group in the House of Commons, which was published by the CPS.[33] His aim was to stimulate public debate about trade union power by raising five key issues:

> 1. Shall we ever cure inflation? 2. Labour's monetarism is the worst of all worlds. 3. Why won't unions bargain responsibly? 4. If unions won't bargain responsibly, why can't we have a strict incomes policy instead? 5. Why must Britain be the odd man out? ... If the debate is to be productive, it must be national and honest, setting the union problem in the context of our economic decline, rather than at the centre of today's crisis. For the problem of the abuse of union power will remain long after today's crisis is over.[34]

With inflation around 8 per cent, Joseph argued: 'Unfortunately the inevitable response of trade unions to an inflation which they did not directly create, makes the cure of inflation more difficult'.[35] He also con-demned Labour's economic strategy under Callaghan and Healey as 'crude monetarism' or as denouncing 'monetarism while practising it'. Similarly, if the powerful unions would not practise wage restraint, tightening monetary control and 'claw-backs' through extra taxation would result in higher taxes, fewer jobs and more bankruptcies. Labour's trade union legislation had provided the unions with 'a militant's charter, as Jim Prior has called it, bred militants and driven moderates underground'. Not surprisingly, Joseph observed that Britain's industrial disputes – including 'picketing of non-involved companies; secondary boycotts' – were 'unique to Britain'. Joseph concluded that Britain stood alone among Western industrial nations – 'there is nothing like it in other countries'.[36]

In her comments on the 'winter of discontent' in her memoirs, Thatcher reviewed the Conservative Party's proposed 'Stepping Stones' programme, the possible vehicle for change which had been assembled by John Hoskyns, a former soldier and computer expert, and his associate, Norman Strauss. Interestingly, the Conservative leader revealed in her memoirs that the first time she had met them to hear their proposals (over Sunday lunch) she was not very impressed.[37] Hoskyns and Strauss urged that the Conservatives would not succeed in any plan for national recovery unless all the party's policies were encapsulated in a single political strategy, worked out in

---

33 Sir Keith Joseph, Solving the Union Problem Is the Key to Britain's Recovery (London: Centre for Policy Studies, 1979).
34 Ibid., p. 2.
35 Ibid.
36 Ibid., p. 3.
37 Thatcher, The Path to Power, p. 420.

advance. In particular, trade union reform could not be avoided. It was central to any Conservative return to power. As head of the party's Policy Unit after 1979, Hoskyns observed: 'I knew that unless the Conservative Government successfully came to grips with a small number of extremely difficult problems that had defeated all its predecessors since the war – monetary policy, union power, public sector pay, public expenditure and borrowing, the nationalised industries – it would fail, as they had failed'.[38]

Yet in late 1977 'Stepping Stones' was viewed as radical thinking from the right of the party – not in tune with the mainstream approach to the trade union question, which was one of caution and avoidance of confrontation. However, Thatcher later claimed that she 'was warming to this analysis' and said as much on meeting Hoskyns and Strauss at the House of Commons at the end of November 1977. As a result, she established a 'Stepping Stones Steering Group' and arranged for small numbers of shadow ministers and others to progress the new strategy in speeches and publications. At the same time, a 'Policy Search' group of senior shadow ministers was set up to develop new policy initiatives in association with Hoskyns and Strauss.[39]

The fifty-first meeting of the Leader's Steering Committee on 30 January 1978 considered two papers, 'Stepping Stones' and 'Implementing Our Strategy'. Thatcher later recalled: 'we argued ourselves to a standstill. Colleagues vied with each other in praising the "Stepping Stones" paper, but then warning against doing anything to follow it up – a well-known technique of evasion.'[40]

Those critical of the 'Stepping Stones' approach included John Davies, who argued that the economic prospects were improving and that the party should be very careful in trying to separate trade union members from their leaders. He noted that the 'Stepping Stones' document did not seek to involve the unions in the economic management of the country, through bodies such as the National Economic Development Council. He was supported by Lord Thorneycroft, who pointed out that the 'Stepping Stones' approach was hostile to trade unionism. On the other hand, Sir Geoffrey Howe remained pessimistic about Britain's economic future and thought union leaders should be challenged about closed-shop arrangements. Thatcher, in turn, questioned Davies's economic analysis. The Conservatives should be able to appeal to union members over the heads of their leaders.[41] The detailed work carried out on 'Stepping Stones' was kept secret. This right-wing political strategy for the Conservative Party

---

38 John Hoskyns, *Just In Time: Inside the Thatcher Revolution* (London: Aurum Press, 2000), p. xii.
39 Thatcher, *The Path to Power*, pp. 422–3.
40 *Ibid.*, p. 421.
41 Minutes of Leader's Steering Committee, 51st Meeting, 30 January 1978, Margaret Thatcher Foundation.

was never published in the 1970s, though Thatcher appointed Hoskyns as the head of the Policy Unit when the Tories regained power in 1979.

To return to office required a careful and cautious approach that included winning trade unionists' votes. In 1974 around 24 per cent of trade unionists voted Conservative, a figure which increased to 33 per cent at the 1979 general election. Thatcher's speeches at the annual party conference from 1975 to 1978 demonstrate her attention to this important constituency of voters. After becoming Conservative Party leader, she declared at the 1975 conference in Blackpool:

> When the next Conservative Government comes to power many Trade Unionists will have put it there ... I want to say to them and to every one of our supporters in industry. Go out and join in the work of your Union. Go to its meetings – and stay to the end. Learn the Union rules as well as the Far Left know them.[42]

At the Brighton conference in 1976 her priority was to create the appropriate environment for successful wage negotiations. 'We want to restore the right of unions and management to make the best bargain they can in circumstances they both know. So do most union leaders.' In particular, she emphasised that union leaders and shop stewards as well as ordinary members, alongside those who did not belong to any union at all – 'all of them should welcome the return of a Conservative government'.[43] In Blackpool at the 1977 party conference, fully aware of the Labour–union alliance, Thatcher tackled head on the popular perception that the Tory party was not the natural home for ordinary working people as union membership soared to record numbers by the late 1970s, reaching over 13 million by 1979:

> The key question I am asked over and over again is 'will the trade unions allow a Conservative Government to govern?' ... [the Labour government] keep repeating: 'The Tories won't be able to work with the unions'... I would like to make two final pints about the Unions. One: a strong and responsible trade union movement is essential.... Two: the belief that those [union] rights take precedence over all other rights, and even the law itself, could be fatal to this country.[44]

In 1978 the annual party conference was held at Brighton again, in somewhat unusual circumstances after Callaghan had unexpectedly deferred the next general election. Thatcher made a direct appeal to trade unionists in what had been anticipated to be an election year:

> For years the British disease has been the 'us' and 'them' philosophy.... Now, you the trade union leaders have great power.... You want higher wages, better pensions, shorter hours, more government spending, more investment. There

---

42 See www.margaretthatcher.org/document/102777.
43 See www.margaretthatcher.org/document/103105.
44 See www.margaretthatcher.org/document/103443.

is no more ... there won't be unless we all produce it ... you are often your own worst enemies ... restrictive practices rob you of your productivity....

Of course, we in Britain see the German success and want it here ... [but] in Germany [there] is strict control of the money supply, no rigid incomes policy, less state control ... lower personal tax and unions which are on the side of the future, not refighting the battles of the past.... If you demand too much you will bargain your firm into bankruptcy and your members on to the dole.... That is our message to the unions. You can hear the same message in country after country ... distant echoes even from Labour Ministers.[45]

At the 1978 conference, Thatcher also reminded her audience that avuncular Jim Callaghan in Harold Wilson's Cabinet had undermined Barbara Castle's trade union reform proposals, *In Place of Strife*, 'tooth and nail' in 1969. 'The unions did not like it. Mr Callaghan saw it straight into the waste paper basket. The road to Blackpool [defeat of Labour's 5 per cent pay policy party conference] was opened in 1969 Mr Callaghan.'[46]

Like most of the Conservative Party, Sir Geoffrey Howe was surprised when Callaghan passed up the opportunity to call a general election in autumn 1978. The shadow Chancellor of the Exchequer recalled that the subsequent months, dominated by the 'winter of discontent', were a turning point in Conservative Party fortunes.[47] As he put it:

The 'national party of government' started six months of transformation into the party that gave us the Winter of Discontent. This last catastrophic phase of Labour rule was to prove decisive in paving the way for Conservative government under Margaret Thatcher's leadership.[48]

Norman Tebbitt took some pleasure in the fact that the Callaghan government received its retribution and that the unions were attacked on all sides – by the government, the opposition and the general public. In particular, the industrial troubles of the winter of 1978–79 unified the Conservatives. The 5 per cent pay norm was undeliverable by the unions and unenforceable by the government. Tebbitt played an important role in the last weeks of 1978 as one of a number of Conservative backbenchers who harried the Callaghan government over its industrial relations policy. In his view the Labour Party, from January to March 1979, reaped the whirlwind during the 'winter of discontent' from its support for union industrial action in 1973–74. As Tebbitt observed:

The sheer viciousness and nastiness of the unions such as NUPE in the hospital service was displayed day after day on every TV screen in the land as the sick, the old and little children were kicked around in a dirty fight

---

45 See www.margaretthatcher.org/document/103764.
46 Cited in Saunders, 'Crisis? What crisis?', pp. 36–7.
47 Geoffrey Howe, *Conflict of Loyalty* (London: Macmillan, 1994), pp. 93–4.
48 *Ibid.*, p. 97.

between the Government and the trades union wings of the Labour Party. And to top it all, there was James Callaghan's famous remark, 'Crisis? What Crisis?' – which – while he may never have actually used those precise words, and certainly had not intended to refer to hospital closures – was hung permanently round his neck because it fitted him so well.[49]

In his memoirs Willie Whitelaw struck a more subdued tone, simply observing that Callaghan had missed his opportunity by postponing the general election in the autumn of 1978, only to be brought down by the action of the trade unions in the 'winter of discontent' that followed. While his account omits the details of the industrial action and its impact in 1979 on the general public, he attributed the Conservatives' victory in the May 1979 general election mainly to the Conservative Party's proposals for trade union reform.[50] It was with the impact of the 'winter of discontent' that Thatcher and her shadow Cabinet first realised their electoral chances had improved. By deferring the general election the previous September, Callaghan had taken his administration into another parliamentary term without TUC support. Then, his government, beset by an accumulation of strikes that affected the general public, became increasing unpopular. Labour's claim to work successfully with the unions, as symbolised in the social contract, was seriously undermined. As Hugo Young observed, the 'winter of discontent' settled the Conservatives' 'main policy dispute' –

> the great undecided question of whose instincts should prevail, Jim Prior's or Margaret Thatcher's coupled with those of Hoskyns and Joseph, in the matter of trade union reform.... From being a liability to the Tories, the union issue became through this 'winter of discontent' a potential election winner, so long as it was properly handled.[51]

On 5 December 1978 Sir Terence Beckett, chairman and managing director of the Ford Motor Company, forwarded Thatcher a copy of his speech at the Savoy Hotel in accepting the Hambro award of 'Businessman of the Year 1978'. He told J. P. Stanley MP, Thatcher's parliamentary private secretary: 'I want to thank her for what she has done in the questions she has asked in the House these last two weeks [about the Ford strike], which have really brought out some of the issues on sanctions in a most effective way'.[52] As we have seen, following the settlement of the nine-week Ford strike, with a wage increase of 17 per cent that breached the government's 5 per cent pay policy, the Conservatives successfully opposed the government's attempt to secure parliamentary approval for the use of its discretionary powers against the company. However, Jim Prior had emphasised that the Conservative Party was at one with the government in its

---

49 Norman Tebbitt, *Upwardly Mobile* (London: Weidenfeld & Nicolson, 1988), pp. 160–1.
50 William Whitelaw, *The Whitelaw Memoirs* (London: Aurum Press, 1989), pp. 96–7.
51 Young, *One of Us*, pp. 126–7.
52 Sir Terence Beckett to J. P. Stanley, 5 December 1978, Thatcher papers, THCR 261/154.

aim of conquering inflation and that responsibility in pay bargaining was essential. Yet the use of discretionary powers by the government to enforce its pay policy was opposed as arbitrary, incompatible with the rule of law and unjust.[53]

At Westminster, Thatcher castigated the government's attempt to penalise the profitable Ford Company – a major exporter – as 'blatant injustice'. The Callaghan administration suffered a six-vote defeat – only to continue as a minority administration by winning a vote of confidence the next day.[54] In many respects, the debate in Parliament concerned the quasi-legal grounds for sanctions against Ford. It was the lull before the gathering storm. From January 1979 Thatcher's leadership of the opposition had a far more robust stance during the 'winter of discontent' as she reaped the full benefit of the hostile media coverage of the government's ineffective handling of industrial unrest in Britain. Thatcher later recalled the industrial difficulties – particularly the road hauliers' strike and the beginning of the public sector strikes – that resulted in Britain being paralysed: 'What was more damaging even than this to the Labour Government, however, was that it handed over the running of the country to local committees of trade unions'.[55] On 7 January, she was interviewed by Brian Walden on the ITV programme *Weekend World*. In this exchange with the former Labour MP, she was still circumspect on the subject of trade union reform. Previously, she had been in favour of state funding for union elections and strike ballots on a voluntary, not compulsory, basis. In addition, withdrawing social security benefits from strikers was a possibility, if no ballot had been held, as well as preventing the right to strike in essential services. John Campbell, her biographer, has noted: 'Public opinion was the key. Mrs Thatcher was still determined not to commit herself to any confrontation with the unions without first making sure that the public would be on her side.'[56]

Thatcher was well briefed by the Confederation of British Industry (CBI), and other informants, who supplied her office with regular situation reports which revealed the widespread industrial action comprising strikes, overtime bans, work-to-rules and similar stoppages. In particular, forceful

---

53 In the case of Ford, the Conservative opposition argued, *inter alia*, on the grounds of the government's unjust action against the private company: 'Ford management ... bargain[ed] responsibly within the guidelines ... their initial 5 per cent offer triggered a massive walk-out ... a nine-week strike, costing £450 million in lost output and causing disruption to Ford throughout Europe.... When management made an offer acceptable to the workforce, the Government impose[d] sanctions ... Ford suffered the same fate [as other companies] last year ... unable to reach a settlement within the guidelines and having *no* [original emphasis] choice but to suffer either prolonged strike action ... or be blacklisted, or a combination of both.' *The Unjust and Arbitrary Use of Sanctions on Industry* (London: Conservative Research Department, December 1978), p. 6, Thatcher papers, THCR 261/154.

54 For discussion of these events, see chapter 3, pp. 55–8.

55 Thatcher, *The Path to Power*, p. 420.

56 Campbell, *Margaret Thatcher, Volume One*, pp. 419–21.

picketing, including stories of associated intimidation and violence, evoked memories of the militancy of the miners' strikes during the Heath government and the Grunwick dispute in 1977.[57]

Just before her PPB on 17 January, Thatcher learned of the anti-British feeling in Sweden generated by the large contingents of motor vehicle parts, worth nearly £1 million and destined for Volvo and Saab, that were held up by the road hauliers' dispute on the docksides at Immingham, Boston and Southport: 'Volvo and Saab … will have to cease production this week because components … are not getting through from British suppliers'. In the north-west, dockers refused to handle important export cargo which had escaped the pickets' notice while, in Manchester, the strike committee of the Transport and General Workers' Union had voted to increase picketing, thereby blocking food supplies.[58]

The next day, a detailed strike report comprising summaries from East Anglia, Birmingham, Scotland, Bristol and the south-west, Newcastle, Northern Ireland, different parts of Yorkshire and Humberside landed on Thatcher's desk. Picketing and lay-offs appeared widespread throughout Britain. In Bristol and the south-west, for example, Thatcher was advised: 'Secondary picketing continued, and severe, though patchy and selective…. Pickets are modelling their activities on those of the pickets during the miners' strike, but do respond to official pressure from other unions.'[59]

Within a few days, the position appeared to have escalated. Examples of secondary picketing in north-west England included complete blockades at the Liverpool Central Oil Company. 'Pickets are not allowing anything in or out; Van de Berg and Jeurguans, food manufacturers, Bibby, Intex Yarn (Manchester) and commercial vehicle manufacturer Seddon Atkinson (Preston) – no engines being made, nothing allowed in'. In addition, at the Heinz factory 3,000 had been laid off.[60]

These situation reports indicate the scale and extent of the number of workers who were not on strike but had been laid off as a consequence of the industrial action. There were also possible incidents of intimidation and violence on the picket lines. In Northern Ireland, 15,000 lay-offs were 'expected to escalate rapidly to 40–50,000 by the middle of next week'.

---

57 For discussion of the Grunwick dispute, see chapter 1, pp. 13–14. Shirley Williams, Fred Mulley and Denis Howell, MPs sponsored by the APEX union, joined the picket line at Grunwick, drawing national media attention. Thatcher and Williams clashed in the parliamentary debate on16 January 1979 over allegations of provoking violence on the picket line. Williams recalled: 'Failure to anticipate what the Tory press might make of my intervention was one of the biggest mistakes of my career.' Shirley Williams, *Climbing the Bookshelves: The Autobiography* (London: Virago, 2009), pp. 237–8. Interview: Baroness Shirley Williams, House of Lords, 12 October 2008.
58 CBI memorandum, 16 January 1979, Thatcher papers, THCR 261/148.
59 Strike report no. 11, 17 January 1979, Thatcher papers, THCR 261/148.
60 William Graham (CBI) to Richmond Ryder, 22 January 1979, Thatcher papers, TCHR 261/148.

Secondary picketing was holding up 'essential supplies' and the local strike committee was giving clearance tickets to companies – 'They may have to stand in line for up to four hours before their case is heard'. In addition, drivers were reported to be turning back at picket lines, owing to 'intimidation and veiled threats from pickets'.[61] These daily briefings provided the platform for a major assault on the Callaghan government and its industrial relations policy.

In Parliament, the opposition devoted one of its supply days to debate what Thatcher described as 'a very grim picture indeed', notably the widespread problems arising from picketing in the road hauliers' national strike. She told Parliament and the nation:

> The strikes today are not the only ones we have experienced recently. The tanker drivers' strike, thank goodness, is over. We have had the bread strike, hospital strikes, strikes at old people's homes, strikes in the newspapers, broadcasting, airports and car plants. Many people who thought previously that strikes were a characteristic only of large firms and that most firms were strike free, received a rather rude shock from a new piece of work by the Social Science Research Council, a Government financed body which found that nearly half of our factories had some form of industrial conflict, stoppages, overtime bans and go-slows in the past two years; and nearly all suffered from all-out strikes.... If the Prime Minister will do something to reverse the effect of the 1974 and 1976 Act which his Government and his predecessor's Government enacted, we shall support him....
>
> Are there not other unions whose members' work is so essential that one would expect them to be prepared to enter into no-strike agreements.... What I am suggesting to the Prime Minister is that he enter into negotiations with some of the unions to see whether he could get a no-strike agreement in return for a different method of bargaining which they would find satisfactory. Again, if he does that we will support him....
>
> ... while we are critical of much of his political philosophy, if he will take steps to deal with the situation of trade union power and consider new laws and new practices against picketing, of alleviating the effect of the closed shop and of trying to achieve more secret ballots so that people do not go on strike before they have been consulted ... if he will agree to take action ... we will support him through and through.

The Tory leader concluded with a *coup de grâce*:

> We believe that this is a matter of great significance for democracy and a free society and we will support him.... May I point out that this is a more generous offer than he ever made to us ... I hope he does take those steps. If he does not, I hope he will step aside for a party that will.[62]

---

61 Philip Ditton to Director General (CBI), Situation report (13), 18 January 1979, Thatcher papers, TCHR 261/148.
62 *Parliamentary Debates* (House of Commons), fifth series, vol. 960, 16 January 1979, cols 1524–6, 1538–9, 1540, 1541.

It was a speech that struck a chord with many in Britain, including an increasing number of trade unionists who less than four months later would vote for Thatcher and the Conservatives at the polls. Thatcher's three proposals to limit union power – funded secret ballots, ending secondary picketing and no-strike agreements in the public utilities – were turned down by the Prime Minister in his reply in Parliament.[63] In her memoirs, Thatcher revealed that Callaghan's initial response took her by surprise: 'I congratulate the Right Honourable Lady on a most effective Parliamentary performance. It was in the best manner of our debates and the style in which it was delivered was one of which the Right Honourable Lady can be proud.'[64] However, he reminded her of the scourge of 'running inflation'.[65] Callaghan also pointed out that 'in the current pay round there were forty-five major wage agreements, of which thirty (covering 800,000 employees) were within the Government's guidelines. However, eight settlements (involving over 500,000 workers) broke the pay policy, although mostly in single figures.'[66]

A few days before this parliamentary debate, Peter Hall, director of Britain's National Theatre (about to move from the Old Vic to its new three-auditorium site on London's South Bank), faced considerable difficulties, including a strike. This conflict appeared in effect a microcosm of wider industrial unrest in Britain. On 12 January 1979, he noted that a productivity deal, arranged with the unions after two months of negotiations, had been 'thrown out this week by the works committee'.[67] The following day, he penned a deeply sombre diary entry:

> The country is gradually coming to a standstill. There are to be two days
> of rail strikes, timed so that the system will be paralysed for a week but the
> men will lose only two days pay. We are a society of greed and anarchy: no
> honour, no responsibility, no pride. I sound like an old reactionary, which
> I'm not, but what we have now....

Normally a Labour voter, Hall revealed he intended to vote Tory at the next election.[68] As we shall see, he was to be joined at the polls by those sharing similar views who supported Thatcher and the Conservative Party's manifesto for trade union reform, particularly after the difficulties encountered by the Callaghan government during the 'winter of discontent'.

---

63 *Ibid.*, col. 1541.
64 Thatcher, *The Road to Power*, p. 429.
65 *Parliamentary Debates* (House of Commons), fifth series, 16 January 1979, vol. 960, cols 1541–2.
66 *Ibid.*, col. 1551.
67 John Goodwin (ed.), *Peter Hall's Diaries: The Story of a Dramatic Battle* (London: Hamish Hamilton, 1983), p. 407 (diary entry: 12 January 1979).
68 *Ibid.*

Chapter Eight

Political aftermath

On 4 May 1979 Margaret Thatcher entered 10 Downing Street as Britain's first woman Prime Minister. Her victory, with a comfortable overall majority of 43, ended an indecisive period of minority government in Westminster politics and paved the way for 18 years of unbroken Tory rule. On 28 March 1979, with the turmoil of the 'winter of discontent' virtually at an end, the Callaghan government had been defeated over a vital vote of confidence by the narrowest of margins – a single vote (311 to 310). It was only the second occasion in twentieth-century British politics a government had lost office over a vote of confidence.[1] Moreover, the Callaghan government had been brought down not by the 'winter of discontent' but over the question of devolution for Scotland and Wales.

Yet if Jim Callaghan had called the general election in October 1978, as widely anticipated at the time, Labour might have won, rather than having to endure a winter of industrial unrest and then be forced to seek re-election in 1979, in very difficult circumstances after losing the crucial vote of confidence on 28 March 1979. Following the 'winter of discontent' the 1979 general election defeat became a major turning point in Labour's history. For 11 of the 15 years from 1964 to 1979, Labour had held office. After five years of largely minority government from 1974, the outcome of the 1979 election was a critical setback. In particular, the inevitable post-mortems over Labour's defeat were accompanied by a turbulent period of fratricidal war between left and right in the struggle for the soul of the party.

When the former Labour Cabinet met for the first time on 9 May, Tony Benn persistently raised the question of the election defeat. Jim Callaghan responded brusquely: 'I'll tell you what happened. We lost the election

---

1   In 1924 Ramsay MacDonald's first Labour government was defeated over a crucial vote of confidence after 287 days in office as a minority administration. See John Shepherd and Keith Laybourn, *Britain's First Labour Government* (Basingstoke: Palgrave Macmillan, 2006).

because people didn't get their dustbins emptied, because commuters were angry about train disruption and because of too much trade union power. That's all there is to it.'[2]

As we have seen, Larry Lamb, the editor of the *Sun*, is usually credited with coining the phrase 'the winter of discontent' for the industrial and political disorder that heralded the fall of the Callaghan government.[3] Crucially, that disorder seriously undermined Labour's historic relationship with the trade union movement from which the party had been born in 1900. Yet the 'winter of discontent' also transformed Conservative fortunes. It built up Margaret Thatcher's stature as an alternative Prime Minister, whose mission in government would be to curb union power by legislation and success-ful confrontation with the trade union movement, particularly during the miners' strike of 1984–85. The unions, credited and blamed by their op-ponents for bringing down three governments – Wilson in 1970, Heath in 1974 and Callaghan in 1979 – were marginalised during the Thatcher years. When Labour finally returned to office after 18 years as New Labour, it was under a new young leader, Tony Blair, who had no particular links with, and little sympathy for, the British trade union movement. New Labour had been carefully and thoroughly distanced from the 'winter of discontent' and the events leading up to it. Blair resolutely declared there would be no return to that chaotic chapter in Labour's recent past.[4]

Yet, over 30 years on, the 'winter of discontent' remains firmly entrenched in the folk memory and still continues to resonate in British politics. In the years after 1979, like the ghost of Hamlet's father, memories of the 'winter of discontent' again and again haunted Jim Callaghan's Labour successors. Their Conservative opponents – aided by their allies in the media – never dawdled in keeping alive the popular memory of 'crisis Britain' under Labour rule during the late 1970s. This chapter, which examines the last days of the Callaghan government in 1979, from the vote of confidence on 28 March to polling day on 3 May, has two main purposes. First, it ques-tions how far the turbulent events of the 1978–79 winter contributed to the downfall of the Callaghan administration in March 1979 and Labour's subsequent defeat in the 1979 general election. Second, the chapter also explores why the 'winter of discontent' in the years after 1979 has remained so prominent in British politics.

In 1979 Callaghan and his former ministers were certainly convinced that the industrial strife of the 'winter of discontent' was the major factor that culminated in Labour's loss of office. A dejected Callaghan acknowl-edged: 'Memories of the winter [strikes] have been too great for many

---

2 Tony Benn, *Conflicts of Interest: Diaries 1977–80*, edited by Ruth Winstone (London: Arrow Books, 1991), p. 499 (diary entry: 9 May 1979).

3 For further discussion of the origins of the appellation 'winter of discontent', see pp. 1–2.

4 John Shepherd, 'Labour wasn't working', *History Today*, vol. 59, no. 1, January 2009, p. 49.

people and undoubtedly that handicapped us … I have a feeling that people voted against last winter, rather than *for* the Conservative proposals'.[5] In fact, Callaghan was only confirming the axiom in politics that it is governments that win or lose general elections, not oppositions.

Shirley Williams, who had been Secretary of State for Education, later recalled the 'winter of discontent' in graphic terms, albeit with some exaggeration. In her autobiography she penned:

> In the winter all hell broke loose. Lorry drivers, school caretakers, local government workers and many others joined in a massive protest against the incomes policy. Newspapers carried pictures of mountains of rubbish in the streets. Worse still were the reports of the dead that lay unburied in hospital morgues *up and down the country*. The strikes turned into a kind of frenzy, *in which otherwise decent men and women outdid one another in their callousness towards the public they were meant to serve.* [Emphasis added][6]

Other members of the Callaghan government generally agreed with this verdict in apportioning blame for the 'winter of discontent'.[7] In his assessment, Peter Shore, Environment Minister before the general election, rigorously defended the Prime Minister, who, in his opinion, was not to blame for the 'winter of discontent':

> it was a nightmare. No one, in their wildest dreams, could have predicted such collective barbarity in advance of the actual event … with a General Election certain to be held at the latest in eight months' time and the fiercely anti-trade union Mrs Thatcher waiting to pounce, self-interest alone should have made certain that the winter was one in which the trade unions and their members would have exercised maximum restraint.[8]

Yet, shortly after the 1979 election, Shore had set to paper his impressions of the various views circulating within the Labour Party about the defeat. There was a general consensus that the postponement of the general election in October 1978 was a significant reason, particularly as local parties had been geared up for the contest. In addition, the government had failed to implement or commit to radical socialist measures when

---

5 George Clark, 'The nation's choice: a Conservative woman Prime Minister', in *Times Guide to the House of Commons, May 1979* (London: Times Books), p. 26.

6 Shirley Williams, *Climbing the Bookshelves: The Autobiography* (London: Virago, 2009), p. 249.

7 One exception was Michael Meacher, the left-wing Labour MP and a junior minister in the Wilson and Callaghan governments, who asked directly after the 1979 election defeat: 'Was it really the winter of discontent that lost Labour the election?' In his view, little attention had been given to the causes of the industrial unrest, largely attributable to the government's inflexible and stringent 5 per cent pay policy at a time of falling living standards, as well factors such as underinvestment in the British economy. Michael Meacher, 'Was it really the winter of discontent that lost Labour the election?', *Tribune*, 18 May 1979. See also the reaction of delegates at the 1979 Labour Party conference at Brighton, which is discussed below.

8 Peter Shore, *Leading the Left* (London: Weidenfeld & Nicolson, 1993), pp. 118–19.

in office. In particular, Shore noted the strong feelings concerning the government's handling of the industrial strife:

> the 'winter of discontent' could have been avoided. However the Labour Government insisted on imposing an unrealistic/impossible 5% which inevitably put it into damaging conflict with the unions and the Party. The Labour Government thus divided the broad Labour Movement and the bitterness of subsequent events could not be patched over in time to avoid handing Mrs Thatcher the election on a plate…. The Labour Government showed itself to be out of touch with the views and aspirations of the Party.[9]

As we have seen earlier, David Owen, Foreign Secretary at the time, was precise in attributing Labour's downfall to the 'winter of discontent', starting with the Ford nine-week strike in the car industry. The company's wages agreement of 17 per cent breached the official 5 per cent pay policy and the government therefore sought to invoke 'discretionary action', although this would require parliamentary approval. Yet on 12 December, the crucial date in the Foreign Secretary's view, the Prime Minister had decided not to make the Westminster debate on sanctions against the Ford Motor Company a vote of confidence. Callaghan's decision proved fatal, as the government was defeated by a combined opposition with abstentions by Labour's Tribune group of MPs.[10] On that occasion the government survived by successfully moving a vote of confidence the next day, which the Labour Tribune group fully supported. However, at the height of the 'winter of discontent', in early 1979, Callaghan failed to declare a state of emergency or to seize the opportunity of a television broadcast to the nation to forcefully counter the strike action. Somewhat removed as Foreign Secretary from the day-to-day handling of the industrial troubles, Owen noted:

> Jim admitted, rather poignantly at one stage, that there was not a single night when he did not consider going on television but then asked himself if anything would be different the next day. I felt he underestimated his own personal authority and the strength of the office he held … I saw perhaps more clearly that we were witnessing the terminal stages of the Government. In a strange way, Jim knew it too. I felt that he had resigned himself to electoral defeat and only had one objective, the perfectly honourable one of keeping the Labour Party together.[11]

Lord Owen later noted that the debilitating effect of the strains and stress on the Prime Minister in coping with the 'winter of discontent' during the

---

9 Peter Shore, 'Antagonism towards the last Labour government and the "why we lost" debate' (n.d., 1979), Lord Peter Shore papers, British Library of Political Science, 12/146.
10 Callaghan's decision not to make the parliamentary debate on sanctions on 12 December 1978 a vote of confidence is discussed in more detail on pp. 56–8.
11 David Owen, *Time to Declare* (London: Penguin, 1992), pp. 408–9.

last months of government contrasted markedly to 'the measured and struc-
tured style of leadership' he had observed James Callaghan adopt earlier
as premier.[12]

With the party conducting an acrimonious inquest into its electoral
defeat, Denis Healey had few doubts about why Labour had lost in 1979.
In his autobiography he wrote: 'all the evidence suggested we had lost
the election mainly because the "Winter of Discontent" had destroyed the
nation's confidence in the Labour Party's ability to work with the unions; it
had also turned large numbers of people against their own trade union representatives'.[13] With hindsight, Healey believed that Labour's unattainable
5 per cent pay policy meant that the eventual downfall of the government
was almost predestined, like a plot in an ancient classical play. He observed:
'Our hubris in fixing a pay norm of five per cent without any support from
the TUC [Trades Union Congress] met its nemesis, as inevitably as in a
Greek drama'.[14]

However, what brought about the downfall of the minority Labour
government was not the 'winter of discontent' but the long-running constitutional question of devolution for Scotland and Wales, which Healey also
readily acknowledged was 'the issue which caused us the greatest trouble'.[15]
During 1974–79, devolution, which internally divided both the Labour
and Conservative parties, often on unconventional lines, was a constant
problem for the Wilson and Callaghan governments, challenged by the rise
of the Scottish National Party (SNP) and Plaid Cymru (PC). After earlier
devolution bills had failed, two separate Devolution Acts for Scotland and
Wales had been passed in 1978, which included the provision of holding
a referendum in each country. What became known as the 'Cunningham
amendment' – passed on Burns' Night, 28 January 1978 – required the 'yes'
vote in the referenda on devolution to constitute at least 40 per cent *of the
total electorate* (not 40 per cent of the total votes cast) in each country.[16] In
effect, this became a ticking time-bomb for the Callaghan government in
its last weeks in office.

On 1 March 1979 the referenda on devolution in Wales and Scotland
took place. In Wales, where there had been far less support for this measure,
devolution was overwhelmingly rejected – with a vote of approximately

---

12 David Owen, *In Sickness and in Power: Illness in Heads of Government During the Last 100
   Years* (London: Methuen, 2008), p. 257; Interview: Lord David Owen, House of Lords,
   16 November 2011.

13 Denis Healey, *The Time of My Life* (London: Penguin, 1990), p. 467.

14 *Ibid.*, p. 462.

15 *Ibid.*, p. 459.

16 This amendment against the Labour government, which was introduced by a hostile
   opponent of devolution, George Cunningham, the Scottish Labour MP for Islington
   South, passed by 166–151 votes. Kenneth O. Morgan, *Michael Foot: A Life* (London:
   HarperCollins, 2007), p. 357.

four to one against, and less than 12 per cent of the electorate voting 'yes'.[17] In Scotland, the 'yes' vote was smaller than expected, at 32.8 per cent of the total electorate, compared with the 'no' vote of 30.8 per cent (with 36.4 per cent not voting). Because less than 40 per cent of the eligible Scots voted for the Scotland Act, the Secretary of State for Scotland, Bruce Millan, was required to lay a repeal order before Parliament.[18]

From January 1979, support for devolution had collapsed, particularly in Scotland, as the referenda campaigns took place against the discordant background of the 'winter of discontent'. The government's popularity took a severe blow, owing to the impact of the national road haulage dispute (which had started in Scotland on 3 January) and the effects of the strike action by the public service workers. On 2 February the *Scotsman* reported:

> selective strike action by public service workers started with a vengeance in Scotland yesterday. Raw sewage was being pumped into the River Clyde, drinking water had to be boiled in West Lothian and refuse collections were halted at Ayr and Prestwich Airport. NUPE, representing 61,000 public sector workers in Scotland's health service and local government, outlined strike plans at a press conference in Edinburgh yesterday.[19]

The Welsh result was probably no surprise to the government, but opinion polls in Scotland shortly before the referendum revealed a majority of nearly two to one in favour of devolution. Yet devolution was closely associated with the troubled Labour government. The Prime Minister had made only one visit to Scotland during the referendum campaign. The 'winter of discontent' was a significant factor in a disappointing pro-devolution vote.[20]

Publishing the outcome of the referendum, the *Scotsman* declared:

---

17 In Wales, five south Wales Labour MPs opposed devolution, including the vociferous young Labour backbencher and future leader of the Labour Party Neil Kinnock. His wife, Glenys, a Welsh-speaker from Holyhead, Anglesey, was a fierce opponent of Plaid Cymru. Morgan, *Michael Foot*, p. 356. Interview: Lord Neil Kinnock, House of Lords, 2 November 2011.

18 William L. Miller, *The End of British Politics? Scots and English Political Behaviour in the Seventies* (Oxford: Clarendon Press, 1981), pp. 248–51.

19 *Scotsman*, 2 February 1979, p. 1, n. 19. The paper's correspondence columns were full of comment on industrial action. See 'STRIKES: an avenue of escape', including, for example, J. M. Matheson, President of the British Medical Association, Lothian Division, Edinburgh: 'The distress caused by these industrial activities to innocent victims, the suffering of patients and their relatives, is shared by doctors whose frustration increases daily'. An editorial concluded: 'No doubt the present dispute, if action is stepped up against essential services, will inconvenience, infuriate and even endanger the public. But among the victims will be members of the unions involved, and their families.' *Scotsman*, 8 February 1979, p. 12.

20 Dick Leonard, 'The Labour campaign', in Howard R. Penniman (ed.), *Britain at the Polls 1979: A Study of the General Election* (Washington, DC: American Enterprise Institute for Public Policy Research, 1981), p. 103.

the devolution referendum battle has left the Labour Government danger-ously exposed and hopes for a Scottish Assembly gravely wounded. Even the Scotland Act's most dedicated supporters now believe it will bleed to death in Parliament. And if the Prime Minister cannot construct a survival plan for his Government then Britain could face a General Election in a matter of weeks.[21]

As the Conservatives were now determined to bring down the Callaghan government after the SNP motion withdrew support from Labour, the balance of power was now held by a motley group of Welsh and Scottish nationalists, Ulster Unionists and other Northern Ireland MPs and 11 Liberal MPs. After the Scottish referendum result, the SNP no longer had any reason to support Labour at Westminster and declared they would vote against the government. Though the votes of the Plaid Cymru MPs, the two Scottish Labour MPs and two Ulster Unionists could be relied upon by Callaghan and his Labour whips, the survival of the government was on a knife edge as Margaret Thatcher moved the vote of no confidence.

In the House of Commons, at 3.34pm on 28 March 1979, Thatcher moved 'That this House has no confidence in Her Majesty's Government'. She opened by blaming the 'Government's inept handling of the result of the referendums on the Scotland and Wales Acts'. She then censured the Callaghan government on its record – its concentration on increasing state control, its failure to create wealth, or to deal with trade union power and the rule of law. She declared:

> The Prime Minister could have taken action [on union reform] with our support. He chose not to do so. He is the prisoner of his own history in this matter. The unions were his stepping stones to power, and they know it. So be it. Changes will have to be made by another Government, and I believe they will have the overwhelming support of the people, including the majority of trade union members.[22]

Thatcher also accused Callaghan of giving insufficient government support for the rule of law and drew on examples from the 'winter of discontent'. The Attorney-General's description of picketing as 'lawful intimidation' had produced the following response from one trade union leader: 'My advice is to carry on picketing. I cannot see union members accepting the court decision. They will inevitably act in such numbers that the authori-ties will have to use football stadia for detention centres.'[23]

More references to the strikes in public services followed as examples of a lack of law and order: 'It means that citizens expect and are not getting an ordered or orderly society. They expect the rubbish to be cleared, the

21 *Scotsman*, 3 March 1979, p. 1.
22 *Parliamentary Debates* (House of Commons), fifth series, 28 March 1979, vol. 965, col. 468.
23 *Ibid.*, col. 469.

schools to be open and the hospitals to be functioning. They are not.... They expect bargains to be kept between trade unions and employers. Finally, they expect Ministers to support them in these views.'[24]

Callaghan's response to Thatcher was to focus on the new agreement, the St Valentine's Day Concordat, between the government and the TUC. Its main features included TUC guidance on industrial relations, with strikes as a last resort, a firm recommendation for strike ballots and a review of closed-shop procedures. One new departure was a national 12-month economic assessment for the economy, involving the participation of the Confederation of British Industry (CBI) as well as the TUC. In particular, discussions would be held on increases in production, 'labour costs' and a 'bold and ambitious target … of working to get inflation down below 5% in the next three years'. Callaghan also announced the establishment, under the chairmanship of Professor Clegg, of a new Standing Commission on pay comparability between different groups of workers, particularly in the public sector.

Callaghan concluded in a determined fashion:

> I am certain that it is a better way forward – far better than the opposi-tion's plan, which seems to dust off some of their more ancient pieces of artillery left over from 1970 and make a planned industrial offensive … for Conservatives to highlight and exploit individual cases as a means of driving the trade union movement, in general, into a corner, tarring all 11 million members of unions with the same brush is a dangerous miscalculation.... The agreement with the TUC will not be perfect, but it is an important step towards industrial peace and steadier prices.[25]

In closing for the opposition, William Whitelaw made numerous refer-ences to the Labour government's industrial relations policy to counter Callaghan's charge that Tory policy under Thatcher's leadership was based on confrontation. Whitelaw observed that the Prime Minister had 'waxed eloquent about support, not sabotage'. Yet 'he was the man who sabotaged his own colleagues over *In Place of Strife* in 1969 and he incited the miners at Aberdare in 1974 during the Heath Government'.[26] Whitelaw challenged Callaghan by referring directly to the 1979 public servants' industrial action: 'What has the Prime Minister's Government been involved in this winter, with the lorry drivers, with the ambulance men, with the gravediggers and with the hospital workers; what are the Government involved in now with the Civil Service, if it is not confrontation?'[27] Michael Foot closed for the government in what his biographer has described as 'a brilliant, if rambling final speech to wind up the debate'. The deputy leader compared

---

24 *Ibid.*, col. 469.
25 *Ibid.*, cols 476–8.
26 *Ibid.*, col. 569.
27 *Ibid.*

the SNP – Callaghan had called them 'Turkeys voting for Christmas' – with the gladiators before their Emperor in ancient Rome: 'We, who are about to die, salute you'. Famously, Foot described David Steel, the Liberal Party leader, as 'the boy David' – having 'passed from rising hope to elder statesman without any intervening period whatsoever'.[28]

In the end, after what was, according to Michael White of the *Guardian*, one of the most exciting and tense debates witnessed by those present, the hapless and worn-out Callaghan government lost the vital vote of confidence by a single vote (311–310).[29] The Wilson–Callaghan governments of 1974–79 had been minority administrations for nearly five years (for about six months there had been a majority of three). For three years the Callaghan administration had battled unparalleled inflation and increasing unemployment, had survived the crisis of 1976 involving the intervention of the International Monetary Fund, by-election losses, parliamentary defeats and the breakdown of the social contract. While the industrial confrontations of the 'winter of discontent' had caused serious economic and political difficulties, the administration's downfall was over devolution. As Foot recalled, the fall of the administration 'was truly the result of the Referendum which led to the government's defeat within the same month of March'.[30]

According to Bernard Donoughue, during the final days before the vital vote at Westminster, it seemed that Labour might lose by two or three votes. At this point, until the pressure of his closest advisers persuaded him to alter course, the Prime Minister actually stopped his whips and ministers in the usual ritual of trading for votes. Of those present in the House of Commons on 28 March, two in particular have left detailed accounts of the comings and goings that day: Mitchell and Hattersley. Austin Mitchell, Labour MP, who had been returned for Tony Crosland's Grimsby constituency at the 1977 by-election, 14 years later brought to mind the fall of the Labour government as a 'night to remember' in febrile terms reminiscent of the sinking of the *Titanic*. He wrote:

> Every string was being pulled. Rumours abounded, Clement Freud [Liberal MP] was to be offered the passage of his Freedom of Information Bill and would miss the train back from Liverpool. The Welsh Nationalists would support us in return for help with disabled miners. The Unionists would stay home, the press were describing Jim Callaghan as some Tammany tyrant....[31]

---

28 Morgan, *Michael Foot*, p. 368.
29 Interview: Michael White, Westminster, London, 11 April 2011.
30 Michael Foot had proposed to Callaghan without success various tactical ploys to conciliate the SNP before the vote of confidence but, as he noted of the Prime Minister, in the end 'his patience *had* snapped'. 'How governments fell: a few brief notes', Michael Foot papers, Labour Archive and Study Centre, MF/c11/1.
31 Austin Mitchell, 'A night to remember. More like a night to forget', *House Magazine*, vol. 18, no. 162, 1993.

Roy Hattersley later recalled that on the day of the vote of no confidence in Parliament, he did not realise that he was witnessing 'the last rites
of "Old Labour"', the party of nationalisation, redistributive income and
trade union power. His role included guarding two Unionist MPs – John
Carson and Harold McCusker – to secure their votes for Labour with an
unlikely promise to tackle inflation. Yet Callaghan apparently turned down
outright a possible deal with Enoch Powell for Ulster Unionist abstentions
in exchange for the promise of a gas pipeline to Northern Ireland –
probably another sign of the Prime Minister's fatigue and lack of willingness
to continue the travails of minority government. The two Northern Irish
Catholic MPs, Gerry Fitt and Frank Maguire, on this occasion had flown
from Belfast to make a point of abstaining. In the debate, Fitt – normally
a supporter of the Labour administration – explained his utter disillusion-
ment with the government's conduct of Irish policy under the Secretary of
State for Northern Ireland, Roy Mason.[32] Both Catholic Northern Ireland
MPs who abstained were under threats from the Irish Republican Army
not to back the Callaghan government.[33]

In retrospect, Mitchell also recognised that the Labour administration
'had been skating on thin ice for so long that few of us realised there was
no ice left'. The minority government's survival from 1976 owed much
to the work of the Labour whips team at Westminster. 'We also ascribed
miraculous powers to those presiding genii of British politics [Michael]
Cocks [chief whip] and Walter Harrison [deputy chief whip]. A double act
who had become legends in their own time. Surely they could pull another
body out of the hat?' However, this was not possible. Sir Alfred Broughton,
the long-serving Labour MP for the Yorkshire constituency of Batley and
Morley, was mortally ill and remained at home. Desperate attempts to

---

32 The socialist and nationalist Gerry Fitt was one of the most well known Northern
    Ireland MPs. He had been the founder and first leader of the Social Democratic and
    Labour Party (SDLP) and had backed the Wilson and Callaghan governments. However,
    on 28 March 1979 he was adamant in his refusal to support the government on the
    vote of confidence, owing to the Irish policies of the Northern Ireland Secretary, Roy
    Mason. *Guardian*, 27 August 2005; *Daily Telegraph*, 27 August 2005. Frank Maguire (a
    former member of the IRA) was the Independent Republican MP for Fermanagh and
    South Tyrone. Elected in October 1974, he usually supported Labour on key votes.
    However, as the owner of a public house, Frank's Bar, in Lisnaskea, County Fermanagh,
    he was often away from Westminster. On the crucial vote of confidence on 28 March
    1979 he explained that he had journeyed to the Commons to 'abstain in person'. *New
    York Times*, 6 March 1981.
33 Interview: Walter Harrison (Labour deputy chief whip in 1979), Wakefield, 5 March
    2012. Interview: Lord Ted Graham (Labour MP for Edmonton and government whip in
    1979), House of Lords, 26 July 2007. Interview: Roy Hattersley, Victoria, London, 25
    June 2009. Roy Hattersley, *Who Goes Home? Scenes from a Political Life* (London: Little,
    Brown, 1995), pp. 208–11.

persuade Maguire not to abstain to keep the Callaghan administration in office were to no avail.[34]

In 1979 there was a long (five-week) general election campaign, partly because the Labour government hoped that the electorate's memories of the industrial strife would fade. In reviewing the Conservatives' advertising campaign, Tim Bell of Saatchi and Saatchi admitted that Callaghan's decision to defer the general election in September 1978 had caused them difficulties as they were prepared for an autumn contest. However, the 'winter of discontent' was critical in allowing the Conservatives to regain the advantage. Bell commented:

> it gave us the opportunity to heighten public dissatisfaction with the government, an opportunity which might not have arisen but for the industrial unrest in the country at the time.... Everything we did was directed towards increasing the salience of the dissatisfaction; towards transforming a vague dislike of the circumstances in which people were living into a burning issue for them ... oppositions win elections by ensuring governments lose – and that is the opportunity with which we were presented by the winter of discontent.

He also observed, as the winter proceeded, the increasing disillusion of the electorate with a minority government. This led to the Conservative poster 'CHEER UP! LABOUR CAN'T HANG ON FOREVER', followed by Margaret Thatcher's famous election broadcast at the peak of the industrial unrest on 17 January, when she was able to present the Conservatives as the 'party of the nation'. In summarising the Conservative advertising campaign, Bell concluded: 'Our contribution on its own did not win the

---

34 Sir Alfred Broughton MP (1902–79), a former medical doctor, while suffering from poor health nonetheless still voted at Westminster on a number of occasions. On 28 March 1979, even though gravely ill, he was willing, against medical advice, to be taken from Yorkshire to Parliament by ambulance to be 'nodded through' on the crucial no-confidence vote. In the end, the deputy chief whip, Walter Harrison, a fellow Yorkshire MP, after extensive discussions with the Broughton family, decided at 1.20pm on the day of the vote not to call 'Doc' Broughton to Westminster. However, possibly the Prime Minister had a late change of mind. Outside the Commons chamber, Callaghan told Bernard Donoughue: 'they cannot get "Doc" Broughton here. He is too ill. We will lose [the vote].' Afterwards, at a sombre meeting in the Labour whips' office, there were bitter recriminations between the chief whip, Michael Cocks, and Bernard (now Lord) Donoughue about Callaghan's intransigence over possible deals on offer that would have secured victory for the government. Bernard Donoughue, *Downing Street Diary, Volume Two: With James Callaghan in No. 10* (London: Jonathan Cape, 2008), pp. 470–3. The next day 'Doc' Broughton heard of the downfall of the Labour government by a single vote. He died four days later. In 2012 Walter Harrison, at 91, still valued Callaghan's personal letter about 'Doc' Broughton: 'I want you to be positively sure that I know you did the right thing at the time, and I have never changed my mind since'. James Callaghan to Walter Harrison, 6 April 2004. Interview: Harrison. Interview: Lord Ted Graham, House of Lords, 26 July 2007. Interview: Baroness Ann Taylor (Labour MP and Labour whip in 1979), House of Lords, 20 June 2011. I am grateful to Baroness Taylor for putting me in touch with Walter Harrison.

campaign. In a sense, the Labour government lost the election by not holding it earlier. In May 1979 the campaign was taking place against the backdrop of the "winter of discontent" and of Mrs Thatcher's broadcast at that time....'[35]

According to the Nuffield study of the 1979 general election, the Conservatives had declined the *Weekend World* invitation on 30 March for a television debate involving the three main party leaders. The Conservative response was: 'we wanted the election to be about the winter [of discontent], not about a TV programme'. Instead, Thatcher's broadcast on 2 April (delayed a day owing to the assassination of Airey Neave) opened the Tory election campaign with the Conservatives' winning card. She commenced with:

> We have just had a devastating winter of industrial strife ... perhaps the worst in living memory, certainly the worst in mine. We saw the sick refused admission to hospital. We saw people unable to bury their dead. We saw children virtually at the mercy of secondary pickets and strike committees and we saw a government apparently helpless to do anything about it ... I think we all know in our hearts it is time for change.[36]

By contrast, Tim Delaney, creative designer at Leagas Delaney Advertising, who was Labour's adviser and advertising consultant in the 1979 election campaign, recalled that the central issue for Labour was 'the management of the economy; which included industrial relations'. He explained that although he had put an election strategy paper to the Labour Party *before* the winter of 1978–79, 'there was no evidence that the issues changed after this time. If anything, the issue of economic management became even more important after the "winter of discontent" than before it' and he had little to say about the 'winter of discontent' itself. Instead, his review of the 1979 campaign finished with an amazingly gloomy conclusion: 'without a more professional approach in the Labour Party to the problems of political communication, one party will be talking through Saatchi & Saatchi to the people while the other will basically be talking to itself'.[37]

References to the 'winter of discontent', and the events that had led to it, were prominent at the Labour Party conference held in Brighton,

---

35 Bell believed the Saatchi and Saatchi poster 'LABOUR ISN'T WORKING', depicting a long line of people outside an unemployment office (the dole queue actually consisted of Young Conservatives from South Hendon and not the advertising agency's employees), 'will probably go down in history as one of the most effective political posters ever produced'. Tim Bell, 'The Conservatives' advertising campaign', in Robert M. Worcester and Martin Harrop (eds), *Political Communications: The General Election Campaign of 1979* (London: George Allen & Unwin, 1982), pp. 12, 16, 22, 25.

36 David Butler and Dennis Kavanagh, *The British General Election of 1979* (London: Macmillan, 1980), pp. 167–8.

37 Tim Delaney, 'Labour's advertising campaign', in Robert M. Worcester and Martin Harrop (eds), *Political Communications: The General Election Campaign of 1979* (London: George Allen & Unwin, 1982), pp. 27–8, 30–1.

1–5 October 1979. It proved a stormy occasion, with bitter recriminations concerning Labour's defeat in the general election, as typified by the blistering and fighting opening address by the party chairman, Frank Allaun MP: 'the real issue behind all the constitutional reforms to be debated … was that Mrs Thatcher had won the election because Labour leaders had ignored the grass roots'.[38] Allaun added: 'a year ago the TUC conference almost unanimously rejected the rigid and inflexible 5 per cent wage ceiling. The Labour Party Conference a month later voted equally solidly. But the Cabinet majority took no notice. Hence the troubles of January and February (*Applause*).'[39]

A typical protest from the conference floor came from Peter Sandland-Nealson (Worcester Constituency Labour Party), the defeated candidate at Oswestry, who declared:

> The Tories in the General Election preached a free market economy financed by capitalism, driven by personal greed, callous indifference and self-interest and that is what the electorate expected a Tory campaign to do.… In no General Election has a more fundamental and ideological challenge ever been thrown down by the Tories … *The Times,* with the help of their pals in the radio, TV and press, threw down the ideological gauntlet.… But where was our response to that?[40]

Bob Wareing, Liverpool, Edge Hill, prospective parliamentary candidate, referred directly to the 'winter of discontent' among the 'reasons why the Labour Party lost the election on Merseyside, [and] why there was a drop in support in Merseyside':

> It is not just because of a winter of discontent, but because of the years of discontent following the throwing out of the industrial strategy upon which this party was elected in 1974 (*applause*) so that there was in fact a league list of big business on Merseyside – Plessey, Lucas, British Leyland, GEC, Dunlop – all of these have made their closures during the last five years, despite the fact that the Labour Government did throw £500 million into the area, saving and creating about 50,000 jobs. But far more jobs were lost.[41]

The former MP for Birmingham Selly Oak, Tom Litterick, melodramatically cascaded National Executive Council (NEC) papers and election leaflets from the conference hall gallery as he protested: 'Governments and only Governments win or lose elections. Oppositions do not. It follows therefore that the Labour Government lost the last election, and it is our business this week to understand how that election was lost.' Litterick's explanation was that Callaghan's influence had dominated 'that fatuous Party

---

38 *Guardian,* 2 October 1979; *Morning Star,* 2 October 1979.
39 *Report of the 78th Annual Conference of the Labour Party 1979,* Brighton, 1–5 October 1979, p. 168.
40 *Ibid.,* p. 184.
41 *Ibid.,* p. 185.

Election Manifesto of 1979. "Jim will fix it" they said.... Our common
sense tells us that Jim cannot fix it. And we should not expect him to fix
it.' Litterick closed by quoting the Irish MP Gerry Fitt, 'the most loyal
supporter ever of the Labour Government', who spoke on behalf of his
constituents: "'It is their voice saying that because of what the Government
have done in the past five years, I cannot go into the lobby with them
tonight." [It] could be an epitaph for the Labour Government (*applause*).'[42]

In response, Ron Hayward (General Secretary of the Labour Party), in
a stirring speech about the divisions clearly visible within the party, in an
appeal to conference asked with reference to the election defeat:

> Can we get it off our chests once and for all.... So are we going to have 50
> more speeches this week about it? If we are going to have speeches from
> the platform or from the floor, I say now what I said then, eight days after
> polling day, at my first meeting, the Northern Regional Conference. If it
> is to be said – and it has to be said – that we lost the election because of
> the winter of discontent – it has been said that Alan Fisher's lads and lasses,
> David Basnett's lads and lasses and Moss Evans lost us the election with the
> winter of discontent – if that is it, you have got to ask the first question: why
> was there a winter of discontent? (*Applause*). The reason was that, for good
> or ill, the Cabinet supported by MPs ignored Congress and Conference
> decisions. It is as simple as that. (*Applause*).[43]

How far did the 'winter of discontent' contribute to the Labour defeat
in 1979? Six months before his 1979 election defeat, on 19 September
1978, Jim Callaghan had scribbled on his notepad in Cabinet: 'I have been
written off more times than I care to remember'. He listed the various
dates when his parliamentary opponents and a hostile press had unsuccess-
fully predicted the downfall of his administration and his political demise.[44]
Less than a year later, it had become quite clear to the majority of the
former Callaghan Cabinet why Labour had been defeated in the May 1979
general election. On 4 May, on leaving 10 Downing Street for the last time,
Callaghan declared: 'The people wanted a change'. The only former trade
union official to become Prime Minister added: 'the unions did it: people
could not forget what they had to suffer from the unions last winter'.[45]

On a turnout of 76 per cent, the Tory share of the vote in 1979 (43.9
per cent) was significantly less than it had been in the Conservative victories
in 1951 (48.0 per cent), 1955 (49.7 per cent) or 1959 (49.4 per cent). In
numerical terms Labour had recorded close to the number of votes in the
February and October 1974 general elections, but its share of the poll had
slumped to 36.9 per cent. Above all, Labour had failed to secure even 40.0

---

42 *Ibid.*, p. 186.
43 *Ibid.*, p. 189.
44 James Callaghan, 'PM's notes for future policy initiatives meeting', 19 September 1978,
   The National Archives PREM 16/1667.
45 Donoughue, *Downing Street Diary, Volume Two*, p. 503.

per cent at the polls for the third successive time. In this respect, it was the worst Labour performance since the 1931 debacle. Given the fact that 56 per cent of voters in 1979 did not choose a Conservative candidate, the 1979 general election could be seen as a prime example of a government losing an election rather than an opposition winning it.[46]

On the main election issues the Conservatives scored over Labour, particularly those where the electors felt their party had believable and workable proposals or possessed a very sound record. In a BBC Gallup survey, conducted on the eve of polling, the issues frequently mentioned in 1979 were prices, unemployment, taxes, strikes and law and order. While Labour led the Conservatives on prices and unemployment, the Conservatives scored far higher on taxes and law and order. However, many electors supported Labour's objectives of securing a 5 per cent rate of inflation within three years (as in Labour's St Valentine's Day Concordat with the TUC) and of securing an enduring pact with the unions on wages. Understandably, polling revealed there was considerable doubt in electors' minds after the 'winter of discontent'. Palpably, these proposals were not solely within a Labour government's gift, whereas the Conservative proposals on income tax reduction were measures well within a new administration's jurisdiction.[47]

In 1979, psephologists and political commentators all drew attention to Labour's dwindling support made apparent by the election result. Peter Kellner's verdict was that 'Labour had suffered not merely a defeat but a disaster' at the hands of the electors on 3 May. In achieving its lowest share of the vote since 1931, the 'winter of discontent' cannot be discounted. Yet the corrosion in Labour's core voters had been longstanding, originating well before the winter of 1978–79. It raised the critical question in 1979 of whether the Labour Party might ever regain a working majority at Westminster again.[48]

Among other immediate post-mortems on Labour's election defeat, Anthony King analysed the widening chasm between Labour's policies and its traditional supporters. There had also been a remarkable turn-around of fortunes between the two major parties. Twelve months before, according to NOP's regular monthly survey, Labour led by 4.5 per cent; the parties were neck and neck in November 1978, but by early February 1979 the Tories had a staggering 19 per cent margin.[49] This could be attributed directly to the 'winter of discontent', though over the weeks up to the election Labour regained much of the Tory lead in the polls. King went on to observe:

---

46 Ivor Crewe, 'The voting surveyed', in *The Times Guide to the House of Commons May 1979* (London: Times Books, 1979), p. 249.
47 Leonard, 'The Labour campaign'.
48 Peter Kellner, 'Not a defeat, a disaster', *New Statesman*, 18 May 1979.
49 Anthony King, 'The people's flag has turned deepest blue', *Observer*, 6 May 1979.

Put simply, the message of all the available evidence is that the British people deeply resent trade union power, increasingly dislike having to pay for even higher levels of government spending (except for a few of the basic social services) and not least are profoundly suspicious of nationalisation and government intervention in the economy generally. Labour's misfortune is that these are precisely the causes that the Party has stood for over the years.[50]

As we have seen, at the Conservative Party conference at Blackpool in 1985, Thatcher, in addressing her Tory audience and the nation, famously asked: 'Do you remember the Labour Britain of 1979? It was a Britain in which union leaders held their members and our country to ransom … a Britain that was known as the sick man of Europe'.[51] It was perhaps one of the clearest examples of why the 'winter of discontent' continued to resonate in British politics. This was true especially at election times, when Thatcher never campaigned without a portfolio of evidence, including 'copies of the newspaper headlines from the "winter of discontent", which she would then hold up as a warning of the consequences of voting Labour'.[52]

As leader of the opposition from 1975, Thatcher had adopted a pragmatic approach to industrial relations, as typified by her general support for Jim Prior, the Conservative Party's employment spokesman. As we have observed, the advent of the 'winter of discontent' gave her the political opportunity to offer Callaghan support for legislation on postal ballots (for union elections and strikes), no-strike agreements in essential public services and amending the law on the closed shop and picketing.[53]

The Conservative manifesto for the May 1979 general election was prepared for 'a great country which seems to have lost its way'. It was relatively modest in measures to deal with trade union power. It nonetheless presented a grim picture: 'During the industrial strife of the last winter, confidence, self-respect, common sense and even our common sense of humanity were shaken. At times this society seemed on the brink of disintegration.'[54]

In the parliamentary debate on 27 January 1978, Prior confirmed the Conservative Party policy on industrial relations and labour law: 'When we return to office, we shall not undertake sweeping changes in the law'.[55] His position had reflected a prominent view within the ranks of the opposition

---

50 *Ibid.*
51 *Daily Telegraph*, 12 October 1985.
52 John Whittingale quoted in James Thomas, 'Bound by history: the winter of discontent in British politics, 1979–2004', *Media, Culture and Society*, vol. 29, no. 2, March 2007, p. 273.
53 Peter Riddell, *The Thatcher Government* (Oxford: Basil Blackwell, 1985), pp. 36–7.
54 'Conservative Party election manifesto 1979', in Iain Dale (ed.), *Conservative Party General Election Manifestos 1900–1997* (London: Routledge and Politico's Publishing, 2000), pp. 265–6.
55 *Parliamentary Debates* (House of Commons), fifth series, 27 January 1978, vol. 842, col. 1847.

that, following the unmitigated failure of the Heath government's 1971 Industrial Relations Act, the Conservatives should proceed with caution and moderation.

However, the industrial strife that had paralysed Britain during the 'winter of discontent' had hardened views within the Conservative Party and dramatically changed attitudes and philosophy. It increased the demand for robust legislation for union reform. Prior recalled that: 'During the winter of 1978–9, the Labour Government's "Winter of Discontent", it became clear that the unions were far exceeding their proper role'.[56] Yet Prior, who conceded that some legislation was necessary, continued to stand out against the diehards within the Conservative ranks.

After taking office in 1979, the Thatcher government enacted a series of legislative measures that transformed trade union law in the 1980s, albeit in piecemeal stages. As Simon Auerbach observed in 1990: 'Today, we find that peaceful industrial action is liable to be unlawful if its secondary or sympathetic action concerns a union membership or recognition issue, involves persons picketing away from their place of work, lacks the support of a majority of those involved in a ballot or one of possibly a set of ballots, is regarded as politically inspired, or otherwise falls outside a narrow range of legitimate topics for a dispute.'[57] Following the collapse of the Callaghan government's incomes policy that culminated in the 'winter of discontent', the year 1979 represented a turning point. As John Hendy QC has written: 'A press campaign of vitriolic and dishonest invective against trade unionism … had created the climate for an attack on unions seen as over-powerful and responsible for Britain's economic decline'.[58]

During the 1980s and early 1990s the Conservative governments enacted nine major pieces of employment legislation.[59] As Hendy observed: 'Elected in 1979 and re-elected 3 times since then, they have, in practice, brought about the most radical package of changes of employment law ever seen in the history of English law'.[60] This legislation created a fundamental, far-reaching legal structure in complete contrast to the policies and tenets of the post-war consensus. Critics claim that a new and hostile legislative framework was established that is distinct from that in other European countries. Supporters of the Conservative legislation believe order was

---

56 James Prior, *A Balance of Power* (London: Hamish Hamilton, 1986), p. 155. Interview: Lord Jim Prior, Beccles, 11 November 2011.

57 Simon Auerbach, *Legislating for Conflict* (Oxford: Clarendon Press, 1990), p. 2.

58 John Hendy, *A Law Unto Themselves. Conservative Employment Laws: A National and International Assessment* (London: Institute of Employment Rights, 1993), p. 20.

59 These nine Acts were: Employment Act 1980; Employment Act 1982; Trade Union Act 1984; Wages Act 1986; Public Order Act 1986; Employment Act 1988; Employment Act 1990; Trade Union Reform Act 1993; and Employment Rights Act 1993. Some of the earlier legislation was codified in the Trade Union and Relations (Consolidation) Act 1992.

60 Hendy, *A Law Unto Themselves*, p. 20.

restored to industrial relations and the 'British disease' of strikes was cured, while unions were made more democratic.[61]

As Margaret Scammell has noted, in 1979 the Conservatives 'were handed the weapon of the winter of discontent'.[62] Saatchi and Saatchi, which had been appointed by Gordon Reece, Thatcher's director of publicity, in 1978, had prepared the Conservative Party's 1979 election broadcasts and still created the programmes for the 1983 election.[63] As David Butler and Dennis Kavanagh observed in the 1983 Nuffield study, important decisions had to be considered in producing party election broadcasts owing to developments in television that offered the elector the option to change channel. For the new-style election broadcast, the iconic images of the 1979 industrial unrest provided valuable propaganda material. The authors commented: 'At its most effective, this gave a sequence of the "winter of discontent" in which, to the accompaniment of a funeral dirge and a doom-laden voice asking "Do you remember?", shots cut rapidly between angry picket lines, paralysed industry and the alarmist front pages of the period.' This high-paced Saatchi and Saatchi presentation was akin to the contemporary television commercial without the normal restraints. By contrast, a global comparison of unemployment in Britain, Germany and Japan was not as effective as the confrontational events of the winter troubles of 1979.[64]

Iconic images of the 'winter of discontent' continued to appear in the right-wing press during the 1983, 1987 and 1992 Conservative election campaigns. On Thursday 9 April 1992, general election day, the *Daily Mail* published 'a warning from 13 years ago'. The newspaper carried an article about the Callaghan government's failure to curb militant trade unions and its refusal to declare a state of emergency in the face of the widespread industrial chaos that paralysed the nation. For those voters too young in 1992 to remember at first hand the last Labour government, the *Daily Mail* reporter, Tracey Harrison, wrote: 'The sick were turned away from hospitals, streets were piled high with stinking rubbish and the dead could not be buried. This was Britain only 13 years ago in the wretched months of the 1978–9 Winter of Discontent … in freezing weather it was the sick who suffered. The patients, the old, the children.'[65]

61 Simon Auerbach, 'Mrs Thatcher's labour laws: slouching towards utopia?', *Political Quarterly*, vol. 64, no. 1, January–March 1993, p. 37.

62 Margaret Scammell, 'The phenomenon of political marketing: the Thatcher contribution', *Contemporary Record*, vol. 8, no. 1, summer 1994, p. 20.

63 For the 1979 general election campaign, see Ivan Fallon, *The Brothers: The Rise and Rise of Saatchi & Saatchi* (London: Hutchinson, 1988), pp. 163–8.

64 David Butler and Dennis Kavanagh, *The British General Election of 1983* (London: Macmillan, 1984).

65 Tracey Harrison, 'The winter of shame', *Daily Mail*, 9 April 1992, p. 5.

In similar vein, the *Sun* a day earlier had printed a full one-page spread, with the headline 'LEST WE FORGET' linked to the subheading 'Hell caused by last Labour Government'.[66] In addition, a side-bar in the *Sun* on union power carried four images of the paper's front pages as examples of 'Jim Callaghan's last Labour government … ruled by an iron fist – by tyrant union bosses'. The main photograph depicted piles of uncollected rubbish in a London street in 'crisis Britain' held to ransom by greedy unions. One caption stated: 'strike caused an invasion of rats', which typified the style and tone of the exaggerated reporting. While the *Sun* reminded its readers of ' these horrors' that seemed 'a lifetime away', the feature's purpose in relation to the forthcoming general election was enforced in the headline 'Nightmare on Kinnock Street'.[67]

Chris Harrigan also produced a 'union bashing' piece to support the *Daily Star's* story that 'Neil Kinnock has dropped the gaffe of the [1992] election campaign by revealing his plans to go easy on the unions if he gets into Number 10'. The *Daily Star* was founded at the start of the 'winter of discontent', with its first issue appearing on 1 November 1978. The Harrigan article during the 1992 election campaign outlined the 1978–79 industrial unrest with its slanted revelation 'How the unions crippled Britain'.[68]

During the 1992 election campaign, Labour held a small and consistent lead over the Conservatives in the polls, which worried some of the broadsheets. On election day the *Financial Times*, with a large number of Conservatives among its business and financial readers, advised its readership to vote Labour. At the same time, *The Times* and *Sunday Times* also expressed concerns about the Conservative campaign. Yet it is the tabloids that arguably had more sway over voting behaviour – if it is the case that the press exercised influence over how people voted. An American journalist from the *Washington Post*, commenting on the bias of tabloid media coverage of British politics, observed: 'In the tabloids, virtually every Tory has the stature of Winston Churchill, every Labourite is a lying Leninite and every "fact" is a lethal weapon'.[69]

In 1992, Prime Minister John Major won against the odds, which was reflected in the last-minute endeavours of the tabloid press to secure the return of the Conservative government. The 1992 headlines of the popular dailies indicate the final line of the anti-Labour attack, including direct invocations of the 1979 'winter of discontent':

---

66 *Sun*, 8 April 1992.

67 *Ibid.*

68 Christopher Harrigan, 'The real truth of life under Labour', *Daily Star*, 25 March 1992.

69 Quoted in 'Did the tabloids destroy Kinnock?', *Independent*, 15 April 1992, p. 15, in Kenneth Newton, 'Caring and competence: the long, long campaign', in Anthony King, Ivor Crewe, David Denver, Kenneth Newton, Philip Norton, David Sanders and Patrick Seyd, *Britain at the Polls, 1992* (New York: Chatterton House, 1992), p. 156.

Daily Mail, 21 March: 'Major defies London mobs'
Daily Mail, 24 March: 'Threat of return to picket terror'
Daily Mail, 1 April: 'The secret tax that will allow Labour to reward its union paymasters'
Daily Mail, 9 April: 'The winter of shame: this was the face of Britain the last time Labour ruled'
Daily Express, 9 April: 'A vote for Ashdown will let Kinnock into No. 10, vote Conservative'

In particular, on election day the *Sun* notoriously carried a negative image of the Labour leader, Neil Kinnock, with the infamous caption: 'If Kinnock wins today will the last person to leave Britain please turn off the lights'.[70]

In 1997, Tony Blair opened his general election campaign with the outright declaration that there would be no turning back to the 1970s decade of strikes and industrial unrest that had undermined the Callaghan administration's economic strategy and failed attempt at corporatist government. The young leader of New Labour attacked the union scare stories emanating from the Conservative camp as 'just Tory lies' and made clear that, if elected, his government would not be changing the Thatcher union legislation of the 1980s. Blair was at pains to emphasise this: 'Let me state the policy clearly, so that no-one is in any doubt. The essential elements of the trade union legislation of the 1980s will remain. There will be no return to secondary action, flying pickets, strikes without ballots, the closed shop and all the rest.'[71]

He made a number of similar statements on unions and industrial relations policy. Three years before, his declaration 'unions know and accept that from a Labour government they can expect fairness not favours' was published in his book in which he outlined how he envisaged the future.[72]

In the autumn 1989 shadow Cabinet elections, Blair had secured fourth place. In appointing him shadow Employment Secretary, in place of Michael Meacher, Kinnock gave Blair virtual *carte blanche* to push industrial relations reform on apace.[73] In taking up this challenge, Blair sought advice from leading authorities on industrial relations. Among those consulted was Jon Cruddas, at the time a postdoctoral student at the University of Warwick, who from 1997 to 2001 was to work for Blair at Downing Street as deputy political secretary, essentially as a link person with the unions (Cruddas entered Parliament at the 2001 election as Labour MP for Dagenham). He

---

70 *Ibid.*, pp. vii, 157.
71 Tony Blair, 'We won't look back to the 1970s', *The Times*, 31 March 1997.
72 Tony Blair, 'Unions 1994 conference, London, 19 November 1994', in Tony Blair, *New Britain: My Vision of a Young Country* (London: Basic Books, 1994), pp. 136–7.
73 Kinnock told Blair: 'If anyone asks, "Are you speaking for Kinnock? ... answer "Yes" ... if you are not sure ... come and see me and I'll make it abundantly clear to anyone that I am behind you.' Anthony Seldon with Chris Ballinger, Daniel Collins and Peter Snowden, *Blair* (London: Free Press, 2004), pp. 103–4.

had previously worked at Labour Party headquarters as assistant to General Secretary Larry Whitty and to his successor, Tom Sawyer. Labour Party modernisation comprised primarily dispelling 'negatives' – 'tax and spend', nationalisation and memories of the 'winter of discontent' – which the Conservative Party and the right-wing press recycled during the 1980s and early 1990s.[74]

What concerned Blair were the powerful negative images in popular memories of trade union bosses and unbridled trade union power that faced Labour on its path back to power. New Labour broadly accepted the view of the 'winter of discontent' and provided no alternative narrative of the events during the Callaghan government.[75] Instead, a line was drawn between New Labour and Old Labour. Peter Hyman, who became Blair's chief speech-writer before departing Downing Street for a career in secondary education, in 2005 put it succinctly with a brilliant extended metaphor:

> In the eyes of this generation [of Blair and Brown] the Labour Party had been like a restaurant that had poisoned its guests. The effect of the Winter of Discontent, the piles of rubbish, the dead not buried, the economic incompetence, the high taxes, the unilateral disarmament policy was to poison the electoral bloodstream.
>
> Think of that restaurant … if you had been violently ill for a week, what would make you return? In the end a combination of new chef, redesigned restaurant, opened under a new name would be needed, and even then you would only consider it at the point when you were getting bored or had been turned off other restaurants … that is how Tony saw the Labour Party.[76]

---

74 Interview: Dr Jon Cruddas MP, Portcullis House, London, 18 February 2010.
75 See, for example, Ross McKibbin, 'Homage to Wilson and Callaghan', *London Review of Books*, vol. 19, no. 7, 3 April 1997.
76 Peter Hyman, *1 Out of 10: From Downing Street Vision to Classroom Reality* (London: Vintage, 2005), pp. 53–4.

Chapter Nine

In conclusion: the 'winter of discontent' – views from abroad

On 6 January 1979, the *New York Times* carried the headline 'Britain will sell fighters to China, Callaghan says at summit meeting'. The paper reported that, at the four-power meeting in St Francois, Guadeloupe, the British Prime Minister had revealed his government's intention to sell Harrier fighter planes – renowned for their short-run or vertical take-offs – to China. Callaghan emphasised it was part of a \$2 billion trade package, which included coal-fired plants, steel plants, various trade deals and academic exchanges. The next day, four world leaders – President Jimmy Carter (United States), Chancellor Helmut Schmidt (West Germany), President Valery Giscard d'Estaing (France) and Jim Callaghan concluded two days of wide-ranging official talks. In the light of steps by the United States towards a new strategic arms agreement on nuclear weapons with the Soviet Union, their discussions covered international politics, potential world crises in 1979 and global security.[1]

For a few days, the British Prime Minister had left behind the growing industrial strife of the 'winter of discontent', on which the US media remained understandably mainly silent (focusing instead on the normalisation of US–Chinese relations and the détente between the United States and the Soviet Union).[2] Callaghan's absence received a hostile press back in Britain, 4,000 miles away – though in Guadeloupe, as a world leader and NATO ally, he played honest broker at times between Carter and Schmidt. The day after his return, Callaghan reported to his Cabinet concerning the Guadeloupe summit on relations with the Soviet Union and China, the Strategic Arms Limitation Talks (SALT II) and likely world flashpoints.

However, it was the current industrial situation, including the full-scale oil tanker drivers' strike and the state of emergency in Northern Ireland,

---

1 *New York Times*, 5, 6 January 1979, p. 1.
2 Drew Middleton, 'Major issue at Guadeloupe: U.S. stand on NATO defense', *New York Times*, 5 January 1979, p. A3.

that took precedence on the Cabinet's agenda.[3] The Guadeloupe inter-
lude reveals how much the industrial unrest and pay policy dominated the
government's thinking, to create almost a bunker mentality in Whitehall
in the final weeks of the Callaghan administration. Tony Benn recorded
the exchange at the Cabinet meeting between the Lord Chancellor, Elwyn
Jones, and the Prime Minister:

> Elwyn Jones said, 'I wish the importance of these Guadeloupe discussions
> could be understood and explained to the public because you, Jim, had a
> very bad press when you were away.' Prime Minister: 'I had expected that. I
> tried to explain to the public that I didn't think there was a crisis when I got
> back but got kicked in the shins for it.'[4]

There was not always an absence of news in the American press on
the British industrial scene. On 25 January, the *Washington Post* carried an
interesting piece on the public sector strikers during the 'National Day of
Action', held three days earlier. The paper informed its readers:

> several hundred thousand garbage collectors, school janitors, hospital kitchen
> help and other low-paid local government blue-collar workers staged what
> had been planned as a one day walk-out. A substantial although unknown
> number ignored their leaders' plan and insisted on staying out for the rest
> of the week or even indefinitely, until they got something resembling their
> demand for a minimum wage of 120 dollars a week.[5]

This piece by the London correspondent of the *Washington Post*, the
distinguished American journalist and author Bernard D. Nossiter, also
gave particular attention to the British media coverage of the widespread
industrial strife:

> In this election year, the media has become almost hysterical about the
> daily effects of the strikes. Headlines have shrieked 'Famine Threat', 'The
> Road To Ruin', 'Chaos' and 'No Mercy'. Business leaders predicted that

---

3   Cabinet conclusions, The National Archives (henceforth TNA) CAB 128/65. For the
    Guadeloupe summit, see TNA PREM 16/2050, 11 January 1979; also Kenneth O.
    Morgan, *Callaghan: A Life* (Oxford: Oxford University Press, 1997), pp. 616–19.
4   Tony Benn, *Conflicts of Interests: Diaries 1977–80*, edited by Ruth Winstone (London:
    Arrow Books, 1991), p. 434 (diary entry: 11 January 1979).
5   Bernard D. Nossiter, 'British strikes risk greater inflation, end of Labor rule', *Washington
    Post*, 25 January 1979, p. A17. Bernard D. Nossiter MA (1926–92) was born in New
    York City. Among his various posts in journalism he was the first London correspondent
    of the *Washington Post*, from 1971 to 1979. During this assignment, he published his
    most controversial book, *Britain: A Future That Works* (London: Andre Deutsch, 1978),
    which challenged conventional views of British trade unions and economic problems
    In 1976 Peregrine Worsthorne of the *Sunday Telegraph* described the book as 'facile,
    starry-eyed indulgence of Britain's shortcomings'. He later acknowledged Nossiter may
    have been led 'to a sounder estimate of Britain's future than those much more penetrat-
    ing prophets of gloom'. For further information, including Worsthorne's comments, see
    Bernard D. Nossiter, 'The battle of Britain', *Washington Post*, 28 January 1979, p. C3.

the truckers would throw two million out of work. Spokesmen for big farmers cried that pigs, cattle, chicken would be cannibalising each other for lack of food. Now, apologetic business leaders put strike-caused lay-offs at a maximum of 200,000 – one tenth the panic estimate – or about one half of one per cent of the labour force. The press has looked but cannot find animals that have eaten each other.[6]

Norrister's perceptive reporting for the *Washington Post* highlighted several key aspects of the causes and much of the character of the British 'winter of discontent'. He observed the outburst of industrial unrest 'powered by worker resentment against three years of pay austerity'. In his view, many of those on strike regarded their wage restraint over three years as 'a wasted sacrifice in the battle against inflation'.

Moreover, the public sector strikes amounted to more of a 'peasants' revolt' than normal industrial stoppages.[7] On this occasion, union leaders, conventionally described as 'power-mad bosses' by an overwhelmingly Tory media, had little control. Contrary to accepted wisdom, the 'winter of discontent' revealed the *weaknesses* of the fragmented British trade union movement rather than its usual depiction as trade unionists 'displaying industrial muscle'.[8] As a result, the *Post*'s London correspondent under-lined the significance of the right-wing political shift in the later 1970s in the British media, particularly the tabloid press. According to Nossiter, the *Guardian* – 'one of the two politically uncommitted national news-papers' – reported that 'The more lurid forecasts of ten days ago have come spectacularly unstuck'.[9]

Another view of the British 'winter of discontent' was provided from the other side of the world – Australia. In 1978, Ralph Willis made a fact-finding visit to Britain to discuss industrial relations policies with members of the Callaghan government and senior trade union leaders. As Australian shadow Minister for Economic Affairs, the main objective was to report back on the Callaghan government's policies in action. Over 30 years later, Willis, who was to be one of the main architects of the Australian Accord, recalled:

---

6   Nossiter, 'British strikes risk greater inflation'.
7   In a chapter headed 'The peasant's revolt', Andy Beckett accurately describes January and February 1979 as the 'two most militant months' of the 'winter of discontent'. 'Almost 30 million working days were lost, more than three times as many as the previous year.... On 22 January, the winter of discontent's single most militant day, 1.5 million public sector staff refused to work. But the winter of discontent was not really about such carefully choreographed, centrally directed "days of action". It was more shapeless and anarchic. Many of the strikes were unofficial without the approval of the union hierar-chies.' Andy Beckett, *When the Lights Went Out: What Really Happened to Britain in the Seventies* (London: Faber & Faber, 2009), p. 465.
8   Nossiter, 'British strikes risk greater inflation'.
9   *Ibid.*

I had been thinking about a credible anti-inflation policy ... when I was a backbencher. The Whitlam government [Gough Whitlam, Australian Labour government 1972–75] had no credible anti-inflation policy. It led me to think we should develop a social contract ... my British visit increased my view that we should have an Accord ... we needed a comprehensive agreement [with the unions] ... we made ours a prices and incomes policy ... not [absolute] price control but some control.[10]

Ken Morgan has noted the likeness of the St Valentine's Day Concordat to the Australian Accord, in which the unions worked in harmony with the government in determining the basis of economic policy and controlling strikes. He has written: 'It was the kind of permanent agreement which underlay the "Accord" between the Australian trade unions and the Labour governments of Hawke and Keating ... [which] helped ensure well over a decade of Labour rule from 1983 to 1996, although admittedly it was bolstered by the much stronger tradition of arbitration in pay awards present in Australia'.[11]

Willis observed in Britain a social contract that was to fall apart in the 'winter of discontent', primarily as a result of an unrealistic and inflexible 5 per cent pay policy. He noted: 'My general impression was that the British government was trying to impose something that was impossible.'[12] Willis was determined the mistakes made by the Callaghan government would not be repeated in Australia.

As Robert Taylor wrote in 1978 (before the winter of discontent), the social contract between the Labour government and the unions had been a considerable achievement and should not be regarded as a scapegoat for British post-war decline: trade union leaders 'are not the guilty men, as often portrayed by economic commentators. The Conservatives have launched a bitter, often hysterical attack against the trade unions for their alleged domination.' Instead, as Taylor observed, the social contract remained the best hope for Britain's future: 'All over north-western Europe, particularly in Germany and Scandinavia, social democratic parties and trade unions are working together in harmony to create richer, fairer societies for all their people. The social contract happens to be the British way in what has become a recognisable development over large parts of the continent.'[13]

Up to 1977, Labour's social contract (or what was sometimes known as 'the wider social contract') with the unions was considered relatively

---

10 Interview: Ralph Willis, by telephone, Melbourne, Australia, 8 August 2012. See also Gough Whitlam, *The Truth of the Matter* (Harmondsworth: Penguin, 1979).

11 Kenneth O. Morgan, *Callaghan: A Life* (Oxford: Oxford University Press, 1997), p. 672.

12 As a young MP, Ralph Willis had been in Britain during the 'three-day week' of 1974, and he recalled the civil servants could not put the lights on for him to read some documents in Whitehall. Interview: Willis (also meeting in Melbourne, 28 October 2012).

13 Robert Taylor, *Labour and the Social Contract*, Fabian Tract no. 458 (London: Fabian Society, 1978), pp. 1–2.

successful, despite the crisis involving the intervention of the International Monetary Fund (IMF) and the subsequent public expenditure cuts. With Jack Jones of the Transport and General Workers' Union working closely with Len Murray of the Trades Union Congress (TUC), the unions had delivered nearly three years of responsible wage restraint, which reduced the rate of inflation in Britain from around 27 per cent to about 8 per cent. However, it was clear that when incomes policies were introduced in post-war Britain by either Conservative or Labour governments to maintain full employment and to fight inflation they usually had on average about a two-year life span.

By the end of 1978 there were significant milestones on the way to the 'winter of discontent', primarily Callaghan's decision to postpone an election that autumn, his dogmatism and inflexibility over the 5 per cent policy, the failure of the government and trade union negotiations to achieve some kind of rapprochement after intense negations that ended in the split vote 14–14 at the TUC General Council on 14 November, followed by the Ford settlement at 17 per cent (over three times the government's guideline) and the parliamentary defeat of the government's sanctions strategy against Ford and other firms that breached the government's pay policy.[14]

According to Bill Rodgers, Jim Callaghan had shown considerable skill in the first two years of his premiership, particularly in handling the IMF crisis and the 'stagflation' that beset his administration. However, the disastrous Heathrow conference on his return from the Guadeloupe summit in early 1979 was, in the view of his Minister of Transport, 'the third serious misjudgement Jim Callaghan had made in six months'.[15] In Cabinet, Rodgers was one of the ministers who had earlier queried imposing the fatal 5 per cent norm rather than a higher figure to avoid a confrontation with the unions in the annual wage round. Rodgers had also taken for granted that Callaghan was going to call a general election in October 1978 – a view shared by many people, especially among the Labour Cabinet and trade union leaders. However, it had been a crucial decision that the Prime Minister had kept virtually to himself. The TUC conference in Brighton had almost been the start of the general election campaign. Two days later, the Prime Minister informed his Cabinet of his decision, ruling out any discussion. As Rodgers observed in his memoirs: 'When he [Callaghan] said that, to the contrary, he proposed to carry on, we almost rose from our chairs in astonishment'.[16]

---

14 Peter Dorey, *Wage Politics in Britain: The Rise and Fall of Incomes Policies Since 1945* (Brighton: Sussex Academic Press, 2001), pp. 2–3, 227–29.

15 Bill Rodgers, *Fourth Among Equals* (London: Politico's, 2000), p. 178. Two years after the 'winter of discontent', Rodgers left the Labour Party with Roy Jenkins, Shirley Williams and David Owen as one of the 'Gang of Four', to form the short-lived Social Democratic Party.

16 *Ibid.*, p. 179.

Why did the social contract fail but the Accord succeed for nearly 13 years in Australia? In the end, the social contract, particularly after the IMF crisis and the public expenditure cuts, became little more than a mechanism for wage restraint. Jack Jones and Len Murray in alliance delivered nearly three years of wage restraint but could not deliver beyond phase 2 of the social contract. The adoption of the 5 per cent norm for a fourth round in 1978–79 spelt disaster, at a time when the unions were demanding a return to free collective bargaining. However, Roy Hattersley recalled a dinner party with trade union leaders (who included Moss Evans, Alf Allen and Len Murray) in which he and Denis Healey were told by Len Murray (about the 5 per cent pay norm): 'Look none of us can carry this in our unions. But if you *blind it through*, you'll get away with this' (original emphasis). The fact that Murray said this 'influenced an entire policy ... and that is what we did – come what may, the decision was made'.[17]

Ralph Willis's report on his visit to Britain fed into debates within the Australian Labour Party (ALP) on industrial relations (when the ALP was in opposition) that eventually developed into the Accord. There were constructive aspects of government cooperation, as also evidenced in Britain, that could be adopted and incorporated into a more widely based and all-embracing policy. From 1983 to 1996 this comprehensive and long-lasting policy agreement on wages, prices, social welfare and employment became the successful foundation stone of incomes policy and associated issues of the Bob Hawke and Paul Keating Labour governments. Part of its early success was the bringing together of the trade union and ALP wings of the Australian labour movement, symbolised, in particular, by Bob Hawke and Ralph Willis, who had held office in Australian trade union and parliamentary politics. The Accord evolved through eight versions that stressed policy flexibility and international competitiveness in the changing global world of the 1980s.[18]

Britain never developed a similar relationship between government and unions to that achieved in Scandinavia and West Germany (a relationship Callaghan admired and which he often referred to). Instead, after 1976, the social contract was little more than a mechanism for wage restraint. By 1978, wage restraint had become a spent force. Jack Jones and Hugh Scanlon, among union leaders the main supporters of the Labour government, were very close to retirement and to being replaced by Moss Evans

17 Interview: Lord Roy Hattersley, Victoria, London, 25 June 2009.
18 Interview: Rt Hon. Bob Hawke, Sydney, Australia, 15 August 2009. Interview: Willis. Interview: Patricia Hewitt, Camden Town, London, 23 June 2010; Interview: Nick Martin, Australian Labour Party, Sydney, 16 October 2012. Andrew Scott, *Running on Empty: 'Modernising' the British and Australian Labour Parties* (Annadale: Pluto Press, 2000), pp. 231–7; Gwynneth Singleton, *The Accord and the Australian Labour Movement* (Carlton: Melbourne University Press, 1990), pp. 155–67.

and Terry Duffy, who had a different agenda and who were considered by some to be of lesser calibre.

Bernard Donoughue has provided perhaps one of the most well known quotes about the end of the Callaghan government. Nearing Downing Street in the official Rover car during the 1979 election campaign, Donoughue mentioned a recent improvement in the opinion polls and the possibility of a narrow Labour victory. The Prime Minister famously replied:

> I should not be too sure. You know there are times, perhaps once every thirty years, when there is a sea-change in politics. It then does not matter what you say or do. There is a shift in what the public wants and what it approves of. I suspect there is now such a sea-change and it is for Mrs Thatcher.[19]

A slightly different account of the car journey on 12 April is, though, reported by Donoughue in his *Downing Street Diary*. Here, a more upbeat Prime Minister is quoted:

> he was *quite optimistic that we would win*, 'unless there has been one of those sea changes in public opinion towards Thatcher. If the people have really decided they want a change of government, there is nothing you can do.'[20]

However, in his autobiography Donoughue also quotes Callaghan on his last day in Downing Street after the 1979 election defeat, as declaring there was little more they could have done to win: 'the people wanted a change' and 'the unions did it. People could not forget and would not forgive what they had to suffer from the unions last winter'. This is very much in line with Donoughue's final entry in his *Downing Street Diary*.[21]

Denis Healey later portrayed the end of the Callaghan government as a classic drama: 'Our hubris in fixing a pay norm of five per cent without any support from the TUC met its nemesis, as inevitably as in a Greek tragedy'.[22] In this sense there was an inevitability, and an air of fatalism, that hung about the last days of the Callaghan government as the general election approached. The loss of the motion of confidence on 28 March

---

19 Bernard Donoughue, *Prime Minister: The Conduct of Policy Under Harold Wilson and James Callaghan* (London: Jonathan Cape, 1987), p. 191. This is confirmed in Donoughue's autobiography where he discusses the 1979 election defeat, and this time cites Callaghan in the following terms: 'Jim had put his finger on it on 12 April.... He said that he was still worried "there has been one of those deep sea changes in public opinion. If people have really decided they want a change of Government, there is nothing you can do about it".' Bernard Donoughue, *The Heat of the Kitchen: An Autobiography* (London: Politico's, 2004), p. 277.

20 Bernard Donoughue, *Downing Street Diary, Volume Two: With James Callaghan in No. 10* (London: Jonathan Cape, 2008), pp. 483–4 (diary entry: 12 April 1979). Emphasis added.

21 Donoughue, *The Heat of the Kitchen*, p. 279; Bernard Donoughue, *Downing Street Diary, Volume Two*, p. 503 (diary entry: 4 May 1979).

22 Denis Healey, *The Time of My Life* (London: Penguin, 1990), p. 462.

by a single vote was a disaster in organisation, particularly surprising by the team of Labour whips who had kept a minority government afloat through more than three years of parliamentary divisions. As in any classical Greek tragedy, you cannot change the end. The 'winter of discontent' led to the 1979 election defeat for Labour, but the memories of the 1978–79 winter have been rekindled by politicians and the media ever since.[23]

---

23 The death of Baroness Thatcher in April 2013 (as this book went to press) witnessed considerable public debate about the 'winter of discontent', the events that led to it and its significance in Thatcher becoming Britain's first woman Prime Minister in 1979.

'Winter of discontent', 1978–79: chronology of key events, including by-elections

1 January 1978   Prime Minister Jim Callaghan, interviewed on BBC radio, says that in 1979 wages and prices are to be held at an annual rate of 5 per cent.

2 March   Redbridge, Ilford North by-election: Labour marginal seat goes to Conservatives. Significant result for minority Labour government and possible general election.

13 April   Glasgow Garscadden by-election: Labour holds seat. Smallest swing against Labour and only 3.6 per cent swing to Scottish National Party.

20 April   Lambeth Central by-election: Labour hold the seat, but there is a nearly 10 per cent swing to the Conservatives.

27 April   Epsom and Ewell and Wycombe by-elections: Conservatives hold both seats with increased majorities.

31 May   Hamilton by-election: Labour secures best result of the Parliament, doubling majority.

July   Government white paper aims to keep pay settlements at 5 per cent to reduce inflation to below 8 per cent.

July   List published of 57 companies which have lost government aid for breaching 1977–78 pay guidelines.

13 July   Manchester, Moss Side, and Penistone by-elections: Labour holds both seats. In Manchester there is a very low swing (less than 4 per cent) to the Conservatives. In Penistone, the Conservative margin is nearly 9 per cent.

24 August   Unions at Ford submit a claim for a 25 per cent pay increase.

1 September   At the TUC Brighton conference the Prime Minister warns that pay rises above 5 per cent will contribute to inflation. The TUC nonetheless overwhelmingly votes against pay limits.

7 September   Callaghan in a television broadcast declares that there will be no autumn general election.

20–21 September   Ford Motor Company strike begins. Workers reject 5 per cent pay offer.

2 October   Labour Party conference votes 4,017,000 to 1,924,000 to reject pay restraint. NUPE's motion for a new national minimum wage of £60 per week in the public sector is carried.

26 October   Pontefract and Castleford, and Berwick and East Lothian by-elections: Labour victories in both. The Conservatives fail to take marginal Berwick and Labour secures a very small swing to the government but at Pontefract there is a swing of nearly 8 per cent to the Conservatives.

14 November   TUC General Council: tied vote 14–14 rejects joint statement with government on economic policy.

22 November   Ford Motor Company strike settlement at 17 per cent pay rise.

November–December   Bakers' strike, with eventual settlement at 14 per cent.

15 December   Government defeated in Parliament by 285 votes to 279 over sanctions against Ford. Six Labour Tribune MPs abstain.

16 December   Government wins vote of confidence by 10 votes.

22 December   BBC technicians/staff win 15 per cent settlement, avoiding threatened Christmas black-out.

December 1978–January 1979   Oil tanker drivers' dispute, with eventual settlement at 13–15 per cent wage increases.

3 January   Road haulage dispute starts in Scotland and spreads to other regions. Robust secondary picketing.

10 January   Prime Minister returns from international summit in Guadeloupe, West Indies. 'Crisis? What crisis?' *Sun* headline the next day.

11 January   Short state of emergency in Northern Ireland.

22 January   Some 1.5 million workers take part in the National Day of Action.

January–March   Public sector strikes, including ambulance crews, local authority manual workers, NHS auxiliary staff, water workers, school caretakers, railway workers.

14 February   'St Valentine's Day Concordat'. Government agreement with the TUC in revised 'social contract'.

February–April   Civil servants' one-day strikes: settlement at 9 per cent, plus £1 per week with later increases (up to 26 per cent) by January 1980.

1 March   Clitheroe and Knutsford by-elections: Conservatives hold seats with swings of almost 10 per cent and over 13 per cent respectively, attributed to the 'winter of discontent'.

7 March   Government establishes new standing commission on pay comparability, chaired by Professor Hugh Clegg.

28 March   House of Commons passes a motion of no confidence in the government, 311 votes to 310.

29 March   Liverpool, Edge Hill by-election: Liberals win Labour seat with remarkable swing of 32 per cent.

3 May   General election. Conservatives win: overall majority, 43: Conservatives 339 (43.9 per cent); Labour 268 (36.9 per cent); Liberals 11 (13.8 per cent).

Bibliography

Unpublished primary sources
    Private papers
    Online sources
    The National Archives (TNA)
    Labour History Archive and Study Centre
    Market and Opinion Research International/Ipsos MORI
    Trade union sources
    Australian collections
Published primary sources
    British parliamentary papers
    Diaries, autobiography, memoirs and biography
General studies
Articles and contributions to books
Biographical dictionaries
Interviews
Newspapers and periodicals
    National newspapers
    Provincial newspapers
    Australian and United States newspapers
    Journals and periodicals
Theses
Symposia
Radio recordings

Unpublished primary sources

Private papers

Lord James Callaghan (Bodleian Library, University of Oxford)
Cllr Johnny Davis (privately held)
Lord Bernard Donoughue (Churchill Archives, Cambridge)
Michael Foot (Labour Archive and Study Centre, Manchester)
Judith Hart (Labour Archive and Study Centre, Manchester)
Bob Hawke (Prime Ministerial Library, University of South Australia, Adelaide; The National Library of Australia, Canberra)
Lord David Owen (Sydney Jones Library, University of Liverpool)
Lord Peter Shore (British Library of Political Science, London)
Baroness Margaret Thatcher (Churchill Archives Centre, Cambridge); Margaret Thatcher Foundation

Online sources

www.margaretthatcher.org/document/102777
www.margaretthatcher.org/document/103105
www.margaretthatcher.org/document/103443
www.margaretthatcher.org/document/103764

The National Archives (TNA), Kew

CAB 128/63 Cabinet conclusions
CAB 128/64 Cabinet conclusions
CAB 128/65 Cabinet conclusions
DEFE 23/189 Aid to civil ministries
DEFE 23/789 Firemen's strike
DEFE 24/445 Contingency planning
DEFE 24/1780 Military aid: civil disputes
DEFE 24/1781 Military aid: oil tankers' dispute
PREM 16/1607 Economic policy
PREM 16/1609 Economic policy
PREM 16/1610 Economic strategy
PREM 16/1611 Economic policy
PREM 16/1612 Economic policy
PREM 16/1613 Economic policy
PREM 16/1621 Election timing
PREM 16/1667 'Forward look'
PREM 16/1702 Ford strike
PREM 16/1707 Oil tanker drivers' action
PREM 16/1708 Ford strike
PREM 16/1770 Nationalised industries
PREM 16/1777 Nationalised industries
PREM 16/2050 Guadeloupe summit
PREM 16/2123 Industrial action by Ford workers
PREM 16/2124 Oil tanker drivers' dispute
PREM 16/2127 Oil tanker drivers and road haulage disputes
PREM 16/2128 Road haulage strike
PREM 16/2188 Nationalised industries

Labour History Archive and Study Centre, Manchester

Judith Hart papers
Michael Foot papers
General correspondence
National Executive Committee minutes
Parliamentary Labour Party minutes
Basnett, David and Geoffrey Goodman, *Royal Commission on the Press: Minority Report*
    (London: Labour Party, 1977).
Report of the 75th Annual Conference of the Labour Party, Blackpool, 27 September–1 October
    1976.
Report of the 77th Annual Conference of the Labour Party, Blackpool, 2–6 October 1978.
Report of the 78th Annual Conference of the Labour Party, Brighton, 1–5 October 1979.
Report of the 110th Annual Trades Union Congress, Brighton, September 1978.
Report of the 111th Annual Trades Union Congress, Blackpool, September 1979.

Market and Opinion Research International/Ipsos MORI Head Office, London

Opinion polls and reports: Campaign Polling Presentations; British Public Opinion September
1978, November 1978, February 1979, March 1979 (general election) 1979; Public Opinion
in Marginal Constituencies 1978; Public Opinion in Marginal Constituencies January 1979;
Labour Party Candidates' and Agents' Assessment of the Election Campaign, 1979.

Trade union sources
Modern Records Centre, University of Warwick
Trade union papers and correspondence
NUPE reports
Winning the Battle Against Inflation, Cmnd 7293, July 1978

Working Class Movement Library, Salford
Black Socialist Alliance, *Why Black People Should Support the Ford Strike* (London: Black
    Socialist Alliance, 1978).
Newspaper collection
Trade union journals: GMWU/GMB; NUPE

Australian collections
Australian trade union and newspaper collections, Noel Butlin Trade Union Centre,
    Canberra.
Bob Hawke papers, trade union collection, National Library of Australia, Canberra.
Bob Hawke papers, Bob Hawke Prime Ministerial Library, University of Australia, Adelaide.

Published primary sources

British parliamentary papers
Parliamentary Debates, fifth series
*The Economy, the Government and Trade Union Responsibilities: Joint Statement by the TUC and
    the Government* (London: HMSO, February 1979).

Diaries, autobiography, memoirs and biography
Ashton, Joe, *Red Rose Blues: The Story of a Good Labour Man* (Basingstoke: Macmillan, 2000).
Barnett, Joel, *Inside the Treasury* (London: Andre Deutsch, 1982).
Bartram, Peter, *David Steel: His Life and Politics* (London: W. H. Allen, 1981).
Beckett, Clare, *Thatcher* (London: Haus, 2006).
Benn, Tony, *Out of the Wilderness: Diaries 1963–67* (London: Hutchinson, 1987).
Benn, Tony, *Conflicts of Interest: Diaries 1977–80*, edited by Ruth Winstone (London: Arrow
    Books, 1991).
Callaghan, James, *Time and Chance* (London: Politico's, 2006, first published 1987).
Campbell, John, *Margaret Thatcher, Volume One: The Grocer's Daughter* (London: Vintage,
    2007).
Campbell, John, *Margaret Thatcher, Volume Two: The Iron Lady* (London: Vintage, 2008).
Castle, Barbara, *Fighting All The Way* (London: Macmillan, 1993).
Cole, John, *As It Seemed To Me: Political Memoirs* (London: Weidenfeld & Nicolson, 1995).
Conroy, Harry, *Callaghan* (London: Haus, 2006).
Davies, Russell (ed.), *The Kenneth Williams Diaries* (London: Harper Collins, 1994).
Davies, Russell (ed.), *The Kenneth Williams Letters* (London: Harper Collins, 1994).
Day, Sir Robin, *Grand Inquisitor: Memoirs* (London: Weidenfeld & Nicolson, 1989).
Donoughue, Bernard, *The Heat of the Kitchen: An Autobiography* (London: Politico's, 2003).
Donoughue, Bernard, *Downing Street Diary: With Harold Wilson in No. 10* (London: Pimlico,
    2006).
Donoughue, Bernard, *Downing Street Diary, Volume Two: With James Callaghan in No. 10*
    (London: Jonathan Cape, 2008).
Edwardes, Michael, *Back from the Brink: An Apocalyptic Experience* (London: Collins, 1983).
Falkender, Marcia, *Downing Street in Perspective* (London: Weidenfeld & Nicolson, 1983).
Goodman, Geoffrey, *From Bevan to Blair: Fifty Years' Reporting From the Political Front Line*
    (London: Pluto Press, 2003).
Goodwin, John (ed.), *Peter Hall's Diaries: The Story of a Dramatic Battle* (London: Hamish
    Hamilton, 1983).
Graham, Lord, *From Tyne to Thames via 'The Usual Channels'* (Durham: Memoir Club,
    2005).

Haines, Joe, *Glimmers of Twilight* (London: Politico's, 2003).

Halcrow, Morrison, *Keith Joseph, A Single Mind* (London: Macmillan, 1989).

Hattersley, Roy, *Who Goes Home? Scenes from a Political Life* (London: Little, Brown, 1995).

Hattersley, Roy, *A Yorkshire Boyhood* (London: Little, Brown, 2001).

Hattersley, Roy, *David Lloyd George: The Great Outsider* (London: Little, Brown, 2010).

Healey, Denis, *The Time of My Life* (London: Penguin, 1990).

Heath, Edward, *The Course of My Life: My Autobiography* (London: Hodder & Stoughton, 1998).

Hollingsworth, Mark, *Tim Bell: The Ultimate Spin Doctor* (London: Hodder & Stoughton, 1997).

Hoskyns, John, *Just In Time: Inside the Thatcher Revolution* (London: Aurum Press, 2000).

Howe, Geoffrey, *Conflict of Loyalty* (London: Macmillan, 1994).

Howell, Denis, *Made in Birmingham: The Memoirs of Denis Howell* (London: Queen Anne Press, 1990).

Hurst, John, *Hawke PM* (London: Angus & Robertson, 1983).

Jones, Jack, *Union Man: The Autobiography of Jack Jones* (Abersychan: Warren & Bell, 2008).

Kaufman, Gerald, *How To Be a Minister* (London: Faber & Faber, 1980).

Lipsey, David, *In the Corridors of Power: An Autobiography* (London: Biteback Publishing, 2012).

Livingstone, Ken, *If Voting Changed Anything, They'd Abolish It* (London: Collins, 1987).

Livingstone, Ken, *You Can't Say That: Memoirs* (London: Faber & Faber, 2011).

Macshane, Denis, *Heath* (London: Haus, 2006).

Martineau, Lisa, *Politics and Power. Barbara Castle: A Biography* (London: Andre Deutsch, 2000).

Morgan, Kenneth O., *Callaghan: A Life* (Oxford: Oxford University Press, 1997).

Morgan, Kenneth O., *Michael Foot: A Life* (London: HarperCollins, 2007).

Neale, Jonathan, *Memoirs of a Callous Picket* (London: Pluto Press, 1983).

O'Farrell, John, *Things Can Only Get Better: Eighteen Miserable Years in the Life of a Labour Supporter* (London: Doubleday, 1998).

Owen, David, *Time to Declare* (London: Penguin, 1992).

Pearce, Edward, *Denis Healey: A Life in Our Times* (London: Little, Brown, 2002).

Perkins, Anne, *Red Queen: The Authorised Biography of Barbara Castle* (Basingstoke: Macmillan, 2003).

Prior, Jim, *A Balance of Power* (London: Hamish Hamilton, 1986).

Radice, Giles, *Friends and Rivals: Crosland, Jenkins and Healey* (London: Abacus, 2002).

Ridley, Nicholas, *'My Style of Government': The Thatcher Years* (London: Hutchinson, 1991).

Rodgers, Bill, *Fourth Among Equals* (London: Politico's, 2000).

Seldon, Anthony, with Chris Ballinger, Daniel Collings and Peter Snowden, *Blair* (London: Free Press, 2004).

Shepherd, John, *George Lansbury: At the Heart of Old Labour* (Oxford: Oxford University Press, 2004).

Shore, Peter, *Leading the Left* (London: Weidenfield & Nicolson, 1993).

Tebbitt, Norman, *Upwardly Mobile* (London: Weidenfield & Nicolson, 1988).

Thatcher, Margaret, *The Path to Power* (New York: HarperCollins, 1995).

Whitelaw, William, *The Whitelaw Memoirs* (London: Aurum Press, 1989).

Williams, Shirley, *Climbing the Bookshelves: The Autobiography* (London: Virago, 2009).

Yarwood, Mike, *Impressions of My Life* (London: Willow Books, 1986).

Young, Hugo, *One of Us: A Biography of Margaret Thatcher* (London: Pan Books, 1990).

Young, Hugo, *The Hugo Young Papers: A Journalist's Notes from the Heart of Politics*, edited by Ion Trewin (London: Penguin, 2009).

General studies

Adeney, Martin, *The Motor Makers: The Turbulent History of Britain's Car Industry* (London: Fontana, 1989).

Addison, Paul, *No Turning Back: The Peacetime Revolutions of Post-War Britain* (Oxford: Oxford University Press, 2010).

Addison, Paul and Harriet Jones (eds), *A Companion to Contemporary Britain, 1939–2000* (Oxford: Blackwell, 2007).

Allen, Joan, Alan Campbell and John McIlroy (eds), *Histories of Labour: National and International Perspectives* (Pontypool: Merlin Press, 2010).

Andrew, Christopher, *The Defence of the Realm: The Authorised History of MI5* (London: Allen Lane, 2009).

Artis, Michael and David Cobham (eds), *Labour's Economic Policies 1974–1979* (Manchester: Manchester University Press, 1991).

Auerbach, Simon, *Legislating for Conflict* (Oxford: Clarendon Press, 1990).

Bacon, Robert and Walter Ellis, *Britain's Economic Problem: Too Few Producers* (London: Macmillan, 1976).

Bailey, Victor, *Forged in Fire: The History of the Fire Brigades Union* (London: Lawrence & Wishart, 1992).

Baird, Marian, Keith Hancock and Joe Isaac (eds), *Work and Employment Relations: An Era of Change. Essays in Honour of Russell Lansbury* (Sydney: Federation Press, 2011).

Baldwin, Nick, *Lorries: 1890s to 1970s* (Oxford: Shire, 2010).

Ball, Stuart and Anthony Seldon (eds), *Recovering Power: The Conservatives in Opposition Since 1867* (Basingstoke: Palgrave Macmillan, 2005).

Bamber, Greg J. and Russell D. Lansbury (eds), *International and Comparative Industrial Relations: A Study of Industrialised Market Economies* (London: Routledge, 1993).

Barnes, Denis and Eileen Reid, *Governments and Trade Unions: The British Experience 1964–79* (London: Heinemann, 1980).

Beckett, Andy, *When the Lights Went Out: What Really Happened to Britain in the Seventies* (London: Faber & Faber, 2009).

Beer, Samuel H., *Britain Against Itself: The Political Contradictions of Collectivism* (New York: W. W. Norton, 1982).

Beers, Laura, *Your Britain: Media and the Making of the Labour Party* (Cambridge, MA: Harvard University Press, 2009.

Bennett, Gill, *A Most Extraordinary and Mysterious Business: The Zinoviev Letter of 1924* (London: Foreign and Commonwealth Office, 1999).

Beynon, Huw, *Working for Ford* (Harmondsworth: Penguin, 1984).

Bingham, Adrian, *Family Newspapers? Sex, Private Life and the British Popular Press, 1918–1978* (Oxford: Oxford University Press, 2009).

Black, Lawrence, Hugh Pemberton and Pat Thane (eds), *Reassessing 1970s Britain* (Manchester: Manchester University Press, 2013).

Black Socialist Alliance, *Why Black People Should Support the Ford Strike* (London: Black Socialist Alliance, 1978).

Blair, Tony, *New Britain: My Vision of a Young Country* (London: Basic Books, 1994).

Bogdanor, Victor (ed.), *From New Jerusalem to New Labour: British Prime Ministers from Attlee to Blair* (Basingstoke: Palgrave Macmillan, 2010).

Booth, Cherie and Cate Haste, *The Goldfish Bowl: Married to the Prime Minister 1955–1997* (London: Vintage, 2005).

Bosanquet, Nick and Peter Townsend (eds), *Labour and Equality: A Fabian Study of Labour in Power, 1974–79* (London: Heinemann, 1980).

Brivati, Brian and Richard Hefferman, *The Labour Party: A Centenary History* (London: Macmillan, 2000).

Broughton, David, David M. Farrell, David Denver and Colin Rallings (eds), *British Elections and Parties Yearbook 1994* (London: Frank Cass, 1995).

Brown, William (ed.), *The Changing Contours of British Industrial Relations* (Oxford: Basil Blackwell, 1981).

Burk, Kathleen and Alec Cairncross, *Goodbye, Great Britain: The 1976 IMF Crisis* (New Haven, CT: Yale University Press, 1992).

Butler, David and Dennis Kavanagh, *The British General Election of 1979* (London: Macmillan, 1980).

Butler, David and Dennis Kavanagh, *The British General Election of 1983* (London: Macmillan, 1984).

Butler, David and Anne Sloman, *British Political Facts, 1900–1979* (London: Macmillan, 1980).

Carpenter, Mick, *Working for Health: The History of the Confederation of Health Service Employees* (London: Lawrence & Wishart, 1988).

Charlesworth, David, David Gilbert, Adrian Randall, Humphrey Southall and Chris Wrigley, *An Atlas of Industrial Protest in Britain 1750–1990* (London: Macmillan, 1996).

Clinton, Alan, *Post Office Workers: A Trade Union and Social History* (London: George Allen & Unwin, 1984).

Coates, David, *Labour in Power? A Study of the Labour Government, 1974–1979* (London: Longman, 1980).

Cockerell, Michael, *Live From Number Ten: The Inside Story of Prime Ministers and Television* (London: Faber & Faber, 1988).

Cole, John, *The Thatcher Years: A Decade of Revolution in British Politics* (London: BBC Books, 1987).

Conservative Research Department, *The Unjust and Arbitrary Use of Sanctions on Industry* (London: Conservative Research Department, 1978).

Coopey, Richard, and Nicholas Woodward (eds), *Britain in the 1970s: The Troubled Economy* (London: University College London Press, 1996).

Crafts, Nicholas, Ian Gazeley and Andrew Newell, *Work and Pay in Twentieth-Century Britain* (Oxford: Oxford University Press, 2007).

Crewe, Ivor and Brian Gosschalk (eds), *Political Communications: The General Election Campaign of 1992* (Cambridge: Cambridge University Press, 1992).

Cronin, James E., *New Labour's Pasts: The Labour Party and Its Discontents* (London: Pearson, 2004).

Cunnison, Sheila and Jane Stageman, *Feminizing the Unions* (Aldershot: Avebury, 1993).

Curran, James and Jean Seaton, *Power Without Responsibility: The Press and Broadcasting in Britain* (London: Routledge, 1997).

Dale, Iain (ed.), *Conservative Party General Election Manifestos 1900–1997* (London: Routledge and Politico's Publishing, 2000).

Dalyell, Tam, *Devolution: The End of Britain?* (London: Cape, 1977).

Darlington, Ralph and Dave Lyddon, *Glorious Summer: Class Struggle in Britain 1972* (London: Bookmarks, 2001).

Denham, Andrew and Mark Garnett, *British Think-Tanks and the Climate of Opinion* (London: University College London Press, 1998).

Deveney, Paul J., *Callaghan's Journey to Downing Street* (Basingstoke: Palgrave Macmillan, 2010).

Dix, Bernard and Stephen Williams, *Serving the Public – Building the Union: The History of the National Union of Public Employees* (London: Lawrence & Wishart, 1987).

Donoughue, Bernard, *Prime Minister: The Conduct of Policy Under Harold Wilson and James Callaghan* (London: Jonathan Cape, 1987).

Dorey, Peter, *The Conservative Party and the Trade Unions* (London: Routledge, 1995).

Dorey, Peter, *Wage Politics in Britain: The Rise and Fall of Incomes Policies Since 1945* (Brighton: Sussex Academic Press, 2001).

Dromey, Jack and Graham Taylor, *Grunwick: The Workers Story* (London: Lawrence & Wishart, 1978).

Drucker, H. M. and Gordon Brown, *The Politics of Nationalism and Devolution* (London: Longman, 1980).

Dunnett, Peter J. S., *The Decline of the British Motor Industry: The Effects of Government Policy, 1945–1979* (London: Croom Helm, 1980).

Elliott, Larry and Dan Atkinson, *Going South: Why Britain Will Have a Third World Economy by 2014* (Basingstoke: Palgrave Macmillan, 2012).

English, Richard and Michael Kenny (eds), *Rethinking British Decline* (London: Macmillan, 2000).

Evans, Brendan, *Thatcherism and British Politics 1975–1999* (Stroud: Sutton Publishing, 1999).

Fallon, Ivan, *The Brothers: The Rise and Rise of Saatchi & Saatchi* (London: Hutchinson, 1988).

Ferguson, Niall, Charles S. Maier, Erez Manela and Daniel J. Sargent (eds), *The Shock of the Global: The 1970s in Perspective* (Cambridge, MA: Belknapp Press of Harvard University Press, 2010).

Field, Frank, *Rising Tide of Poverty: A Challenge to the Political Parties*, Low Pay Paper No. 25 (London: Low Pay Unit, September 1978)

Fielding, Steven, *Labour: Decline and Renewal* (Manchester: Baseline Books, 1995).

Friedman, Henry and Sander Mereedeen, *The Dynamics of Industrial Conflict: Lessons from Ford* (London: Croom Helm, 1980).

Fryer, Bob and Steve Williams, *A Century of Service: An Illustrated History of the National Union of Public Employees, 1889–1993* (London: Lawrence & Wishart, 1993).

Gamble, Andrew and Tony Wright, *Britishness: Perspectives on the British Question* (Brighton: Wiley-Blackwell, 2009).

Geddes, Andrew and Jonathan Tonge (eds), *Labour's Landslide: The British General Election 1997* (Manchester: Manchester University Press, 1997).

General Synod Board for Social Responsibility, *Winters of Discontent: Industrial Conflict. A Christian Perspective* (London: CIO Publishing, n.d. but 1981).

Gould, Philip, *The Unfinished Revolution* (London: Abacus, 1999).

Gourvish, Terry and Alan O'Day (eds), *Britain Since 1945* (Basingstoke: Macmillan, 1991).

Grant, John, *Blood Brothers: The Division and Decline of Britain's Trade Unions* (London: Weidenfield & Nicolson, 1992).

Greenslade, Roy, *Press Gang: How Newspapers Make Profits From Propaganda* (Basingstoke: Macmillan, 2003).

Grundy, Bill, *The Press Inside Out* (London: W. H. Allen, 1985).

Harvie, Christopher, *No Gods and Precious Few Heroes: Scotland 1914–1980* (London: Edward Arnold, 1981).

Hattersley, Roy, *Fifty Years On: A Prejudiced History of Britain Since the War* (London: Abacus, 1998).

Hattersley, Roy, *The Edwardians* (London: Abacus, 2007).

Hattersley, Roy, *Borrowed Time* (London: Abacus, 2009).

Hayter, Dianne, *Fightback! Labour's Traditional Right in the 1970s and 1980s* (Manchester: Manchester University Press, 2005).

Hendy, John, *A Law Unto Themselves. Conservative Employment Laws: A National and International Assessment* (London: Institute of Employment Rights, 1993).

Hilson, Mary, *The Nordic Model: Scandinavia Since 1945* (London: Reaktion Books, 2008).

Hobsbawm, Eric, *The Forward March of Labour Halted?* (London: Verso, 1981).

Holland, Stuart, *The Socialist Challenge* (London: Quartet Books, 1975).

Holmes, Martin, *The Labour Government, 1974–79: Political Aims and Economic Reality* (London: Macmillan, 1985).

Howell, Chris, *Trade Unions and the State: The Construction of Industrial Relations in Britain 1890–2000* (Princeton, MA: Princeton University Press, 2007).

Hyman, Peter, *1 Out of 10: From Downing Street Vision to Classroom Reality* (London: Vintage, 2005).

Hyman, Richard, *Strikes* (Glasgow: Fontana, 1972).

Ironside, Mike and Roger Seifert, *Facing up to Thatcherism: The History of NALGO 1979–93* (Oxford: Oxford University Press, 2000).

Jackson, Tim, *Chasing Progress: Beyond Measuring Economic Growth* (London: New Economic Foundation, 2004).

Jacques, Martin and Francis Mulhern (eds), *The Forward March of Labour Halted?* (London: Verso, in association with Marxism Today, 1981).

Jeffery, Keith and Peter Hennessy, *States of Emergency: British Governments and Strike Breaking Since 1919* (London: Routledge & Kegan Paul, 1983).

Jones, Nicholas, *The Control Freaks: How New Labour Gets Its Own Way* (London: Politico's, 2001).

Joseph, Sir Keith, *Solving the Union Problems Is the Key to Britain's Recovery* (London: Centre for Policy Studies, 1979).

Kaufman, Gerald, *How To Be a Minister* (London: Faber & Faber, second edition 1997).

Kavanagh, Dennis and Anthony Seldon (eds), *The Thatcher Effect* (Oxford: Clarendon Press, 1989).

Kavanagh, Dennis and Anthony Seldon (eds), *The Major Effect* (London: Macmillan, 1994).

Kelly, Michael P., *White-Collar Proletariat: The Industrial Behaviour of British Civil Servants* (London: Routledge, 1980),

Kelly, Paul, *The Hawke Ascendancy: A Definitive Account of Its Origins and Climax 1975–1983* (London: Angus & Robertson, 1984).

Kelly, Paul, *The End of Certainty: The Story of the 1980s* (St Leonards: Allen & Unwin, 1992).

Kessler, Sid and Fred Bayliss, *Contemporary British Industrial Relations* (Basingstoke: Macmillan, 1998).

Kettley, John, *Weatherman* (Ilkley: Great Northern, 2009).

King Anthony (ed.), *The British Prime Minister* (Basingstoke: Macmillan, 1985).

King, Anthony, Ivor Crewe, David Denver, Kenneth Newton, Philip Norton, David Sanders and Patrick Seyd, *Britain at the Polls, 1992* (New York: Chatham House, 1993).

Kramnick, Isaac (ed.), *Is Britain Dying? Perspectives on the Current Crisis* (Ithaca, NY: Cornell University Library, 1979).

Kynaston, David, *The Financial Times: A Centenary History* (London: Viking, 1988).

Lamb, Larry, *Sunrise: The Remarkable Rise and Rise of the Best-Selling Soar-Away Sun* (London: Papermac, 1989).

Le Cheminant, Peter, *Beautiful Ambiguities: An Inside View of the Heart of Government* (London: Radcliffe Press, 2001).

Lipsey, David and Dick Leonard (eds), *The Socialist Agenda: Crosland's Legacy* (London: Jonathan Cape, 1981).

Ludlam, Steve and Martin J. Smith, *New Labour in Government* (Basingstoke: Macmillan, 2001).

Mailly, R., S. J. Dimmock and A. S. Sethi (eds), *Industrial Relations in the Public Services* (London: Routledge, 1989).

Marriott, Ray, *Limping and Waddling to the Revolution: A Memoir of Colin Barnett* (Kirkby Stephen: Hayloft, 2007).

Marsh, David, *The New Politics of British Trade Unionism: Union Power and the Thatcher Legacy* (Basingstoke: Macmillan, 1992).

Mathews, John, *Ford Strike: The Workers' Story* (London: Panther, 1972).

McCaskill, Ian and Paul Hudson, *Frozen in Time: The Years When Britain Shivered* (Ilkley: Great Northern, 2006).

McIlroy, John, Nina Fishman and Alan Campbell (eds), *The High Tide of British Trade Unionism: Trade Unions and Industrial Politics, 1964–79* (Monmouth: Merlin Press, second edition 2007).

McSmith, Andy, *No Such Thing As Society: A History of Britain in the 1980s* (London: Constable, 2010).

Meyer, Henning and Jonathan Rutherford, *The Future of European Social Democracy: Building the Good Society* (Basingstoke: Palgrave Macmillan, 2012).

Middlemas, Keith, *Politics in Industrial Society: The Experience of the British System Since 1911* (London: Andre Deutsch, 1979).

Millar, Ronald, *A View From The Wings: West End, West Coast, Westminster* (London: Weidenfeld & Nicolson, 1993).

Miller, William L., *The End of British Politics? Scots and English Political Behaviour in the Seventies* (Oxford: Clarendon Press, 1981).

Minkin, Lewis, *The Labour Party Conference: A Study in the Politics of Intra-Party Democracy* (Manchester: Manchester University Press, 1980).

Minkin, Lewis, *The Contentious Alliance: Trade Unions and the Labour Party* (Edinburgh: Edinburgh University Press, 1991).

Mitchell, Austin, *Four Years in the Death of the Labour Party* (London: Methuen, 1983).

Mitchie, Andy and Simon Hoggart, *The Pact: The Inside Story of the Lib–Lab Government, 1977–8* (London: Quartet Books, 1978).

Morgan, Kenneth O., *Labour in Power 1945–51* (Oxford: Oxford University Press, 1984).

Morgan, Kenneth O., *Labour People: Leaders and Lieutenants* (Oxford: Oxford University Press, 1987).

Morris, Gillian S., *Strikes in Essential Services* (London: Mansell, 1986).

National Union of Public Employees, *Union Wages Strategy 1978–79* (London: NUPE, 1978).

National Union of Public Employees, Northern Division, *Together We Can Win: The Story of Two NUPE Branches Involved in the Council and Hospital Workers Pay Dispute Winter 1978/79* (Newcastle upon Tyne: NUPE, 1979).

Nossiter, Bernard D., *A Future That Works* (London: Andre Deutsch, 1978).

Owen, David, *In Sickness and in Power: Illness in Heads of Government During the Last 100 Years* (London: Methuen, 2008).

Packard, Vance, *Hidden Persuaders* (Harmondsworth: Penguin, 1981).

Peak, Steve, *Troops in Strikes: Military Intervention in Industrial Disputes* (London: Cobden Trust, 1984).

Penniman, Howard R. (ed.), *Britain at the Polls, 1979: A Study of the General Election* (Washington, DC: American Enterprise Institute, 1981).

Peston, Robert, *Who Runs Britain?* (London: Hodder & Stoughton, 2008).

Pimlott, Ben and Chris Cook (eds), *Trade Unions in British Politics* (Harlow: Longman, 1982).

Piven, Frances Fox (ed.), *Labour Parties in Post-Industrial Societies* (Oxford: Oxford University Press, 1992).

Plant Raymond, Matt Beech and Kevin Hickson (eds), *The Struggle for Labour's Soul: Understanding Labour's Political Thought Since 1945* (London: Routledge, 2004).

Price, Lance, *Where the Power Lies: Prime Ministers v. the Media* (London: Simon & Schuster, 2010).

Pugh, Martin, *Speak for Britain: A New History of the Labour Party* (London: Bodley Head, 2010).

Rallings, Colin (ed.), *British Elections and Parties Yearbook 1994* (London: Frank Cass, 1995).

Ramdin, Ron, *The Making of the Black Working Class in Britain* (Aldershot: Wildwood House, 1987).

Raw, Louise, *Striking a Light: The Bryant and May Matchwomen and Their Place in History* (London: Continuum, 2011).

Richards, Huw, *The Bloody Circus: The Daily Herald and the Left* (London: Pluto Press, 1999).

Richardson, John E., *Analysing Newspapers: An Approach from Critical Discourse Analysis* (Basingstoke: Palgrave Macmillan, 2007).

Riddell, Peter, *The Thatcher Government* (Oxford: Basil Blackwell, 1985).

Riddell, Peter, *The Thatcher Decade* (Oxford: Basil Blackwell, 1989).

Rosen, Greg, *Serving the People: Co-operative Party History From Fred Perry to Gordon Brown* (London: Co-operative Party, n.d.).

Rosen, Greg, *Old Labour to New: The Dreams That Inspired, The Battles That Divided* (London: Politico's, 2005).

Sandbrook, Dominic, *State of Emergency. The Way We Were: Britain, 1970–1974* (London: Allen Lane, 2010).

Sandbrook, Dominic, *Seasons in the Sun: The Battle for Britain, 1974–1979* (London: Allen Lane, 2012).

Sarlvik, Bo and Ivor Crewe, *Decade of Dealignment: The Conservative Victory of 1979 and Electoral Trends in the 1970s* (Cambridge: Cambridge University Press, 1983).

Scott, Andrew, *Running on Empty: 'Modernising' the British and Australian Labour Parties* (Annandale: Pluto Press, 2000).

Seaton, Jean and Ben Pimlott, *The Media in British Politics* (Aldershot: Avebury, 1987).

Sejersted, Francis, *The Age of Social Democracy: Norway and Sweden in the Twentieth Century* (Princeton, MA: Princeton University Press, 2011).

Seldon, Anthony, *How Tory Governments Fall: The Tory Party in Power Since 1783* (London: Fontana Press, 1996).

Seldon, Anthony, *The Blair Effect: The Blair Government 1997–2001* (London: Little, Brown, 2001).

Seldon, Anthony (ed.), *Blair's Britain, 1997–2007* (Cambridge: Cambridge University Press, 2007).

Seldon, Anthony and Stuart Ball, *Conservative Century: The Conservative Party Since 1900* (Oxford: Oxford University Press, 1994).

Seldon, Anthony and Kevin Hickson (eds), *New Labour, Old Labour: The Wilson and Callaghan Governments, 1974–1979* (London: Routledge, 2004).

Shaw, Eric, *The Labour Party Since 1979: Crisis and Transformation* (London: Routledge, 1994).

Shepherd, Janet and John Shepherd, *1970s Britain* (Oxford: Shire, 2010).

Shepherd, John and Keith Laybourn, *Britain's First Labour Government* (Basingstoke: Palgrave Macmillan, 2006).

Singleton, Gwynneth, *The Accord and the Australian Labour Movement* (Carlton: Melbourne University Press, 1990).

Smith, Justin Davis, *The Atlee and Churchill Administrations and Industrial Unrest, 1945–1955* (London: Pinter, 1990).

Smith, Paul, *Unionization and Union Leadership: The Road Haulage Industry* (London: Continuum, 2001).

Steel, David, *A House Divided: The Lib–Lab Pact and the Future of British Politics* (London: Weidenfeld and Nicholson, 1980).

Tanner, Duncan, Pat Thane and Nick Tiratsoo (eds), *Labour's First Century* (Cambridge: Cambridge University Press, 2000).

Taylor, Andrew J., *The Trade Unions and the Labour Party* (Beckenham: Croom Helm, 1987).

Taylor, Robert, *Labour and the Social Contract*, Fabian Tract no. 458 (London: Fabian Society, 1978).

Taylor, Robert, *The Fifth Estate: Britain's Unions in the Modern World* (London: Pan, 1980).

Taylor, Robert, *The Trade Union Question in British Politics: Government and Unions Since 1945* (Oxford: Blackwell, 1993).

Taylor, Robert, *The TUC: From the General Strike to New Unionism* (Basingstoke: Palgrave, 2000).

Thatcher, Margaret, *Speeches to the Conservative Party Conference 1975–1988* (London: Conservative Political Centre, 1989).

Thomas, James, *Popular Newspapers, the Labour Party and British Politics* (Abingdon: Routledge, 2005).

Thornett, Alan, *From Militancy to Marxism: A Personal and Political Account of Organising Car Workers* (London: Left View, 1987).

Thornett, Alan, *Inside Cowley. Trade Union Struggle in the 1970s: Who Really Opened the Door to the Tory Onslaught?* (London: Porcupine Press, 1998).

Thorpe, Anthony, *A History of the Labour Party* (Basingstoke: Macmillan, 1997).

Times Guide to the House of Commons 1979 (London: Times Books, 1979).

Tiratsoo, Nick (ed.), *From Blitz to Blair* (London: Orion, 1998).

Tomlinson, Jim, *The Politics of Decline* (London: Longman, 2000).

Towers, Brian and William Brown, *Employment Relations in Britain: 25 Years of the Advisory, Conciliation and Arbitration Service* (Oxford: Blackwell, 2000).

Trades Union Congress, *A Cause for Concern: Media Coverage of Industrial Disputes, January and February 1979* (London: TUC Publications, 1979).

Tunney, Sean, *Labour and the Press: From New Left to New Labour* (Brighton: Sussex Academic Press, 2007).

Tunstall, Jeremy, *The Media in Britain* (London: Constable, 1983).

Turner, Alwyn W., *Crisis? What Crisis? Britain in the 1970s* (London: Aurum Press, 2008).

Vinen, Richard, *Thatcher's Britain* (London: Simon & Schuster, 2009).

Ward, George, *Fort Grunwick* (London: Maurice Temple Smith, 1977).

Ward, Paul, *Red Flag and Union Jack* (London: Royal Historical Society, 1998).

Ward, Paul, *Britishness Since 1870* (London: Routledge, 2004).

Whitehead, Philip, *The Writing on the Wall: Britain in the Seventies* (London: Michael Joseph, 1985).

Whitlam, Gough, *The Truth of the Matter* (Harmondsworth: Penguin, 1979).

Wickham-Jones, Mark, *Economic Strategy and the Labour Party: Politics and Policy-Making, 1970–83* (London: Macmillan, 1996).

Wilks, Stephen, *Industrial Policy and the Motor Industry* (Manchester: Manchester University Press, 1988).

Williams, Stephen and Robert H. Fryer, *Leadership and Democracy: The History of the National Union of Public Employees. Volume Two, 1928–1993* (London: Lawrence & Wishart, 2011).

Wood, Jonathan, *The British Motor Industry* (Oxford: Shire, 2010).

Worcester, Robert M. and Martin Harrop (eds), *Political Communications: The General Election Campaign of 1979* (London: George Allen & Unwin, 1982).

Wrigley, Chris (ed.), *A History of British Industrial Relations, 1939–1979: Industrial Relations in a Declining Economy* (Cheltenham: Edward Elgar, 1996).

Wrigley, Chris (ed.), *A History of British Industrial Relations: vol. 3, 1939–79* (Brighton: Harvester Press, 1996).

Wrigley, Chris, *British Trade Unions, 1945–1995* (Manchester: Manchester University Press, 1997).

Wrigley, Chris, *British Trade Unions Since 1933* (Cambridge: Cambridge University Press, 2002).

Wring, Dominic, *The Politics of Marketing the Labour Party* (Basingstoke: Palgrave Macmillan, 2005).

Articles and contributions to books

Aitken, Ian, 'The island summit in the full glare of privacy', *Guardian*, 4 January 1979.

Auerbach, Simon, 'Mrs Thatcher's labour laws: slouching towards utopia?', *Political Quarterly*, vol. 64, no. 1, January–March 1993, p. 37.

Bassett, Philip, 'Turning point in industrial relations', *Financial Times*, 15 February 1988.

Bell, Tim, 'The Conservatives' advertising campaign', in Robert M. Worcester and Martin Harrop (eds), *Political Communications: The General Election Campaign of 1979* (London: George Allen & Unwin, 1982), pp. 12–25.

Bilton, Michael and Sheldon Himmelfarb, 'Fleet Street', in David Butler and Dennis Kavanagh (eds), *The British General Election of 1979* (London: Macmillan, 1980).

Black, Lawrence and Hugh Pemberton, 'Reassessing the seventies: the benighted decade', *British Academy Review*, issue 14, November 2009.

Black, Lawrence and Hugh Pemberton, 'The winter of discontent in British politics', *Political Quarterly*, vol. 80, no. 4, October–December 2009, pp. 553–61.

Blair, Tony, 'Unions 1994 conference, London, 19 November 1994', in Tony Blair, *New Britain: My Vision of a Young Country* (London: Basic Books, 1994).

Blair, Tony, 'We won't look back to the 1970s', *The Times*, 31 March 1997.

Booth, Janine, 'Albert Booth 1928–2010: an "Old Labour" man', *Worker's Liberty*, 18 February 2010.

Brown, William, 'Industrial relations', in Michael Artis and David Cobham (eds), *Labour's Economic Policies 1974–79* (Manchester: Manchester University Press, 1991), pp. 213–16.

Burgess, Simon and Geoffrey Alderman, Centre for Political Studies: the influence of Sir Alfred Sherman', *Contemporary Record*, vol. 4, no. 2, November 1990, pp. 14–15.

Clark, George, 'The nation's choice: a Conservative woman Prime Minister', in *Times Guide to the House of Commons, May 1979* (London: Times Books, 1979).

Clegg, Hugh, 'How public sector pay systems have gone wrong before', in John Gretton and Anthony Harrison (eds), *How Much Are Public Servants Worth?* (Oxford: Basil Blackwell, 1982), pp. 7–8.

Cockerell, Michael, 'Reece, Sir (James) Gordon (1929–2001)', in Lawrence Goldman (ed.), *Oxford Dictionary of National Biography 2001–2004* (Oxford: Oxford University Press, 2009).

Coote, Anna, 'Strike havoc probed', *New Statesman*, 26 January 1979.

Crewe, Ivor, 'The voting surveyed', in *The Times Guide to the House of Commons May 1979* (London: Times Books, 1979).

Crewe, Ivor, 'Why the Conservatives won', in Howard R. Penniman (ed.), *Britain at the Polls, 1979: A Study of the General Election* (Washington, DC: American Enterprise Institute for Public Policy Research, 1981).

Dalyell, Tam, 'Albert Booth: principled Labour MP who served as Secretary of State under James Callaghan', *Independent*, 11 February 2010.

Delaney, Tim, 'Labour's advertising campaign', in Robert M. Worcester and Martin Harrop
    (eds), *Political Communications: The General Election Campaign of 1979* (London: George
    Allen & Unwin, 1982), pp. 27–31.
Donoughue, Bernard, 'The conduct of economic policy 1974–79', in Anthony King (ed.),
    The British Prime Minister (Basingstoke: Macmillan, 1985), pp. 70–1.
Dorey, Peter, 'Between principle, pragmatism and practicability: the development of
    Conservative Party policy towards the trade unions in opposition, 1974–1979', in David
    Broughton, David M. Farrell, David Denver and Colin Rallings (eds), *British Elections
    and Parties Yearbook 1994* (London: Frank Cass, 1995), pp. 29–44.
Ferguson, Niall, 'Introduction. Crisis? What crisis? The 1970s and the shock of the global',
    in Niall Ferguson, Charles S. Maier, Erez Manela and Danile J. Sargent (eds), *The
    Shock of the Global: The 1970s in Perspective* (Cambridge, MA: Belknap Press of Harvard
    University Press, 2010), pp. 1–24.
Fielding, Steven, 'The 1974–79 governments and "New Labour"', in Anthony Seldon and
    Kevin Hickson (eds), *New Labour, Old Labour: The Wilson and Callaghan Governments,
    1974–79* (London: Routledge, 2004), pp. 286–7.
Forrester, Tom, 'The bottom of the heap', *New Society*, 18 January 1979, pp. 125–6.
Fountain, Nigel, 'A long, hot winter', *Guardian*, 25 September 1993, pp. 18–19, 22.
Fryer, Robert H., 'Public service trade unionism in the twentieth century', in R. Mailly,
    S. J. Dimmock and A. S. Sethi (eds), *Industrial Relations in the Public Services* (London:
    Routledge, 1989), pp. 47–8.
Fryer, Robert H. and Stephen Williams, 'Dix, Bernard Hubert (1925–1995)', in Keith
    Gildart and David Howell (eds), *Dictionary of Labour Biography* (Basingstoke: Palgrave
    Macmillan, 2010), vol. 13, pp. 88–108.
Gennard, John, 'Chronicle. Industrial relations in the United Kingdom November 1978–
    March 1979', *British Journal of Industrial Relations*, vol. 22, no. 2, July 1984, pp. 268–79.
Goodman, Geoffrey, 'The impact of the media on industrial relations', *Personnel Management*,
    vol. 11, no. 3, October 1979, pp. 44–7.
Goodman, Geoffrey, 'The role of the industrial correspondents', in John McIlroy, Nina
    Fishman and Alan Campbell (eds), *British Trade Unions and Industrial Politics. Volume One:
    The Postwar Compromise, 1945–64* (Aldershot: Ashgate, 1999), pp. 23–36.
Harrison, Brian, 'Joseph, Keith Sinjohn. Baron Joseph (1918–1994)', in H. C. G. Mathew
    and Brian Harrison (eds), *Oxford Dictionary of National Biography* (Oxford: Oxford
    University Press, 2004).
Harper, Keith, 'The justified grievances of Britain's low-paid workers', *Guardian*, 2 January
    1979.
Hattersley, Roy, 'Callaghan, Leonard James (Jim). Baron Callaghan of Cardiff (1912–2005),
    prime minister', in Lawrence Goldman (ed.), *Oxford Dictionary of National Biography
    2001–2004* (Oxford: Oxford University Press, 2009).
Hay, Colin, 'Narrating crisis: the discursive construction of the winter of discontent',
    Sociology, vol. 30, no. 2, 1996, pp. 253–77.
Hay, Colin, 'The winter of discontent thirty years on', *Political Quarterly*, vol. 80, no. 4,
    October–December 2009, pp. 545–52.
Hay, Colin, 'Chronicles of a death foretold: the winter of discontent and construction of the
    crisis of British Keynesianism', *Parliamentary Affairs*, vol. 63, no. 3, July 2012, pp. 446–70.
Hitchens, Christopher, 'The *Daily Mail* does it again', *New Statesman*, 2 February 1979, p. 136.
Hitchens, Christopher, '"Ghost" writing at the *Daily Mail*', *New Statesman*, 9 February 1979.
Institute of Contemporary British History, 'Symposium: the winter of discontent',
    Contemporary Review, vol. 1, no. 3, autumn 1987, pp. 34–43.
Jacques, Martin, 'The Ford strike: where does it take us? An interview with Dan Connor',
    Marxism Today, February 1979, p. 34.
Jenkins, Simon, 'Why *The Times* and *Sunday Times* vanished', *Encounter*, August 1979, pp.
    59–69.
Jordan, David, 'Five year's hard labour', *Low Pay Bulletin*, April/June 1979, p. 2.
Kavanagh, David, 'The making of Thatcherism 1974–1979', in Stuart Bell and Anthony
    Seldon (eds), *Recovering Power: The Conservatives in Opposition Since 1867* (Basingstoke:
    Palgrave Macmillan, 2005), pp. 219–41.

Keegan, William, 'The old bruiser who remained the boy next door', *Observer*, 3 December 2006.

Kellner, Peter, 'Not a defeat, a disaster', *New Statesman*, 18 May 1979.

Kellner, Peter and Robert M. Worcester, 'Electoral perceptions of media stance', in Robert M. Worcester and Martin Harrop (eds), *Political Communications: The General Election Campaign of 1979* (London: George Allen & Unwin, 1982), pp. 57–9.

King, Anthony, 'The people's flag has turned deepest blue', *Observer*, 6 May 1979.

Lancaster, Terence, 'Jim: why I'll carry on', *Daily Mirror*, 8 September 1978.

Langdon, Julia, 'Albert Booth obituary: MP and Employment Secretary in James Callaghan's cabinet', *Guardian*, 10 February 2010.

Law, Christopher M., 'The geography of industrial rationalisation: the British motor car assembly industry, 1972–1982', *Geography*, vol. 70, no. 1, January 1985, pp. 1–6.

Leonard, Dick, 'The Labour campaign', in Howard R. Penniman (ed.), *Britain at the Polls, 1979: A Study of the General Election* (Washington, DC: American Enterprise Institute for Public Policy Research, 1981), pp. 95–116.

Ludlam, Steve, 'The gnomes of Washington: four myths of the 1976 IMF crisis', *Political Studies*, vol. 40, 1992, pp. 713–27.

Ludlam, Steve, '"Old" Labour and the "winter of discontent"', *Politics Review*, vol. 9, no. 2, 2000, pp. 30–3.

Ludlam, Steve, 'Too much pluralism, not enough socialism: interpreting the unions–party link', in John Callaghan, Steve Fielding and Steve Ludlam (eds), *Interpreting the Labour Party: Approaches to Labour, Politics and History* (Manchester: Manchester University Press, 2003), pp. 150–65.

Lyddon, Dave, 'The car industry, 1945–79: shop stewards and workplace unionism', in Chris Wrigley (ed.), *A History of British Industrial Relations, 1939–1979: Industrial Relations in a Declining Economy* (Cheltenham: Edward Elgar, 1996), pp. 198–202.

Martin, Tara, 'The beginning of Labor's end? Britain's "winter of discontent" and working-class women's activism', *International Labor and Working-Class History*, no. 75, spring 2009, pp. 49–67.

McCarthy, William and C. S. Nicholls, 'Fisher, Alan Wainwright (1922–1988)', in H. C. G. Mathew and Brian Harrison (eds), *Oxford Dictionary of National Biography* (Oxford: Oxford University Press, 2004).

McKibbin, Ross, 'Homage to Wilson and Callaghan', *London Review of Books*, vol. 19, no. 7, 3 April 1997.

McKie, David, '"Fact is free but comment is sacred"; or was it *The Sun* wot won it?', in Ivor Crewe and Brian Gosschalk (eds), *Political Communications: The General Election Campaign of 1992* (Cambridge: Cambridge University Press, 1992), pp. 121–36.

Meacher, Michael, 'Was it really the winter of discontent that cost Labour the election?', *Tribune*, 18 May 1979.

Middleton, Drew, 'Major issue at Guadeloupe: U.S. stand on NATO defense', *New York Times*, 5 January 1979.

Mitchell, Austin, 'A night to remember. More like a night to forget', *House Magazine*, vol. 18, no. 612, 1993.

Morgan, Kenneth O., 'James Callaghan, 1976–1979', in Vernon Bogdanor (ed.), *From Jerusalem to New Labour: British Prime Ministers from Attlee to Blair* (Basingstoke: Palgrave Macmillan, 2010), pp. 123–43.

Morgan, Kenneth O., 'Was Britain dying?', in Anthony Seldon and Kevin Hickson (eds), *New Labour, Old Labour: The Wilson and Callaghan Governments, 1974–1979* (London: Routledge, 2004), pp. 303–7.

Newton, Kenneth, 'Caring and competence: the long, long campaign', in Anthony King, Ivor Crewe, David Denver, Kenneth Newton, Philip Norton, David Sanders and Patrick Seyd, *Britain at the Polls, 1992* (New York: Chatterton House, 1992).

Norton, Philip, 'Parliament', in Anthony Seldon and Kevin Hickson (eds), *New Labour, Old Labour: The Wilson and Callaghan Governments, 1974–1979* (London: Routledge, 2004), pp. 190–206.

Nossiter, Bernard D., 'British strikes risk greater inflation, end of Labor rule', *Washington Post*, 25 January 1979, p. A17.

Nossiter, Bernard D., 'The battle of Britain', *Washington Post*, 28 January 1979, p. C3.

Owen, David, 'Stick to your principles and damn your party', *New Statesman*, 24 January 2011.

Pond, Chris, 'The unacceptable face of Labour's pay policy', *New Statesman*, 17 November 1978, p. 565.

Rodgers, William, 'A winter's tale of discontent', *Guardian*, 7 January 1984, p. 11.

Rodgers, William, 'Government under stress, Britain's winter of discontent', *Political Quarterly*, vol. 55, no. 2, 1984, pp. 171–9.

Rose, Clive, 'Symposium: the winter of discontent', *Contemporary Review*, vol. 1, no. 3, autumn 1987.

Rose, Peter, 'The Wilson–Callaghan government of 1974–79: by-elections (eventually) bring down a government', in Chris Cook and John Ramsden (eds), *By-elections in British Politics* (London: University College London Press, 1997), pp. 215–27.

Rutherford, Malcolm, 'Why Mr. Callaghan had cold feet', *Financial Times*, 8 September 1978, p. 17.

Saunders, Robert, 'Crisis? What crisis? Thatcherism and the seventies', in Ben Jackson and Robert Saunders (eds), *Making Thatcher's Britain* (Cambridge: Cambridge University Press, 2012), pp. 25–42.

Scammell, Margaret, 'The phenomenon of political marketing: the Thatcher contribution', *Contemporary Record*, vol. 8, no. 1, summer 1994, p. 20.

Seaton, Jean, 'Trade unions and the media', in Ben Pimlott and Chris Cook (eds), *Trade Unions in British Politics* (London: Longman, 1982), pp. 272–90.

Shepherd, John, 'James Bryce and the recruitment of working-class magistrates, 1892–1894', *Bulletin of the Institute of Historical Research*, vol. 52, no. 126, November 1979, pp. 155–69.

Shepherd, John, 'Labour wasn't working', *History Today*, vol. 59, no. 1, January 2009, pp. 43–9.

Shepherd, John and Keith Laybourn, 'Labour's red letter day', *BBC History Magazine*, vol. 5, no. 12, December 2004, pp. 22–5.

Skidelsky, Robert, 'The worst of governments', Anthony Seldon and Kevin Hickson (eds), *New Labour, Old Labour: The Wilson and Callaghan Governments, 1974–1979* (London: Routledge, 2004), pp. 316–20.

Smith, Paul, 'The road haulage industry, 1945–79: from statutory regulation to contested terrain', in Chris Wrigley (ed.), *A History of Industrial Relations 1939–1979: Industrial Relations in a Declining Economy* (Cheltenham: Edward Elgar, 1996), p. 212–34.

Smith, Paul, 'The winter of discontent: the hire and reward road haulage dispute, 1979', *Historical Studies in Industrial Relations*, vol. 7, spring 1999, pp. 38–44.

State Research Bulletin, no. 4, February–March 1978.

Suddaby, John, 'The public sector strike in Camden: winter '79', *New Left Review*, no. 116, July–August 1979, pp. 83–93.

Taylor, Andrew, 'The party and the trade unions', in Anthony Seldon and Stuart Ball (eds), *Conservative Century: The Conservative Party Since 1900* (Oxford: Oxford University Press, 1994), pp. 499–546.

Taylor, Andrew, 'The "Stepping Stones" programme: Conservative Party thinking on trade unions, 1975–9', *Historical Studies in Industrial Relations*, vol. 2, spring 2001, pp. 109–33.

Taylor, Andrew, 'The Conservative Party and the trade unions', in John McIlroy, Nina Fishman and Alan Campbell (eds), *The High Tide of British Trade Unionism: Trade Unions and Industrial Politics, 1964–79* (Monmouth: Merlin Press, second edition 2007), pp. 151–86.

Taylor, Robert, 'The rise and fall of the social contract', in Anthony Seldon and Kevin Hickson (eds), *New Labour, Old Labour: The Wilson and Callaghan Governments, 1974–1979* (London: Routledge, 2004).

Taylor, Robert, 'When the sun set on Labour the last time', *Tribune*, 19 September 2008, p. 28.

Thomas, James, 'Bound by history: the winter of discontent in British politics, 1979–2004', *Media, Culture and Society*, vol. 29, no. 2, March 2007, pp. 263–83.

Tiratsoo, Nick, '"You've never had it so bad"? Britain in the 1970s', in Nick Tiratsoo (ed.), *From Blitz to Blair: A New History of Britain Since 1939* (London: Phoenix, 1997), pp. 163–90.

Tweedale, Geoffrey, 'Industry and de-industrialisation', in Richard Coopey and Nicholas Woodward (eds), *Britain in the 1970s: The Troubled Economy* (London: University College London Press, 1996), pp. 258–9.

Whelan, Christopher J., 'Military intervention in industrial disputes', *Industrial Law Journal*, vol. 8, no. 4, December 1979, pp. 222–6.

Wood, Frances, 'Scottish Labour in government and opposition, 1964–1979', in Ian Donnachie, Christopher Harvie and Ian S. Wood (eds), *Forward! Labour Politics in Scotland 1888–1998* (Edinburgh: Polygon, 1989).

Worcester, Robert, 'What happened? Post-election aggregate analysis', MORI, *Campaign Polling Presentations* (London: MORI, 1979).

Wrigley, Chris, 'Trade unions, the government and the economy', in Terry Gourvish and Alan O'Day (eds), *Britain Since 1945* (Basingstoke: Macmillan, 1991), pp. 59–87.

Wrigley, Chris, 'Trade unions, strikes and the government', in Richard Coopey and Nicholas Woodward (eds), *Britain in the 1970s: The Troubled Economy* (London: University College London Press, 1996), pp. 273–92.

Wrigley, Chris, 'The winter of discontent: the lorry drivers' strike, January 1979', in Andrew Charlesworth, David Gilbert, Adrian Randall, Humphrey Southall and Chris Wrigley, *An Atlas of Industrial Protest in Britain 1750–1990* (Basingstoke: Macmillan, 1996), pp. 210–16.

Wrigley, Chris, 'Women in the labour market and in the unions', in John McIlroy, Nina Fishman and Alan Campbell (eds), *The High Tide of British Trade Unionism: Trade Unions and Industrial Politics, 1964–79* (Monmouth: Merlin Press, second edition 2007), pp. 55–7.

Biographical dictionaries

Gildart, Keith and David Howell (eds), *Dictionary of Labour Biography* (Basingstoke: Palgrave MacMillan, 2010).

Goldman Lawrence (ed.), *Oxford Dictionary of National Biography 2001–2004* (Oxford: Oxford University Press, 2009).

Mathew, H. C. G. and Brian Harrison (eds), *Oxford Dictionary of National Biography* (Oxford: Oxford University Press, 2004).

Interviews

Jeff Baker, Swansea, 1 May 2012.
Brendan Barber, Congress House, London, 4 August 2008.
Lord Joel Barnett, House of Lords, 2 June 2010.
Tony Benn, Notting Hill, London, 20 June 2011.
Rodney Bickerstaffe, Russell Square, London, 23 June 2009.
Frank Bland, Romford, 29 August 2012.
Professor William A. Brown, Darwin College Cambridge, 13 January 2012.
Jim Clark, Grimsby, 28 August 2012.
Michael Cockerell, Notting Hill, London, 4 April 2011.
Dr Jon Cruddas MP, Portcullis House, London, 18 February 2010.
Cllr John Davis, Dagenham, 2 April 2012.
Lord Bernard Donoughue, House of Lords, 6 July 2010.
John Edmonds, Victoria, London, 17 November 2010.
Geoffrey Goodman, Congress House, London, 22 July 2008.
Baroness Joyce Gould, House of Lords, 12 September 2011.
Lord Ted Graham, House of Lords, 26 July 2007.
Walter Harrison, Wakefield, 5 March 2012.
Lord Roy Hattersley, Victoria, London, 25 June 2009.
Rt Hon. Bob Hawke, Sydney, Australia, 16 August 2009.
Rt Hon. Patricia Hewitt, Holloway, London, 23 June 2010.
Fred Jarvis, Bloomsbury, London, 22 June 2010.
Lord Neil Kinnock, House of Lords, 2 November 2011,

Sir Tim Lankester, Dry Drayton, 30 May 2011.
Lord David Lea, House of Lords, 15 October 2007.
Lord David Lipsey, House of Lords, 9 February 2009.
John Mallinson, Highbury, London, 16 November 2011.
Nick Martin, Australian Labour Party, Sydney, 16 October 2012.
Lord Tom McNally, House of Lords, 23 June 2007.
Lord Matthew Oakeshott, OLIM Ltd, London, 28 September 2011.
Lord David Owen, House of Lords, 16 November 2011.
Lord Jim Prior, Beccles, 11 November 2011.
Lord Giles Radice, House of Lords, 26 January 2011.
Lord William Rodgers, House of Lords, 15 October 2007.
Sir Clive Rose, Lavenham, 24 June 2011.
Lord Tom Sawyer, House of Lords, 12 January 2011.
Robert Shepherd, Gravesend, 20 August 2012.
Baroness Ann Taylor, House of Lords, 20 June 2011.
Brenda Treadwell, People's History Museum, Manchester, 30 September 2012.
Stephen Wade, Dry Drayton, 15 January 2012.
Michael White, Westminster, London, 11 April 2011.
Lord Larry Whitty, House of Lords, 12 January 2011.
Baroness Shirley Williams, House of Lords, 12 October 2008.
Ralph Willis, by telephone, Melbourne, Australia, 8 August 2012.
Sir Robert Worcester, Ipsos MORI Head Office, Borough Road, London, 27 June 2011.

Newspapers and periodicals

National newspapers
Daily Express
Daily Mail
Daily Sketch
Daily Star
Daily Telegraph
Economist
Evening News
Evening Standard
Financial Times
Guardian
Independent
Morning Star
News of the World
Observer
Scotsman
Sun
Sunday Express
Sunday Mirror
Sunday People
Sunday Telegraph
Sunday Times

Provincial newspapers
Cambridge Evening News
Grimsby Evening Telegraph
Liverpool Echo
Northern Echo

Australian and United States newspapers
New York Times
Record

Sydney Morning Herald
Washington Post

Journals and periodicals
BBC History Magazine
Big Flame
Bulletin of the Institute of Historical Research
Contemporary Record
Contemporary Review
Encounter
Geography
Historical Studies in Industrial Relations
History Today
House Magazine
Industrial Law Journal
Labour Review of Books
Listener
Media, Culture and Society
New Left Review
New Society
New Statesman
Parliamentary Affairs
Personnel Management
Political Quarterly
Sociology
Tribune
Workers Liberty

Theses

Ludlam, Steve, 'Labourism and the disintegration of the post-war consensus: disunited trade union economic policy responses to public expenditure cuts, 1974–1979', PhD thesis, University of Sheffield, 1991.

Martin, Tara, '"End of an era?" Class politics, memory and Britain's winter of discontent', PhD thesis, University of Manchester, 2008.

Nelder, Dominic, 'The British winter of discontent 1978–79: the construction of an image', MPhil thesis, University of Cambridge, 1996.

Symposia

British Academy, 'Re-assessing the seventies', 22 January 2009.
Institute of Contemporary British History, 'Winter of discontent', September 1987.

Radio recordings

Winter of Discontent, Archive Hour, BBC Radio 4, 6 September 2008.

Index

CPSIA information can be obtained at www.ICGtesting.com
Printed in the USA
BVOW11s2233111015

421814BV00003B/8/P

9 781784 991159